THE CHALLENGE
OF MAN'S FUTURE

THE CHALLENGE
OF MAN'S FUTURE

An Inquiry Concerning
the Condition of Man
During the Years
That Lie Ahead

THE CHALLENGE
OF MAN'S FUTURE

by Harrison Brown

New York · **THE VIKING PRESS**

FIRST PUBLISHED IN MARCH 1954 BY

THE VIKING PRESS, INC.

625 MADISON AVENUE, NEW YORK, N.Y. 10022

PUBLISHED ON THE SAME DAY IN THE DOMINION OF CANADA

BY THE MACMILLAN COMPANY OF CANADA LIMITED

VIKING COMPASS EDITION MARCH 1956

EIGHTEENTH PRINTING MARCH 1970

SBN 670-21110-9 (HARDBOUND)

SBN 670-00003-5 (PAPERBOUND)

LIBRARY OF CONGRESS CATALOG CARD NUMBER: 54-6422

PRINTED IN THE U.S.A. BY THE COLONIAL PRESS INC.

TO RUDD

ACKNOWLEDGMENTS

Much of the research and study preliminary to writing this book was done while the author was a member of the staff of the Institute for Nuclear Studies of the University of Chicago. The author is greatly indebted to a great many colleagues in various divisions of the university—including the Divisions of Social, Physical, and Biological Sciences, the Oriental Institute, and the Research Institutes—for their help in locating information, for their patient explanations involving fields of inquiry previously unfamiliar to the author, and for their sharp criticism of viewpoints, ideas, and interpretations. The author is also greatly indebted to many of his colleagues at the California Institute of Technology for their help and criticisms during the process of manuscript preparation, and to associates in Europe who made suggestions during the author's four-month stay there in 1950. However, the author takes sole responsibility for whatever errors of fact or interpretation may appear on the following pages.

The author also acknowledges the patient help of Mrs. Ora Coon, who typed much of the first draft of the manuscript, at the University of Chicago; of Mrs. Mary Eiker and Mrs. Evelyn Nelson of the California Institute of Technology, who saw to it that the typing and retyping were carried to completion and who in other ways helped in the preparation of the manuscript; and of Miss Ellen Powelson and Mrs. Charlotte Bjornssen, who prepared the drawings.

Above all, the author expresses his gratitude to Mr. Robert Ballou of The Viking Press for his careful editing. Insofar as some sections of this book are concerned, he deserves to be known as "co-author" rather than "editor."

CONTENTS

CONTENTS

PREFACE

A large part of this book has been written on a porch overlooking Ocho Rios Bay on the island of Jamaica. As I look out over the Caribbean, I can see the white line of waves breaking on the coral reef, which pushes ever upward, only to be ground down by the action of wind and water. The reef is a universe in itself; every crevice is filled with forms of life that are at once strange and magnificent—plants, fish of practically every shape and color, sea urchins with their dangerous black waving sabers Between the reef and the shore dense forests of plants push upward from the ocean floor, and on the sandy beaches ghost crabs scurry to the water's edge, then back to the holes in the sand which are their homes. Beyond the ribbon of beach sand I can see the lush, green cultivated jungles of coconut palms, banana, akee, breadfruit, and pimento. And high above is the John Crow, which soars with seemingly infinite patience, searching for the bodies of dead animals.

To the casual observer who spends a day driving about the island, Jamaica appears to be a tropical paradise where food can be obtained simply by going to the nearest tree or by placing a net or line in the nearest water. Malnutrition would appear to be inexcusable. Yet here, as in practically all places in the world, the struggle for survival goes on. The universe of the island, like the universe of the reef, is filled with battles for food and everlasting struggles against death. Beneath the dense roof of trees there is beauty—but there are also ugliness, starvation, and misery.

Jamaica in a very real sense is a world in miniature. Here one can observe on a small scale the operation of forces identical with those that bring misery and starvation on a large scale to the greater portion of humanity. If one spends sufficient time on the island to become familiar with the enormous changes that have been wrought since the first human being came here, one cannot help wondering about the interrelationships between man and his environment. And one cannot help wondering further about the ultimate fate not only of the island population but of humanity as a whole. Thus this beautiful island, with its strange contrasts, has provided much of the stimulation for the effort which has gone into this inquiry concerning the future.

This book represents an attempt to examine man's past and present and, on the basis of the clues derived from such a study, to examine his future. I have not attempted to predict that future, for the course of events ahead of us depends upon the actions of man himself, which are, in the main, unpredictable. Nevertheless, on the basis of our knowledge concerning the physical and biological world in which we live, we can obtain a clear picture of what *cannot* happen. And we can also obtain pictures of what will probably happen in the event that we behave in any one of a number of specific ways. Thus, during the course of our studies, several possibilities will emerge, some of which are more probable than others, but all of which are possible on the basis of our existing knowledge.

It is difficult for human beings to conceive of a personal death, and it is equally difficult for us to conceive of a time when our nation, our culture, or our species will cease to exist. Yet, just as we know rationally that the time will come when each of us as individuals will perish, so we know that our country, our culture, and our species cannot exist forever. Sometime there must be an end.

Nevertheless, the fact that we know that we as individuals must someday perish does not prevent our attempting to bring as much comfort, security, and happiness into our individual lives as possible. And by studying ways in which men have died in the past and are dying at present, we attempt to lengthen our individual lifetimes—often quite successfully Similarly, most of us like to think in terms of maximum longevity for our civilization and for humanity, and we like to look forward to a world in which most people can be reasonably happy and can live securely and freely without pestilence, war, and starvation.

As we shall see, we are now living in a phase of history which is destined never to be repeated. For the fifth of the world's population that lives in regions of machine culture it is a period of unprecedented abundance. And most of us who are a part of that fortunate one-fifth are so enamored with the achievements of the last century and with the abundance which has been created that we believe the pace of achievement will continue uninterrupted in the future. However, only a cursory investigation of the present position of machine civilization is needed to uncover the fact that it is indeed in a very precarious position. A cosmic gambler, looking at us from afar, would in all likelihood give substantial odds in favor of the probability that it will soon disappear, never again to come into existence.

If machine civilization, which thus far has created more problems than it has solved, disintegrates, humanity as a whole will revert to a way of life not unlike that which existed in Europe in the seventeenth century or that which exists in China today. If, on the other hand, machine civilization is able to survive, the possibilities for human comfort, security, and achievement in the centuries ahead are virtually limitless.

Whether or not it survives depends upon whether or not man is able to recognize the problems that have been created, anticipate the problems that will confront him in the future, and devise solutions that can be embraced by society as a whole. The problems that can be recognized at present are enormous, and great intelligence, vision, and courage are required for their solution. In the light of what we know of the nature of man, it would appear that the possibilities of solution are remote. However, I do not believe that solution is by any means impossible—if I thought so, a book such as this would serve little purpose other than to depress people further at a time when events are depressing enough.

I believe that man has the power, the intelligence, and the imagination to extricate himself from the serious predicament that now confronts him. The necessary first step toward wise action in the future is to obtain an understanding of the problems that exist. This in turn necessitates an understanding of the relationships between man, his natural environment, and his technology. I hope that this study will in some measure contribute to that understanding.

Ocho Rios, Jamaica
April 1953

**THE CHALLENGE
OF MAN'S FUTURE**

THE CHALLENGE
OF MAN'S FUTURE

Chapter I:

EMERGENCE

. . . *What is a man,*
If his chief good and market of his time
Be but to sleep and feed? A beast, no more.
Sure he that made us with such large discourse,
Looking before and after, gave us not
That capability and godlike reason
To fust in us unused. . . .

SHAKESPEARE, *Hamlet,* Act IV, Scene IV

1.

The earth upon which we live is covered with a wondrous film of stuff which we call life. The film is exceedingly thin, so thin that its weight can scarcely be more than one-billionth that of the planet which supports it. If we were to collect all living matter and mold it into a a single lump, it would appear, when placed next to the earth, as a mosquito appears in relation to a melon. So insignificant in size that it would be detectable only with the greatest difficulty by beings on other planets, and would certainly be unnoticeable to observers elsewhere in our galaxy, the living envelope has clung tenaciously to the surface of our planet for hundreds of millions of years. It is insubstantial, flaccid, and sensitive in the extreme to the physical conditions about it—so much so that a slight cosmic ripple would quickly bring extinction. Yet, in an ever-changing way, the envelope of living things, of which we human beings are now a part, has continued to exist for the greater part of earth-history. The lofty and seemingly permanent mountains, which we consider to be such stable features of the earth scene, have lifetimes that are insignificant in comparison.

Although the world's film of life is continuous, the living species

3

within the film have, in the main, been short-lived. Life on earth has consisted of a steady flow of births and deaths not only of individual organisms, but of groups of organisms. These groups have evolved, cut out niches for themselves in the scheme of life, and exploited those niches to the fullest extent until they could progress no farther. They have then become extinct or have ceased to change. The records of the past are filled with the histories of species which came into existence possessing equipment particularly suited to their environments, multiplied rapidly, soon became dominant, lived for a while longer, then disappeared. Frequently a new species arose which was better able to cope with the environment and thus displaced the old. But often the original species was doomed by its own particular specialization, which permitted the exploitation of only a narrow mode of existence. When the environment changed appreciably, the species frequently could no longer flourish and passed out of existence.

Man is the most recent arrival on the evolutionary scene to become dominant among land animals. He appeared in the envelope of living matter equipped with all of the biological advantages characteristic of mammals. But superimposed upon those advantages was a tool that no animal had possessed before him—the power of conceptual thought. The effects of the introduction of this power into the evolutionary scene have been manifold. In particular, in a length of time which is insignificant when compared with that during which living matter has covered the earth, the human population has increased from hundreds to billions. As the reptilian population catapulted upward at the beginning of the Mesozoic, following the evolution of the egg which could survive on dry land, as the mammalian population increased with explosive suddenness at the decline of the Kingdom of the Reptiles, so the population of a still newer form of life—life possessed of the power of conceptual thought—is multiplying about us rapidly today. It is important that we ask, while we are still in the middle of the population upsurge: How far will this new development carry us? How large can the human population become? Is mankind destined, as were the reptiles in times past, for extinction? Or will an equilibrium be developed in which man can live in harmony with his environment?

And finally we may ask: To what extent, if any, does man still possess the power to determine his destiny? Can he willfully create a stable relationship between himself and his environment? Or are his needs and his relationship to the world about him such that he is being swept inexorably toward his end?

2.

In 1798 the Reverend Thomas Robert Malthus published the first edition of an essay which was destined to precipitate one of the longest and at times one of the most heated controversies in history. The publication carried the impressive title *An Essay on the Principle of Population as it affects the Future Improvement of Society, with Remarks on the Speculations of Mr. Godwin, M. Condorcet, and other Writers.* It put forward the view that human populations, if not checked in some way, would increase much more rapidly than would the means of subsistence, and that populations always increase up to the limits imposed by the means of subsistence—that is, until they are prevented from increasing further by insufficient food, and by disease and war.

Malthus foresaw only disaster, and to the end of his days he was profoundly pessimistic concerning the future of humanity. In the second edition of his work he recognized the existence of "moral restraint," by which he meant postponement of marriage and the practice of strict sexual continence, as a possible population check. But to the time of his death he had little faith that the human race could regulate its numbers by the exercise of such measures. He recognized that sexual continence, even as a means of averting disaster, was about the most unpopular idea imaginable, and he dismissed other willful population checks as being immoral.

The disaster which Malthus foresaw for the Western World did not occur. Instead, Western populations grew far beyond the levels he would have considered possible, and the poverty and deprivation so widespread in Malthus's time were enormously decreased. So widely divergent were the predictions from the actual course of events that, if we were to look only at the predictions divorced from the reasoning, we would be inclined to say that he was incompetent. Indeed, during the last few decades he has been held up as a warning and an object lesson to those who would be sufficiently rash to attempt to predict man's future on the basis of existing knowledge.

In retrospect it is clear, however, that both Malthus's reasoning and the principles he enunciated were sound. His extrapolation into the future suffered not from lack of proper reasoning, but from lack of sufficient knowledge of the potentialities of technological development. He was in no position to foresee the enormous influence of the railroad and the steamship upon European populations. He was in no position to foresee that greatly increased numbers of Englishmen would be fed with Australian meat, Canadian wheat, butter from New Zealand, and sugar from the West Indies. He lacked sufficient knowledge to estimate correctly the effect of industrialization upon agricultural production. Further, he could not have foreseen the extent to which the changed way of life in an industrial age would result in drastically declining birth rates coupled with decreasing mortality. In short, the scientific knowledge of his time was too meager to permit his drawing valid quantitative conclusions, no matter how sound his reasoning was.

The Malthusian point of view influenced public opinion during the first half of the nineteenth century, and in particular the "struggle-for-existence" aspect of the *Essay* had considerable effect upon the thinking of Charles Darwin, who read it by chance in 1838. But during subsequent decades it was in large measure disparaged. During the age of colonial expansion and increasing industrialization it appeared that there were no limits to the number of people that could be supported by the resources of the earth.

In recent years discussions similar to Malthus's have developed. On the one hand there have been numerous books and articles warning of possible disaster resulting from our increasing populations, from our misuse of the land, and from our accelerated consumption of resources. The arguments used to bolster this point of view are essentially of a Malthusian nature. On the other hand there are those who point to the spectacular failure of Malthus's predictions and who maintain that the predictions of the modern prophets of doom will similarly be proved false. The proponents of this belief point to the technological developments of the past and insist that the developments of the future will be even more spectacular. They maintain that our science and our ingenuity make possible the clothing, housing, and feeding of far more people than now inhabit the surface of the earth. As evidence they call attention to such wonders as synthetic fabrics, synthetic gasoline, synthetic foodstuffs, plant hormones, soil conditioners, and inexpensive inorganic fertilizers. They point to the vast, relatively thinly populated areas of South America and Africa as the potential living space for additional hundreds of millions of people.

Unfortunately the primary results of the discussions thus far have been the generation of much heated controversy on an emotional level rather than on a logical one, the widespread dissemination of opinion disguised as scientific fact, and the confusion of the majority of the people who have taken the trouble to read the discussions relating to both sides of the argument.

In principle, the vast knowledge we have accumulated during the last 150 years makes it possible for us to look into the future with considerably more accuracy than could Malthus. But in actual fact we are dealing with an extremely complex problem which cuts across all of our major fields of inquiry and which, because of this, is difficult to unravel in all of its interlocking aspects. The complexity of the problem, our confusion, and our prejudices, have combined to form a dense fog that has obscured the most important features of the problem from our view—a fog which is in certain respects even more dense than that which existed in Malthus's time. As a result, the basic factors that are determining the future are not generally known or appreciated.

In spite of the complexity of the problem which confronts us, its overwhelming importance, both to ourselves and to our descendants, warrants our dissecting it as objectively as possible. In doing so we must put aside our hatreds, desires, and prejudices, and look calmly upon the past and present. If we are successful in lifting ourselves from the morass of irrelevant fact and opinion and in divorcing ourselves from our preconceived ideas, we will be able to see mankind both in perspective and in relation to his environment. In turn we will be able to appreciate something of the fundamental physical limitations to man's future development and of the hazards which will confront him in the years and centuries ahead.

The populations of the hundreds of thousands of living species which inhabit the surface of the earth are limited. The limiting factors for any species are numerous and interrelated, but clearly a major one is the food supply. Animals will live, grow, and reproduce only if they can eat. If the food supply disappears, the animals will die.

Relatively simple organisms such as amoebas reproduce by the process of direct cell division. Given an abundant supply of food, a single amoeba will, at the end of about an hour, divide into two amoebas. These two will each divide at the end of another hour and become four. At the end of the third hour we will have eight amoebas; at the end of the fourth hour, sixteen. If this process of division went on indefinitely there would be one pound of amoebas at the end of two days, and a ton before two and a half days had passed. By the fifth day the weight of the amoebas would exceed the combined weights of the oceans of the world, and by the sixth day the amoebas would weigh more than the earth itself!

Clearly, although the reproductive potentials of living organisms are enormous, such huge quantities of living matter cannot exist because of the limitations imposed by the food supply. This can be seen in the laboratory when bacteria are cultured in test tubes. Let us suppose that a nutrient solution is inoculated with a small number of bacteria, and that nutrients are added to the solution at a constant rate. At first the bacteria will multiply at the maximum rate, the number doubling every hour or so. However, after a few hours their number will reach a level at which competition for food becomes significant. The rate of population increase will then become gradually smaller until the death rate becomes equal to the birth rate, after which the population will remain constant. (See Figure 1.) The level which the population attains is determined by the rate at which nutrients are added to the solution—in general, the greater the rate of food input, the greater will be the equilibrium population level which is attained.

Since the primary source of animal food is plant life, the total amount of life which can exist in the animal world is fixed by the rate at which photosynthesis (the process whereby the carbon

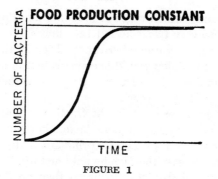

FIGURE 1

dioxide of the air is transformed by the action of solar energy into carbohydrates) takes place. The world-wide rate at which photosynthesis takes place is in turn fixed by such factors as the amount of sunlight, seasonal variations in temperature, and the availability of water and nutrients necessary to plants, such as nitrogen, phosphorus, and sulphur.

Most photosynthesis takes place in the oceans, and thus there is more animal life in the oceans than on land. On the surfaces of most seas we find countless microscopic plants caHed algae. Microscopic animals feed upon the algae and upon one another. In turn, larger animals feed upon the mixture of microscopic plants and animals. The total amount of animal life in the oceans, including all whales, fish, mollusks, and protozoa, is thus fixed by the rate at which the ocean plant life grows. A similar situation exists on the land areas of the earth.

Within the animal world there is unceasing fluctuation. Populations of individual species increase and decrease; new species appear and disappear. Whether or not a species of animal continues to exist depends upon many factors. Ultimately, however, continued existence of a group depends upon the specific rate of production of young and upon the fraction of the young which survive through the breeding age. For a species of animal equally divided between males and females, the population will be stable if two young members enter the breeding period for every two who leave it. If the number entering drops appreciably, the population of the group as a whole will drop rapidly. For example, let us suppose that in a group of dinosaurs of a given kind the number of young which reached breeding age dropped slightly below two for every two who left breeding age—either through death or old age. If the number dropped to 1.9, then an original population of 10 million would become extinct in about 300 generations. Assuming a life of ten years per generation, extinction would take place in 3000 years.

In a given group of animals, the fraction of young which survives to breed depends upon many factors in addition to the food supply and the birth rate. The offspring arising from species that watch over and care for their young until maturity is reached stand a better chance of surviving to breed than do the offspring of other species. The existence of predators decreases the chances of survival. Frequently, within the species, there are threats to existence, involving cannibalism or competition for mates.

The mathematics of the interrelationships between living species is extremely complicated if more than two species are involved. If we consider an idealized case involving only two groups of living things, grass and rabbits, we have the following situation (ignoring, for the moment, seasonal variations): The more grass available, the greater will be the rabbit population. On the other hand, the more rabbits there are, the more rapidly will the grass be consumed. Eventually, if only these two species of living things are involved, an equilibrium will evolve where both the amount of grass and the number of rabbits will remain approximately constant. As the steady state is approached, there will be oscillations around an average population, as shown in Figure 2.

If we now complicate the picture by introducing animals that

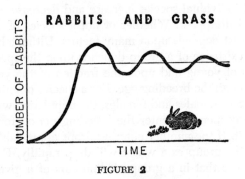

RABBITS   AND   GRASS

NUMBER OF RABBITS

TIME

FIGURE 2

feed upon rabbits—foxes, for example—the situation becomes altered considerably. Here, as before, the greater the amount of grass, the greater the rabbit population becomes, with the modification that the greater the fox population, the smaller will be the number of rabbits. It can be demonstrated that such a system is stable only if rather special uniform conditions exist If the system is appreciably disturbed—as, for example, by an unusually high yield of grass during a given year—the curve of rabbit population might be as shown in Figure 3.

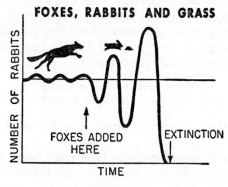

FIGURE 3

Such a system, once disturbed appreciably, would oscillate, and the peaks and valleys would become ever higher and deeper until a valley so low that reproduction could no longer take place would be reached. Briefly, a sudden rise in available grass would result in a larger number of rabbits. With more rabbits available upon which to feed, the fox population would increase rapidly. As the grass supply decreased and the fox population increased, the rabbit population would cease to grow and would then decrease. This would be followed by an increase of grass and a decrease in the number of foxes. The rabbit population would then start to increase. The oscillations would continue either until stability was achieved, or until grass, rabbits, or foxes disappeared.

The actual world of living things is governed by relationships similar to those which determine the populations of rabbits and foxes in the simplified situations cited above. However, most living creatures live in far more complex environments, and as a result the interrelationships between a given species and the living things about it are manifold.

Wherever an existence can in some manner be eked out, an organism can be found which manages to take advantage of the possibility. At any time, every possible niche of life is filled, and the life within each niche is related to the other living groups about it. We see, in the oceans and on the land, vast systems of living things, in each of which the various species are dependent upon one another for their existence. A given system might include a diversity of plant life, bacteria, insects, fish, amphibians, reptiles, and mammals, all living in harmony. While such systems are frequently fairly stable and can exist for long periods of time, if any one of the component groups is disturbed appreciably, all of the others will be affected. The lines

> Thou canst not stir a flower
> Without troubling of a star [1]

express well the delicacy and far-reaching nature of the balance that exists.

During the course of geologic time most living systems that have come into existence have undergone drastic change. Frequently climatic changes have resulted in the disruption of established systems. Another related cause of importance has been the evolution of new species of living things which have been better able than the old to cope with their environments.

4.

The first creatures which can be called "men"—creatures possessed of the power of conceptual thought as well as the ability to learn, to solve problems, and to transmit knowledge to others— appeared upon the earth perhaps 1 million years ago, some 3 billion years after the formation of our planet. Thus, from a geological point of view, man is but an infant among living species. If we were to compress the age of the earth to 1 year, the first creature who possessed the power of conceptual thought would have appeared upon the earth but a scant 3 hours ago.

The first men were the products of a long and tortuous path of

1. Francis Thompson, "The Mistress of Vision."

evolutionary trial and error. By the time they appeared, millions of species of living things had evolved, each of which had found for itself a place in the scheme of life and exploited its opportunity to the fullest until it could progress no further. Evolutionary dead ends awaited the overwhelming majority of the species. But throughout the intricate maze of dead ends there was a devious pathway along which overspecialization was avoided and from which we human beings emerged.

In respect to the general anatomy, the differences between modern men and the other higher primates are not enormous. The evolutionary development which was of overwhelming importance took place in the brain. Almost all parts of the brain became enlarged, but the greatest enlargement of all took place in those regions connected not directly with the sense organs or instinct, but with memory, the ability to solve problems, and the power of speech. These changes brought into the pattern of life on earth a creature which could devise and use tools, could transmit its knowledge to its fellow creatures, to its descendants, and through them to their descendants. Thus there began the transmission of experience from one generation to the next—a process which is cumulative and which was chiefly responsible for the rapid emergence of man as the dominant species among living things.

Men emerged in the world as animals, and for hundreds of thousands of years their lives, as did those of the other animals, consisted largely of finding enough food, of avoiding being killed, and of reproducing. Advances in techniques came slowly. But as time went on, the ever-increasing accumulation of knowledge permitted the new form of life to spread over the greater part of the earth's surface. The controlled use of fire extended the range of things that could be eaten, and thus permitted the existence of higher population densities. It provided warmth and protection, thus extending the range of livable climate and increasing the average human life span. Tools such as axes, spears, bows and arrows, and digging sticks made possible both more efficient accumulation of food and more adequate protection from predators.

As men spread over the earth, geographic isolation led to the evolution of various types of manlike beings which differed from one another in a number of important aspects. But by 50,000 B.C.

The CHALLENGE OF MAN'S FUTURE

all save the direct ancestors of the human race had vanished, leaving the present species, Homo sapiens, as the sole erect-walking, speaking species of animal on the surface of our planet.

Eventually there came a time when the population of human beings could increase no further. Men were then living in every part of the earth where existence was possible, and in most places they were crowded up to the limit of the food supply. In a culture where food is obtained by hunting and by gathering edible vegetation, about two square miles of fertile land in the natural state are required to support a single individual. Further, there are areas of the earth that are barren of both animal and vegetable food because of climatic and other physical conditions. Thus the earth probably could never support a human population of more than about 10 million depending entirely upon hunting and wild vegetation.

Once this point had been reached by men who led a food-gathering existence, further improvements in tools and weapons had but small effect in increasing the human population. To be sure, every improvement made the existence of the species as a whole less precarious, for the population could be restored with increased vigor following a catastrophe. But no matter how efficient the tools, if one kills too much game it will disappear. Nor can one pick more fruit than a tree is able to bear.

5.

A moderately fertile wild region 10,000 square miles in area offers a sufficient abundance of animal and vegetable life to support about 5000 persons who live solely on a food-gathering basis. Let us imagine that a small family group consisting of 10 food-gatherers entered a rich, hitherto uninhabited river valley of about 10,000 square miles during Paleolithic or Mesolithic times. Seeing the abundance of game, vegetation, and water, they settled. Their tools consisted solely of fire, stone implements, spears, and bows and arrows.

In the presence of an abundance of the necessities of life, the family group led a happy existence, and many children were born. There were deaths, of course, resulting from disease and from accidents, but by the time 30 years had passed the colony numbered

20 persons. In 60 years there were 40 people, of which only one, by then a very old man, had been one of the original settlers. During the 90th year of the settlement the population reached 80, and in the 120th year there were 160 persons. By that time the origin of the little colony in the fertile valley was little more than a legend. There were no survivors from the second generation, and there were but 3 survivors from the third.

The radius of operations of a hunting party from its base can be little more than about 15 miles, particularly in the absence of techniques for preserving food. This represents the distance over which a hunting party might travel, capture its prey, and transport the meat to the community without undue spoilage. By the 130th year, the hunters found that they were having increasing difficulty obtaining enough game in such a limited area to feed the larger number of people. Friction and quarreling disrupted the life of the group, and a number of its members left the settlement for other parts of the valley and established communities of their own.

By the 200th year after the first entrance of man into the fertile valley, the population had passed 1000, and there were 10 settlements. By the 225th year, all possible land within the valley had been claimed by family groups, making the creation of new communities impossible, and the population was approaching 2000, divided among 15 settlements. But there was still an abundant supply of food, and by the 240th year the population had reached 2500 and was still increasing.

The people in the various valley communities possessed no elaborate social organizations. All persons shared the work, and all shared the food after it was collected. On occasion two or more communities banded together and formed larger groups for the purpose of hunting a large herd of game, and in such cases organization was necessary—but usually it was of the loosest sort.

The residents of the valley tended to identify themselves very closely with their environment and to regard the wild life in their territory as their own property. They were most careful not to trespass on the territory of their neighbors. They possessed intimate knowledge of the living things among which they lived— the habits of the animals, the properties of the plants, the poisonous or nonpoisonous nature of grubs, termites, lizards, and other potential sources of food. They were keen observers, agile and alert, and frequently they showed an extraordinary ability to mimic animals. They possessed considerable powers of endurance, necessitated by the fact that there were times of scarcity. In times of plenty they gorged themselves. They had little in the way of personal possessions, but treasured those things that were useful in gathering food. As frequent movement from one location to another was necessary, their dwellings were of a temporary nature.

Following the 250th year of the occupation of the valley, the residents encountered increasing difficulties. Populations of animals, which had made up a large part of the diet of the people, dwindled noticeably. New tools were invented to increase the efficiency of hunting, but the quantity of food gathered never seemed quite to equal the demand. The people experimented with new foods. Some, they learned, were fatally poisonous; others they found nourishing, if not satisfying. The list of foods they would willingly eat grew to include a variety of rodents, caterpillars, ants, termites, larvae, snakes, and lizards.

The death rate, particularly that of the children, began to increase. In the 275th year a family group, dissatisfied with life in the valley, headed across the desert into the unknown, in search of a more abundant existence. During the subsequent years and centuries many more family groups were to follow these first emigrants.

Following the 275th year the population continued to increase, but the rate of increase was relatively slow. By the 300th year there were 5000 persons. During the 250 years that followed, the population oscillated between 4500 and 5500, corresponding to periods of scarcity of food and periods of plenty. The meager existence was taken for granted. There existed tribal legends about a time, long before, when food had been abundant and everyone had led a happy, contented life. But few people really believed the legends.

A religion evolved among the people of the valley—a religion that was closely related to their intimate association with animals and to their dependence upon the mysterious powers of nature. They had a god who was all-powerful and who brought thunder and rain, good luck or bad, plenty of food or none. They looked upon the sun, moon, and stars with awe and worshiped them. They respected their dead and viewed the body and the soul as different things. They had magicians and believed that these magicians could bring good or evil to individuals, make rain, and quell certain violent outbursts of nature.

During the 700th year the inhabitants of the valley were struck by disease, which up to that time they had not experienced. For a time there was considerable difficulty; all but 1000 people were killed. However, shortly after the catastrophe the inhabitants entered another age of abundance. The supply of many varieties of edible animals increased, and for 100 years there was ample food. But the population once again reached the limit which the land could support, and the austere life, which had been forgotten, became again a part of normal existence.

Thus life went on in the valley for several hundred more years. For the greater part of the time the population remained stable at about 5000, but fluctuations were frequent, and from time to time a sudden catastrophe reduced the number materially.

Eventually there came a time when new techniques were brought into the valley from the outside. Strangers entered the region, bringing with them some domesticated animals and primitive agricultural techniques. Other wanderers from the outside followed, and gradually animal domestication and agriculture became part of the lives of most of the people of the valley. Two hundred years after the introduction of the new techniques the population of the valley had increased fivefold. By the time another 100 years had passed, it had reached 150,000.

Even with the thirty-fold increase, an abundance of food was achieved by placing more land under cultivation and raising more domesticated animals. For 200 additional years life in the valley was more abundant than it had been since the period, hundreds of years before, when the first family of food-gatherers had entered and made their homes.

Even when conditions for food-gathering had been favorable, the earliest residents of the valley had had little free time. But later, agricultural practices made it possible for one man to feed more than his family alone. With abundant food and a large population, there were many men who were able to think of things other than securing sufficient nourishment. Specialization became possible—some men became tool-makers; others became potters; still others became spinners and weavers. Techniques were improved with increasing rapidity.

As techniques, specialization, and population increased, villages arose in the valley which were of a more permanent nature than had been the relatively temporary quarters of the food-gatherers. As men are fundamentally gregarious and require not only the companionship but the protection provided by their fellows, the greater part of the agricultural workers lived in or near these small communities. The sizes of the villages were severely limited by the fact that the distance from an individual's home to the soil which he tilled could not be excessive. Thus, in an age when walking was the primary means of transport, the sizes of the agricultural villages of the valley had an upper limit of 200 or 300 persons.

Gradually three of the villages were transformed into cities, each built around a temple. The cities came into existence on the river, for only by the use of water transport could an individual city draw upon a sufficiently large area for its food supply. Within the new urban centers of the valley dwelt the craftsmen, and with them dwelt other classes which were created by the new social order—merchants, officials and public servants, soldiers and sailors. The temples became the centers of all major economic activity. The farmers and craftsmen brought their products to the temple and received needed artifacts and foodstuffs from the priests in exchange. Public servants were paid from the common pool of goods.

Largely as the result of the dependence of the new social order upon agriculture, the religious practices of the people in the valley underwent profound transformation. The new religion centered in the worship of a mother goddess and was an expression of the dependence of life upon animal husbandry and plant cultivation. The process of sowing plant seed was looked upon as the impregnation of mother earth by a fertilizing agent. The seminal fluid of the human male or the male domestic animal, the seeds which were planted in the ground, and the rain which caused crops to grow were all regarded by the primitive agriculturists as being analogous. Thus the mother goddess became at once goddess of plant growth, animal reproduction, sexual love, and maternity. The temples which formed the centers of the new urban cultures were built in her honor. The priests who ruled over the temple domains were the cultural descendants of the earlier witch doctors and magicians of the food-gatherers.

The population of the valley continued to increase, and more elaborate public works were required to permit food production to equal need. Irrigation systems were built, and requirements connected with the organization of construction and maintenance brought forth governments that were universal and more highly centralized. Metallurgy was introduced into the valley, and the smith quickly became one of the most respected, yet one of the most fearsome, members of society, creating as he did, in seemingly magical fashion, objects of metal from piles of stones. Writing came into existence. Ships were built, and goods were traded with people from distant lands.

Within a few centuries after the first introduction of agriculture into the valley, and 25 centuries after the first human beings had settled there, the population had reached 1 million. Thus, in a space of time which was but a fleeting instant when compared with the length of time in which man had lived upon earth, a civilization had been created. The cultures of the tribal center, the nomadic camp, and the peasant village had been transformed into the culture of the city. Progress had been given a new form.

6.

The rise of urban culture in the valley was made possible by the great achievements of agriculture and animal domestication, which permitted the production of a surplus of food. This surplus was not a true surplus for any protracted period of time—in the sense that production capacity exceeded demand—for population growth pressed heavily upon the food supply. But from the beginnings of field agriculture in the valley, and in particular following the harnessing of the ox to the plow, agricultural workers could produce more food than they alone required. The surplus, however, was never large. It required the efforts of nine persons working in the fields to produce sufficient surplus to feed one man living in the city.

The lot of the agricultural workers was by no means appreciably improved by the fact that they produced food for the urban workers. In almost every respect the rural people lived much as had the primitive agriculturalists who preceded them. But whereas in pre-city days the rural workers of the valley could live independently and consume all the food they produced, the rise of cities imposed upon them severe controls. There were taxes and obligations to their gods which had to be paid from their crops. Interest had to be paid on loans made by temple officials. A system of private ownership of land came into existence, by means of which all crops over and above the minimum required for a peasant's subsistence could be taken from him. As a result of these developments, the status of the peasants—who comprised the largest fraction of the population of the valley—became essentially one of serfdom.

Class structures developed within the minority of the population that dwelled in the urban centers. With the evolution of the crafts came the craft workers, who were differentiated into highly skilled workers and common laborers. The skilled workers became organized into guilds, which were under the supervision of royal or priestly overseers and which guarded jealously their specialized techniques. There came also the class of businessmen, which gradually took over from the temples the functions involved in economic enterprise.

The industries of the cities of the valley gradually became dependent upon imports for many of the raw materials required for manufacturing. In order to persuade the owners of raw materials to exchange them for manufactured goods, it became necessary to instill in them a desire for the goods, and also to modify their economy so that the new goods could be absorbed. On the other hand, the necessary raw materials could also be obtained by waging war and extracting the needed materials by force. Thus the people of the valley became involved in peaceful trading as well as in imperialistic wars.

War brought into existence the military class and the class of slaves. As the techniques of war became increasingly specialized, the military class became separated from the rest of society by an ever-widening gap. Slavery on a large scale had its beginnings in the valley when captives of war were compelled to work for their conquerors. As time went on slaves came to form a substantial proportion of the total population and engaged in diverse work in the temples, shops, markets, homes, and fields.

Gradually enormous cultural and intellectual cleavages developed between the agricultural workers, the urban workers, and the ruling classes. Class struggles appeared, caused by the exploitation of the masses by the politically strong and by the rivalries between classes for the possession of the economic surplus. It was quite common for the laborers in the valley to work for subsistence. At the other end of the social scale economic gain became a leading compulsion to work. While the right of private property, as it had evolved, compelled many men to work hard for practically no return, it compelled others to work increasingly hard in order to obtain ever greater shares of the economic surplus.

Although the proportion of the population that could live in cities was small, the actual numbers grew increasingly large as the new techniques of food production were extended further. In turn, although the proportion of persons in the higher classes was extremely small, their numbers increased with the general rise in population. With the increase in numbers of skilled craftsmen and educated persons, there came a revolution in knowledge. Writing evolved to the point where it became much more important as an instrument of learning than as a tool of administration; by giving permanent form to religious beliefs, codes, legends, and songs, it contributed more than anything else to social unification. The sciences of mathematics and astronomy were developed to high levels. Standard units of length, weight, and time were established. Art flourished.

Science in the valley bore little resemblance to the science of today, for even the most learned of men believed that magic rather than logic governed the natural world about them. Although they utilized mathematics and measurement for the solution of purely practical problems, they had not yet learned to think in terms of abstract principles. They had little desire to inquire into the "how" and the "why" of the workings of nature, with the result that their highly developed engineering and technology bore little relation to their philosophies of life.

As knowledge and technical ability increased, the population of the valley continued to grow. Irrigation systems became more elaborate. Farming techniques became more efficient. But eventually no more land could be placed under irrigation, and crop yields could not be increased further. Then, slowly but relentlessly, the

death rate began to rise. So slow were the changes that no person
in the valley noticed them. But as time went on more children
died each year, more women died in childbirth, more people died
of disease—particularly in the densely populated cities. When
the population of the valley reached 3 million it ceased to increase
and, as in the time of the food-gatherers who had lived in the
valley many centuries before, began to oscillate, increasing during periods when the water in the river was abundant, and decreasing during periods when the flow of water lessened. Legends
appeared, similar to those that had been repeated by the food-
gatherers long before, of ancient times when everyone had had
enough to eat, when everyone had lived a contented life.

The great empire of the valley continued to exist for many centuries. But the population remained relatively static. In the cities
of the valley, huts were crowded together in such a way that filth
and stench were everywhere apparent. The food allotments to
the workers were barely sufficient to maintain life. Famines spread
over the land at 5- to 10-year intervals. Occasionally the deaths
from famine and disease were so numerous that periods of plenty
followed periods of death—but such relatively good times were
usually of short duration.

Eventually the social upheavals within the valley, and the military pressures from without, brought an end to the civilization
that had been created. Canals filled with silt. Irrigation systems
diminished in extent and in effectiveness. Food supplies lessened,
and the population of the valley decreased. The civilization that
had been spawned by but a handful of people, many centuries before, ceased to exist.

Later in history the age of greatness of the valley was to be
called "the Golden Age." Civilization had in truth brought a
golden age to 3000 nobles and persons of wealth. But the his-
torians, piecing together the history of the valley, did not appreciate that the possessions of kings were not indicative of the
possessions of the population as a whole. They failed to appreciate
that the 3 million peasants, common laborers, and slaves, who
had tilled the fields or lived and worked in the dirty cubicles of
the cities, had been no better off than their neolithic predecessors

7.

When measured in terms of a single human lifetime, urban culture spread slowly over the surface of the earth. But in terms of the geologic time scale, its spread, and the increase in human population that accompanied it, were somewhat like an explosion. So far as can be discerned, six, and possibly seven, great urban cultures arose directly from primitive life. The earliest transitions from peasant-village to city existence took place in Mesopotamia, along the banks of the Tigris and Euphrates Rivers; in Egypt, along the banks of the Nile; and on the mountainous island of Crete. A fourth urban culture arose at an early date in the Indus valley in western India, but scholars disagree as to whether this was an offshoot of the Sumerian culture or an independent emergence from primitive existence. At a much later date civilization arose in the lower valley of the Yellow River. Still later the transition was made by the residents of the tropical forest of Central America and by the inhabitants of the Peruvian coastland and plateau regions.

All of the urban cultures which emerged directly from primitive life had at their roots the great neolithic achievements of agriculture and husbandry and the marked improvements in techniques of making things. But while these achievements were necessary for such a culture, they were by no means sufficient. Environmental factors determined where food could and could not be grown. Human factors determined the levels of creativity that could be reached and the intensity of the dynamic activity that could be attained.

The first cities probably appeared in Egypt and in Mesopotamia about 3500 B.C. During the millennium which followed, the cities of both regions emerged as centers of highly developed industries and extensive commerce. By 2500 B.C. the Sumerians had developed a general system of irrigation and flood control in the lower Tigris-Euphrates valley. Agriculture was highly developed, centered largely on the cultivation of wheat and barley. Cattle were used to pull the plow and to furnish milk, leather, and meat; goats also were milked, and goats and sheep were shorn to provide fibers for the large textile industry, while the hides and meat of both were used for leather and food. A multitude of vegetables and fruit was cultivated. Varieties of tools were manufactured of stone, copper, and bronze.

In Egypt the general development in technics paralleled the Sumerian developments rather closely, with due allowances for availability of raw materials. By 2500 B.C. the Egyptians had accumulated vast experience in many fields of endeavor. Writing had become well established. Art was well developed, and an elaborate religion had evolved. Various fields of learning such as medicine, mathematics, and astronomy were differentiated. Enormous advances had been made in the organization of large-scale engineering and building projects. Mesopotamian and Egyptian cultures had now existed for 1000 years, and the cities of Crete and the Indus valley were nearly 500 years old. But civilization had not spread very far from the centers of origin. The world was still occupied largely by food-gatherers and by groups that were in the process of passing through the various phases of neolithic culture.

Europe, following the breakup of the ice sheet, was on the periphery of the new cultural developments, and by 2500 B.C. Egyptian and Cretan influences had given rise to a neolithic culture in Spain which gradually spread into southern France and the Rhone valley. To the east, peasant-village culture appeared in Greece and Thessaly and spread westward through the Balkans. Settlements appeared in southern Italy and Sicily.

A factor of considerable importance in the further diffusion of the new culture from the areas of origin was the stimulation of trade which resulted from the use of copper. By 2000 B.C. a bronze age had begun in Central Europe and in Britain. The new techniques gradually spread north into northern Germany, Denmark, and southern Sweden. Soon metal trading linked the whole of Central Europe into a single economic unit.

As the new techniques spread over Europe and Asia, human population increased. And associated with the population increases were innumerable migrations, wars, and social revolutions. As the population pressed ever harder against the food supply, land had to be found for the offspring of the peasantry. This land could often be obtained by reclamation, but frequently war, aimed at seizing the land already reclaimed by the citizens of a neighboring area, appeared to be an easier outlet. Many of the early wars between cities were fought over the question of access to water. Others were precipitated by half-starved barbarians who cast envious eyes upon urban wealth and decided to attempt to take it for their own.

The first social revolution of recorded history took place in Egypt, where the food allotments to the workers were barely sufficient to maintain life. An observer wrote:

Why Really, the face is pale. The bowman is ready. Robbery is everywhere. . . .

Why Really, the Nile is in flood, but no one plows for himself because every man says: "We do not know what may happen throughout the land!" . . .

Why Really, many dead are buried in the river. The stream is a tomb, and the embalming-place has really become the stream.

Why Really, nobles are in lamentation, while poor men have joy. Every town says: "Let us banish many from us."

Why Really, . . . dirt is throughout the land. There are really none whose clothes are white in these times. . . .

Why Really, the River is blood. If one drinks of it, one rejects it as human and thirsts for water. . . .

Why Really, laughter has disappeared and is no longer made. It is wailing that pervades the land, mixed with lamentation. . . .

Why Really, the children of nobles are dashed against the walls. The once prayed-for children are now laid out on the high ground. . . .[1]

The populations of the ancient oriental empires were eventually limited by deaths resulting from starvation, disease, and war, and, to a lesser extent, by conscious control of conception, by abortion, and by infanticide. Sanitation measures were seldom taken, except in the homes of the higher classes. Famine surged over the ancient lands at frequent intervals. As the crowded conditions, the filth, and the food situation in the ancient cities worsened, contagious diseases, and with them high rates of infant mortality, prevailed.

"The once prayed-for children are now laid out on the high ground" is clearly a reference to infanticide, which was practiced to some extent in Egypt, and later widely practiced by the Greeks.

1. *Ancient Near Eastern Texts,* edited by J. B. Pritchard (Princeton: Princeton University Press, 1950), p. 442. J. A. Wilson, translator.

A number of methods to prevent conception were used in Egypt, among them a medicated lint tampon. Several methods which were used for family limitation are mentioned in the Bible and in Hebrew law—among them, coitus interruptus, the moistened sponge (possibly having its origin in the Egyptian lint tampon), and the removal of semen from the vagina.

Thus increased mortality and, to a lesser extent, conscious family limitation continuously lowered the rate of population growth in the ancient oriental empires. But in the new regions where urban culture was surging upward, populations grew rapidly. The changes resulted in the destruction of old civilizations and the creation of new ones.

The Egyptians succumbed in turn to the Ethiopians, the Assyrians, and the Persians. The ancient civilization of the Indus valley disappeared, and new urban centers, dominated by Indo-Europeans, arose in the Indus valley, on the divide between the Indus and the Ganges, and on the Gangetic plain. A high level of urban culture arose in China. In Europe the great Minoan civilization, and with it the flourishing cities of Cnossos, Tiryns, Mycenae, and Troy, perished, destroyed by Hellenic tribes. New Greek cities arose—Athens, Sparta, Corinth, Thebes, Samos, and Miletus. To the west, urban centers appeared on the Italian mainland and in Sicily. In northern Italy the Etruscans became dominant, and in Africa, Carthage became powerful. Rome, which had been a minor city when compared with the other centers of Italian urban culture, began its rise to prominence. After thirty-five centuries of Mesopotamian and Egyptian supremacy, the location of the most advanced cultures of the world shifted rapidly northwestward to the European continent.

8.

The spread of urban culture throughout Europe was made possible by the agricultural and technological knowledge that had been accumulated in the ancient oriental empires. By the time Greek civilization appeared, agriculture was already a highly developed art which had behind it millennia of empiric progress. Further improvements in agricultural techniques came very slowly. During the many centuries which intervened between the rise of European civilization and the beginnings of the Industrial Revolution, the rapid increase in European populations resulted less from improvements in agricultural technology than from the simple extension to ever greater areas of the farming methods then known.

Although improvements in agricultural techniques came slowly, related developments accelerated the diffusion of agriculture over the European continent. Perhaps the most important was the introduction of metallic iron. Deposits of iron ore exist in much greater abundance than do deposits of copper ore, with the result that, once the metallurgy of iron was worked out, the use of metals could really become widespread. Immediately there was an increase in the amount of land that was farmed, and in the population.

Throughout all of the early days of European population expansion we see evidences that the numbers of human beings kept abreast of existing food supplies. Indeed, in two localities, Greece and Italy, the populations actually exceeded the maximum numbers that could be supported by local agriculture—eventually with disastrous results.

Greek civilization, upon which so many of the foundations of Western culture were laid, evolved in a region where only 20 per cent of the land area could be cultivated and which lacked adequate raw materials for industrial production. As the Greek population pressed more heavily upon the food supply, further agricultural improvements appeared. The principles of fertilizing soil were discovered empirically, and the spreading of animal manure and the rotation of crops began to be practiced. Nitrates and lime were spread upon the soil.

But Greek food production could not keep pace with requirements. By 600 B.C. the new civilization was flourishing under an economy that was largely dependent upon commerce. At home the Greeks specialized in the cultivation of the grape and the olive, the products of which were traded for grain. Later they started manufacturing industrial articles in order to augment further the food supplies that were necessary for the growing population. Trading in specialized agricultural products became so profitable that large landowners gradually gave up grain cultivation entirely and replaced it with the cultivating of more specialized exportable foodstuffs. Thus Greece grew to depend almost entirely upon food imports for its survival.

For a while the Greeks were able to produce sufficient specialized agricultural products and industrial goods to pay for their requirements of food and raw materials. But eventually industrial competition from other areas, such as Rome, coupled with the disruption in trade caused by wars and social upheavals, brought on a crisis that could not be surmounted.

In Italy, as in Greece, population growth outstripped increases in supplies of food and raw materials. During the second century A.D. the population of Italy reached about 14 million persons, over 1,200,000 of whom lived in Rome. The large landholders of Italy, like those of Greece before them, specialized increasingly in cultivating the grape and the olive, with the result that grain-growing declined and importation of food became essential. Rome became so dependent upon imports that she had to go to great lengths to encourage trade.

With the decline of grain production in Italy, the commodity was produced in increasing quantities in other areas, especially in Gaul, North Africa, and Syria, and shipped to the capital of the empire. But as time went on the grain supplies of the Italian cities became insufficient. Rome was forced to issue an edict to the effect that all exported Egyptian grain was to be shipped to the capital of the empire.

Eventually the production of the Roman granaries could no longer keep pace with demand. According to Simkovitch:

Province after province was turned by Rome into a desert, for Rome's exactions naturally compelled greater exploitation of the conquered soil and its more rapid exhaustion. Province after province was conquered by Rome to feed the growing proletariat with its corn and enrich the prosperous with its loot. The only exception was Egypt, because of the overflow of the Nile. . . . Latium, Campania, Sardinia, Sicily, Spain, Northern Africa, as Roman granaries, were successively reduced to exhaustion. Abandoned land in Latium and Campania turned into swamps, in Northern Africa into a desert. The forest-clad hills were denuded.[1]

1. V. G. Simkovitch in *Toward the Understanding of Jesus, and Other Studies* (New York: The Macmillan Company, 1921).

During the third century A.D. there was a marked decline in the population of the Roman Empire brought about by wars, plagues, inadequate food supplies, and, related to these factors, a reluctance to raise children. By the end of the fifth century A.D. the empire had disintegrated.

In the civilizations of Greece and Rome, as in those which preceded them, and in ours today, few persons thought of the world in terms of populations, technics, and resources. Generally changes take place so slowly in relation to a single human lifetime that a given trend, which may have enormous long-range significance, goes unnoticed. But although the trends may escape observation, their consequences are felt by society as a whole and are reflected in various manifestations of culture—in philosophy, in custom, and in law.

Thus the population problems of the ancient empires, although they were not in general looked upon as problems, were reflected in the cultures. An individual would not ask, "Can my country feed more mouths?" But he would ask, "Can I personally feed another mouth?"

We see in Hebrew law changing attitudes, tending in general to liberalization, toward methods of family limitation. Plato and Aristotle permitted abortion. Nor was the practice condemned by any law in Greece or the Roman Republic. Infanticide was widely practiced in Greece, where the head of the family could dispose of his children as he wished. Generally, on the fifth day after birth, the father publicly proclaimed whether he would keep the child or not. Aristotle did not look with favor upon infanticide in his ideal legislation, but he treated it in a matter-of-fact way:

As to the exposure and rearing of children, let there be a law that no deformed child shall live, but that on the ground of an excess in the number of children, if the established customs of the state forbid this (for in our state population has a limit), no child is to be exposed, but when couples have children in excess, let abortion be procured before sense and life have begun; what may or may not be lawfully done in these cases depends on the question of life and sensation.

In Rome infanticide appears to have been in general use, although an old law enjoined the father to bring up all male children and at least the eldest female. Abortion appears to have been more widely practiced in Rome than in Greece.

Although few of the early writers and philosophers discussed the question of human populations in its broadest aspects, the early Christian writer Tertullian, a Carthaginian who had lived in Rome, wrote the following remarkable passage early in the third century A.D.:

We find in the records of the Antiquities of Man that the human race has progressed with a gradual growth of population. . . . Surely it is obvious enough, if one looks at the whole world, that it is becoming better cultivated and more fully peopled than anciently. All places are now accessible, all are well known, all open to commerce; most pleasant farms have obliterated all traces of what were once dreary and dangerous wastes; cultivated fields have subdued forests; flocks and herds have expelled wild beasts; sandy deserts are sown; rocks are planted; marshes are drained; and where once were hardly solitary cottages are now large cities. No longer are savage islands dreaded, nor their rocky shores feared; everywhere are houses, and inhabitants, and settled government, and civilized life. What most frequently meets our view is our teeming population; our numbers are burdensome to the world, which can hardly supply us from its natural elements; our wants grow more and more keen, and our complaints more bitter in all mouths, whilst nature fails in affording us her usual sustenance. In very deed, pestilence, and famine, and wars, and earthquakes have to be regarded as a remedy for nations, as a means of pruning the luxuriance of the human race.

Tertullian anticipated Malthus by nearly sixteen centuries. But as he wrote the above words, even he probably did not appreciate in full measure the difficulties in which the Roman Empire would soon find itself. Already Rome was wasting away. The effects of ruthless exploitation of soil and resources were beginning to take their toll. The economic decline had begun.

9.

During the dim days of pre-history, when most men were food-gatherers, the population of the small island we now call Great Britain probably did not exceed a few hundred individuals. The lands were then covered with dense forests and with marshes.

which effectively inhibited the development of agriculture. "The untamed forest was king," says Trevelyan.

Its moist and mossy floor was hidden from heaven's eye by a close-drawn curtain woven of innumerable treetops, which shivered in the breezes of summer dawn and broke into wild music of millions upon millions of wakening birds; the concert was prolonged from bough to bough with scarcely a break for hundreds of miles over hill and plain and mountain, unheard by man save where, at rarest intervals, a troop of skin-clad hunters, stone-axes in hand, moved furtively over the ground beneath, ignorant that they lived upon an island, not dreaming that there could be other parts of the world besides this damp green woodland with its meres and marshes, wherein they hunted, a terror to its four-footed inhabitants, and themselves afraid.[1]

Long before the beginnings of Rome, traders from the ancient oriental empires came to the island of Britain and found there pearls, copper, gold, and tin. The primitive natives learned the art of smelting, and by 2000 B.C. an age of bronze had begun. Trade routes appeared, connecting widely separated tribes. Ports grew up, tiny centers of trading with Ireland to the west, and with the European continent to the east. The plow was introduced, but for many centuries it could be utilized only in a few carefully chosen localities. The forests and the marshes remained inviolate.

When agriculture was first practiced on the island, probably no more than a few thousand persons lived there. But as farming slowly progressed, and as the areas under cultivation expanded, particularly after the introduction of iron, about 1000 B.C., the population increased.

After 600 B.C. a succession of people came to Britain from the European continent—Celts, Romans, Saxons. The Celts brought with them their own skills in ironwork and in arts and crafts, but they were not primarily an agricultural people. There was no significant development of urban culture in Britain until the Roman occupation, which started in the first century A.D. and lasted for about 250 years. However, when the occupation ended, the Roman-imposed urban culture ended with it, and the primary social units were once again the tribal center, the nomad camp, and the peasant village. Not enough people of Roman stock had come

1. G. M. Trevelyan, *History of England* (London: Longmans, Green and Company, 1926).

to Celtic Britain to change the island culture except superficially.

The area of agriculture and the area of land reclaimed from the forests and the marshes were both extended in Roman times. But it remained for the Nordic people, who displaced the Celts from the richest agricultural regions of the island between 300 A.D. and 1020 A.D., to make really major efforts to reclaim land for agricultural purposes. By the time of the Norman conquest in the eleventh century, about 20 per cent of the land area of the island was being farmed, and the population had risen to well over 1 million persons.

The rise continued during the twelfth and thirteenth centuries, apparently more rapidly than the gain in area resulting from deforestation and reclamation. By the middle of the fourteenth century the population was in the neighborhood of 4 million, and there was clearly a surplus of individuals, relative to the land that was farmed.

The situation was altered considerably by the appearance of plague, the Black Death, in 1348. This scourge, which wiped out about one-quarter of the population of Europe in a short time, reduced the population of England by one-third or one-half in less than 2 years. Subsequent recurrences of the disease prevented a return to the pre-Black-Death level until the beginning of the sixteenth century.

Urban developments came slowly. The towns and cities of fourteenth-century England were still, in the main, agricultural communities, and even the inhabitants of London led a half-rural existence. Pestilence hit the urban communities more heavily than the more sanitary rural ones and inhibited rapid city development. By the middle of the sixteenth century London appears to have contained about 100,000 persons. But by the opening of the seventeenth century urban communities were on the increase—in spite of recurrent visits of the Black Death—and the population of London had reached about 200,000.

During these early stages of urban developments there was increased use of non-human and non-animal energy. By the end of the eleventh century there were 5000 water-mills in England. During the twelfth century use of the windmill spread rapidly over Europe, and soon hundreds of the machines were in operation on the island. The new techniques of using water and wind power accelerated the development of both mining and manufacturing, and to some extent the windmill aided in the reclamation of the English fens.

By the sixteenth century the island, which had once been in large measure covered with a roof of trees, was experiencing a shortage of timber. Deforestation had continued at a rapid pace, both to increase the area of agricultural land and to provide wood for building and heating houses, fuel for the growing industries, and charcoal for the production of metallic iron. So severe did the shortage of wood become that in some regions families were deprived of the fire that had warmed the dwellings of their ancestors for so long, and which had, until then, been taken for granted.

Increased use was made of "sea-coal"—so named because it was brought to London by ship. As early as 1234 the freemen of Newcastle were given a charter to mine coal, and by the fourteenth century the fuel was being shipped to London in substantial quantities from Durham and Tyneside. There was, however, considerable prejudice against the use of coal as domestic fuel. Residents of London complained of "the stench of burning sea-coal," and an attempt was made to regulate the coal nuisance by ordinance.

As the wood shortage became more acute, prejudice gave way to necessity, and coal consumption increased rapidly. By 1550 approximately 50,000 tons of the fuel were being mined annually. Soon most of the surface coal was consumed, and the black seams were followed deeper into the earth. By the seventeenth century men were working 400 feet underground. By 1680 coal was being produced at a rate of 280,000 tons per year.

By the end of the seventeenth century the population of the island had grown to about 7 million persons, and London, in spite of plague and fire, had become a city of 674,000 inhabitants. Improved farming practices and an enormously increased trade had created a larger economic surplus than had previously existed. The new knowledge disseminated during the European Renaissance had struck the island with full impact and resulted in the emergence of scientists such as Gilbert, Napier, and Harvey; then Boyle, Hooke, and Newton. The Royal Society was founded in 1662, and it quickly became a world center of scientific activity. Exploration, colonization, trade, and exploitation brought wealth from the outside. The Guinea Company, the Levant Company, the East India Company, and the Hudson's Bay Company flourished.

During the early eighteenth century industry, agriculture, and commerce continued to expand. Harvests were good, food was cheap, and the people were in the main contented. Agriculture, industry, and commerce were in harmony. The peasants and craftsmen were better off than they had ever been, for the expanding trade was providing new markets for their products. Indeed, so fundamentally good and harmonious was life at that time that a modern Englishwoman writes:

Only the most prejudiced can deny that the eighteenth century, and especially the reign of Queen Anne, was for all classes one of the best times to have been alive in this country. It is idiocy to pretend that to live in a lovely countryside, to handle only comely things, and to know that only comely things will issue from your hands is of no importance when set beside the amount of cash in your purse. It was a great time, for reason was still living on the fertility of the Great Goddess. . . .[1]

But the "Golden Age of Anne" was not to last for long. Unknowingly, the people of the island were living on the edge of a new era. The scientists, the craftsmen, the engineers, and the manufacturers were, unaware of the consequences, laying the foundations for a sequence of developments that were destined to affect human society more drastically than any since the beginnings of primitive agriculture. Within a few brief decades the island would be transformed to an extent undreamed of by peasant, king, genius, or madman.

10.

The production of metallic iron from ore requires the use of carbon of high purity. For many centuries charcoal, prepared from wood by heating, constituted the only satisfactory source of carbon. As the wood shortage became more acute the iron industry of the island faced increasing difficulties. Smelting plants had to follow the timber and waterpower into the mountain districts. Seldom did locations of timber and ore coincide, and this situation gave rise to grave transportation problems.

1. Jacquetta Hawkes, *A Land* (New York: Random House, 1951).

Many attempts were made to substitute coal for charcoal in the production of iron, but until the eighteenth century little progress was made. The sulphur fumes given off by most coal continued to spoil the iron.

By 1709 Abraham Darby had learned to drive off the volatile fumes from coal by preheating, thus converting the fuel into "coke." The product, although usable for iron production, was not entirely satisfactory. Further experiments by Darby's son resulted in improved methods, and by 1753 the right kind of coke could be produced in quantity for the blast furnaces. The development came just in time. The younger Darby's wife wrote: "The Iron Trade of our own produce would have dwindled away, for wood for charcoal became very scarce, and landed gentlemen rose the prices of cord wood exceeding high. But from pit coal being introduced in its stead, the demand of wood charcoal is much lessened and in a few years I apprehend will set the use of that article aside."

Underground water was one of the major limiting factors in coal mining. In 1705 Thomas Newcomen and John Calley designed a steam engine that could furnish the power to pump water from the mines. A company was formed in 1716 to promote application of the machine, and soon the engines were used for draining a number of mines. By 1765 approximately 100 Newcomen engines were in use in the Wear and Tyne districts. As a result, coal production increased rapidly from 2,500,000 tons annually in 1700 to 4,500,000 tons annually in 1750. By that year practically all of the present English coal fields were in operation.

In 1764 Hargreaves constructed his "spinning jenny," a combination of many spindles into a single machine that could be run by one operator. The following year Watt constructed a steam engine which required only one-third the coal consumed by a Newcomen engine. In 1768 Arkwright and Kay produced the "water frame." By 1785 the steam engine was used to drive both the new spinning machines and power looms. These developments quickly led to the consolidation of small industries into larger factories. In 1782 there were two textile factories in Manchester. Twenty years later fifty-two such factories had appeared. By 1813 there were 2400 power looms in operation in England.

Each development catalyzed innumerable others. By the beginning of the nineteenth century men had conceived of the screw-propeller steamboat, the threshing machine, and the sewing machine. A chemical industry had appeared. Maudslay had developed the screw-cutting lathe, which made possible the automatic production of screws, bolts, and nuts, and standardization of such items.

As development followed development, demands for steel increased. Production jumped from 70,000 tons per year in 1788 to 250,000 tons per year in 1806. Demands for coal likewise increased rapidly. Production rose from 4,500,000 tons in 1750 to 10,000,000 tons in 1800 and 16,000,000 tons in 1829.

Simultaneously with the appearance of the new industrial machinery, improvements appeared both in agriculture and in public-health techniques. Smallpox inoculation was introduced from Turkey. In the period between 1720 and 1745 five major hospitals were founded in London. Between 1700 and 1825 over 150 hospitals and dispensaries were established in Britain. The practice of midwifery was revolutionized. Principles of hygiene based upon scientific observation were introduced into the armed forces, and from there they were diffused and influenced the habits of the general public. Steps were taken to decrease infant mortality among the poor. Bastard children, previously left by the roadside to die, or abandoned in rooms or on the street, were taken to foundling hospitals.

During the course of the eighteenth century approximately 2 million acres were added to the agricultural land of England and Wales by further conversion of waste and woodland. Scientific methods were applied to agriculture. The owners of many large estates set examples by holding demonstrations for their tenants for the purpose of teaching them proper farming methods. Crop yields increased to the point at which the output of wheat and barley was sufficient to feed the population at home and at the same time permit export of substantial quantities of cereals. Grass and root crops were raised to feed the cattle and sheep through the winter, thus putting to an end the traditional fall slaughters. Increased attention was paid to stock breeding, with the result that the cattle and sheep sold at one of the major island markets doubled in average weight between 1710 and 1795. Scurvy, which had previously been common even among the well-to-do, almost disappeared as a result of the changed diet.

Throughout the greater part of the eighteenth century death rates dropped significantly. With their decrease, and with but slightly changed birth rates, the population of the island increased rapidly. During the reign of a single king, George III (1760–1820), it rose in England and Wales from 7½ million to 14 million (see Figure 4).

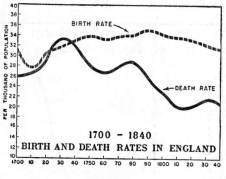

1700 – 1840
BIRTH AND DEATH RATES IN ENGLAND

FIGURE 4

The combination of increasing numbers of available jobs in the rapidly industrializing cities, improved transportation, and a population growth which exceeded by far the increase in the conversion of land to cultivation, led to large movements of workers from rural to urban districts. As early as 1771 the situation was deplored by an observer, who wrote:

To find fault with good roads would have the appearance of paradox and absurdity; but it is nevertheless a fact that giving the power of expeditious travelling depopulates the Kingdom. Young men and women in the country villages fix their eyes on London as the last stage of their hope. They enter into service in the country for little else but to raise money enough to go to London, which was no such easy matter when a stage coach was four or five days in creeping an hundred miles. The fare and the expenses ran high. *But now!* a country fellow, one hundred miles from London, jumps on a coach box in the morning, and for eight or ten shillings gets to town by night, which makes a material difference; besides rendering the going up and down so easy, the numbers *who have seen London* are increased tenfold, and of course ten times the boasts are sounded in the ears of country fools to induce them to quit their healthy clean fields for a region of dirt, stink and noise.

But the movement from country to city went on relentlessly. Although the population of the island as a whole was increasing, during the first part of the nineteenth century that of several rural areas actually began to decrease. By the middle of the nineteenth century half the people of the island lived in cities—a situation which at that time was unique in world history.

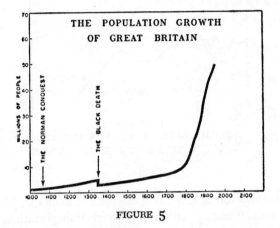

FIGURE 5

Invention followed invention, discovery followed discovery, and the island became one of the major workshops of the world. By the middle of the nineteenth century the world had seen, on the industrial side, the coming of railroads, the planing machine, Portland cement, the high-pressure steam boiler, the high-speed sewing machine, elevators, the electric battery, the dynamo, the telegraph, the vulcanization of rubber, steel cables, the electric engine, practical wood-pulp paper, the pneumatic tire, the rotating cylinder press, and the electric locomotive. On the medical and public-health side, there had appeared the stethoscope, anesthetics, and filtration plants for water. Food canning was beginning to shape future eating habits. Mechanical plowing and the mechanical reaper had begun to influence the future course of Western agriculture.

By 1850 the population of the island had reached 20 million.

Goods poured out of the factories and were shipped to the far reaches of the earth. Food and raw materials poured into the island cities from India, China, Egypt, America, the West Indies, Australia, and New Zealand. Death rates continued to decrease, and the population continued to rise rapidly. An increasingly large fraction of the people lived in cities.

Although foodstuffs were imported, the island was basically self-sufficient nutritionally until 1875. In that year the island civilization succumbed to the temptations that had faced the Greeks and the Romans before them. Food could be obtained less expensively outside the island, notably from America, than it could be produced at home. Local agriculture declined, and the people of the island became largely dependent upon food imports for their survival.

From 1875 onwards the catastrophe set in [says Trevelyan]. A series of bad seasons aggravated its initial stages, but the cause was the development of the American prairies as grain lands within reach of the English market. The new agricultural machinery enabled the farmers of the Middle West to skim the cream off virgin soils of unlimited expanse; the new railway system carried the produce to the ports; the new steamers bore it across the Atlantic. English agriculture was more scientific and more highly capitalized than American, but under these conditions the odds were too great. Mass production of crops by a simpler and cheaper process undercut the elaborate and expensive methods of farming which had been built up on well-managed English estates during the previous two hundred years. The overthrow of the British landed aristocracy by the far-distant democracy of American farmers was one outcome of this change of economic circumstance. An even more important consequence has been the general divorce of Englishmen from life in contact with nature, which in all previous ages had helped to form the mind and the imagination of the island race.[1]

II.

While Abraham Darby was experimenting with the production of metallurgical coke, and Newcomen engines were being installed in English coal mines, the colonies that had been established on

[1] G. M. Trevelyan, *English Social History* (London: Longmans, Green and Company, 1942).

the eastern coast of North America were growing rapidly. Man had brought European agricultural methods to the vast new continent which possessed such apparently limitless resources and which had previously been occupied only by primitive people living at the low population densities characteristic of predominantly food-gathering groups. Although life in the newly settled areas was rugged, the vast supplies of fresh fertile land made it relatively easy to produce an abundance of the basic necessities of life, with the result that the colonial population doubled about every 25 years. Peter Kalm, a Swedish observer of the colonial scene, wrote:

It does not seem difficult to find out the reasons why the people multiply more here than in Europe. As soon as a person is old enough, he may marry in these provinces without any fear of poverty; for there is such a tract of good ground yet uncultivated, that a new married man can, without difficulty, get a spot of ground, where he may sufficiently subsist with his wife and children. The taxes are very low, and he need not be under any concern on their account. The liberties are so great, that he considers himself a prince in his possessions.

Kalm spoke further of two women of New England, one of whom "has brought sixteen children into the world; and from seven of them only, she had one hundred and seventy-seven grandchildren and great-grandchildren." The second woman, at death in her hundreth year of age, "could count altogether five hundred children, grandchildren, great-grandchildren, and great-great-grandchildren."

Life in the colonies was predominantly rural, and England did everything possible to keep it so by forbidding the exportation of manufactured goods from the colonies to England or to other colonies, and by forbidding the erection of furnaces for making steel or mills for rolling or slitting iron. The new colonies existed primarily for the advancement of the mother country—they were expected to send raw materials to England and be a market for finished English goods.

England's attempts to enforce her mercantile policy in America led to growing friction, and eventually to the War of Independence. By 1789 the constitution of a new nation, the United States of America, was in effect; it bound together under a common government a population of somewhat less than four million persons, over 95 per cent of whom lived east of the Alleghenies. The vast majority were attached to the land, devoting most of their time to agriculture. There were but 6 cities with a population of 8000 or more, and a mere 3.3 per cent of the people lived in them. This was the scene into which the Industrial Revolution was introduced, some 50 years after it had started to transform English life.

Great Britain attempted to prevent knowledge of her new machinery from being carried abroad by enacting legislation preventing emigration of machine operators and export of textile machinery or plans or models of such machinery. But by 1791 a spinning mill was in operation in the United States. It contained spinning machines which had been built from memory by Samuel Slater, who had come to America in 1789. By 1810 there were 269 cotton mills and 87,000 spindles in the United States. In 1814 machinery was set up in Waltham, Massachusetts, where for the first time spinning and weaving were brought together in one factory.

Once the machine age got under way in America, developments followed each other rapidly. Metals industries were established in the middle states, where major deposits of iron and coal were located. Stoves, iron rails, and farm tools were manufactured. Americans turned to inventing, and during the decade 1850–1860 approximately 28,000 patents were recorded. Increased industrialization brought with it increased urbanization, with the result that by 1860 over 16 per cent of the expanded population was living in cities of over 8000 persons.

By 1860 the population of the United States had increased eightfold over that which had existed in 1790. The territorial limits of the country had been expanded over threefold as the result of the Louisiana and Florida Purchases, the annexations of Texas and the Oregon Country, and the Mexican Cession. One-half of the population lived west of the Alleghenies, and the number of cities and towns of over 8000 persons had increased to 141. Some of the cities had grown to substantial size: New York had passed the million mark; Philadelphia and Baltimore had 565,000 and 200,000 inhabitants respectively.

Most of the farm machinery in use today had been invented by 1860, and the agricultural revolution was under way—speeded

by cheap land and expensive labor, which hastened mechanization. With an increasingly effective transportation system which
expedited the export of agricultural products, farm production increased rapidly. The Civil War gave further impetus to agriculture, and during the war years the wheat crop was greater than
at any previous time. Wool production rose from 40 million to
140 million pounds.

The Civil War also gave enormous impetus to factory production. During the period 1860 to 1870 the number of manufacturing
establishments increased by nearly 80 per cent, and the number
of wage earners by 56 per cent. Energy consumption increased—
in part to heat the homes of the larger population, and in part to
turn the wheels of the newly founded industries.

In 1820 only 300 tons of bituminous coal were mined. By 1860
coal production had reached 15 million tons annually. By 1870
it had increased almost another threefold. Use of waterpower had
increased sixfold over the 1800–1809 level of consumption. As
wood resources in the eastern part of the country declined dan-
gerously, consumption of fossil fuels increased rapidly. The
striking of oil in Pennsylvania in 1859 gave rise to a new industry
that was destined to have enormous influence upon both the
nation and the world.

Consumption of wood for fuel reached its peak in the 1870s,
and by the 1880s the United States was obtaining more energy
from coal than from any other source. By 1900 coal consumption
had passed 240 million tons annually—greater than that of the
United Kingdom—and pig-iron production was greater than 15
million tons annually. By 1910 there was more railroad mileage
in the United States than in all of Europe.

The first century of the existence of the United States as a
nation was characterized by an unrestrained scramble for wealth
—a situation which led John Stuart Mill, as early as 1848, to point
to the nation as a horrible example of a society in which material
progress is the ultimate goal and where "the life of the whole of
one sex is devoted to dollar-hunting, and of the other to breeding
dollar-hunters." In 1860 there were probably no more than 3
millionaires in the country, but by 1900 the number had jumped to
about 3800. It is estimated that by 1900 only 10 per cent of the
people owned 90 per cent of the nation's wealth.

By the turn of the present century the population of the United States had reached 76 million, and the shift from rural to urban existence had reached the point where over 40 per cent of the population were town and city dwellers. Mechanical power was beginning to transform farm life rapidly and already provided approximately one-fifth of the farm power. The nation as a whole was on the threshold of a period characterized by the development and rapid expansion of electricity and of the internal combustion engine. Already 1 million telephones were in use. The project of harnessing Niagara had been accomplished. More than 2000 electrical power stations had come into existence.

The developments during the first 50 years of the twentieth century produced changes at an unprecedented rate. The automobile revolutionized both transportation and production techniques. Electricity made possible the design of production and control systems of previously unsuspected efficiency and versatility. Production per man-hour, both in the factory and on the farm, climbed ever higher.

By 1950 the shift to machine power had changed America from a rural agricultural nation to an industrial colossus in which the individual inhabitants had more material possessions than the inhabitants of any previous or any other contemporary society. Productivity per man-hour had climbed to more than five times the level that had existed a century previously. Three-quarters of the population of 150 million persons were urbanites. Less than 13 per cent of the labor force was engaged in agricultural work. Human and animal power, both on the farm and in the factory, had become insignificant when compared with the huge amount of mechanical power available.

The colossal industrial machinery of the nation consumed vast quantities of energy and of raw materials. By 1950 per capita consumption of energy had risen to the equivalent of nearly 10 tons of coal per person per year. Iron ore was being removed from the ground at the rate of nearly 1 ton per person per year. Consumption of other materials such as copper, lead, sulphur, and phosphates had risen to levels that would have seemed fantastic 50 years previously.

Already there were rumblings that supply might not fulfill demand indefinitely. In 1947 the United States became a net importer of oil—i.e., more petroleum products were imported than were exported. Long previously she had become a net importer of manganese, chromium, nickel, tin, mercury, cobalt, and bauxite. Yet it was predicted that during the period 1950 to 1975 both population and per capita consumption would expand further,

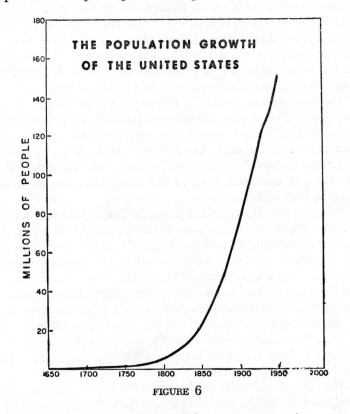

FIGURE 6

resulting in greatly increased total consumptions of most raw materials. It was predicted that although the population might increase only an additional 25 to 30 per cent during that period, consumption of electrical energy would increase nearly fourfold, consumption of petroleum would more than double, steel production would increase 50 per cent, aluminum production might increase fivefold, and demands for copper and zinc might increase another 80 per cent.

It was admitted that the United States would have difficulty meeting these demands with her own resources. Already copper ores containing only 0.7 per cent copper were being mined. Major plans were under way for processing relatively low-grade iron ore. It was believed that manganese and lead imports might increase 60 per cent, copper and zinc imports might double, cadmium imports might increase fivefold.

There were other rumblings. The United States was still self-sufficient agriculturally, and there was good reason to believe that she could remain self-sufficient for centuries. But deforestation, the mining of soil, and general abuse of the land had resulted in a series of catastrophes ranging from floods to dust bowls. Top soil was being washed into the sea at an enormous rate. Streams were being polluted by industries. Ground water was being pumped at rates which were greater than rates of replenishment.

In the meantime people in other areas of the world saw the vast quantities of material possessions in the hands of the people in Western Europe and the United States, and wanted similar possessions for themselves. Industrialization spread to Japan and to the Soviet Union. Signs of impending major attempts to industrialize could be seen in Southern Asia and in South America. By 1950 it seemed likely that industrialization, like agriculture, might one day become world-wide.

Yet already the first of the great industrial powers was on the decline. Great Britain could no longer feed her expanded population, nor could she provide herself with raw materials to feed her industries. In order to obtain food and raw materials she had to export manufactured goods. Yet her markets for manufactured products were steadily dwindling. And her people wondered if Great Britain—like Egypt, Greece, and Rome in times long past —was destined for oblivion.

Chapter II:

STATUS QUO

> *All civilization has from time to time become a thin crust over a volcano of revolution.*
> HAVELOCK ELLIS

1.

As we have seen, man emerged in a universe of other biological creatures, but he was superior to other creatures in that he was endowed with a vastly improved brain which permitted him to solve relatively complex problems and to speak—abilities which in turn permitted him to invent tools for accomplishing specific tasks, to consult with his fellow men, and to transmit his experience to his offspring. Following the initial use of controlled fire, which extended the range of his foods and tools, and thus compensated for his lack of such biological weapons as claws and fangs, the number of human beings on the earth's surface, after reaching about 10 million, probably remained more or less stationary for many millennia. The population was then limited by the extent to which accessible edible vegetable and animal life existed in nature, and by man's ability to compete with other animals for food.

Eventually man learned how to encourage the growth of edible plants and to domesticate animals that would provide food or perform useful work. Populations then started to increase rapidly, for a given area, when placed under cultivation, will support far more persons than will an area left in a natural state. The new techniques spread most rapidly in those areas which could be cultivated readily—primarily the great river valleys, which were endowed with both ample water and naturally recurrent fertilization.

The spread of agriculture made it possible for one man to grow sufficient food to feed more than his family alone. There arose, as a consequence, first the peasant village and then the city, within which lived those persons who were not directly connected with the production of foodstuffs. And with the cities there gradually emerged a vast fabric of knowledge that permitted man to extend his techniques to new areas. He learned to irrigate, to cut forests, to fertilize, and to cross the seas in search of additional food and raw materials. He learned to extract metals from ores and to fashion them into tools and weapons to aid him in those tasks.

As the agricultural revolution spread over a large part of the world, and as the urban revolution followed in those regions where transportation permitted, human populations increased. Except on rare occasions, population increases kept pace with the limits of land productivity under the conditions then prevailing. Occasionally a new technique or the spread of old techniques to new lands, or a catastrophe, relieved the pressure temporarily. But the periods of respite were short when compared with the span of human history. In practically all times in practically all places, some human beings have lived on a marginal subsistence basis, and, either rapidly or slowly, they have starved.

Long before the urban revolution had spread over the entire globe, man learned how to harness non-animal energy. He first harnessed falling water and the winds, but eventually he learned to make machines that could convert the energy of wood and coal into useful work. Soon a man working in a machine-powered factory could produce far more goods than could a man attempting to fabricate the same goods by hand. Equally important, machines made possible the fabrication of articles which otherwise could have been made only with the greatest difficulty. The new power also enabled one man working on a farm to feed several men working in the city, in addition to his own family.

Man learned that he could understand nature, and by understanding it he could control many natural phenomena. He experimented and formulated laws which enabled him to predict the behavior of physical systems. He learned to fabricate an ever-greater diversity of machines and products. He learned something of the behavior of biological systems and soon was able to breed plants and animals which possessed characteristics better fitted to his needs than were those which he had found in their natural states. His knowledge of biological systems enabled him to control many diseases which threatened his existence.

The new machines and products, coupled with the new knowledge, made possible increases in crop yields and extension of agriculture to more difficult areas. The new developments made possible the transportation of food rapidly over long distances from regions of agricultural surplus to regions of agricultural deficiency. Thus, in the part of the world which possessed the new machines and the new products, famine was in large measure eliminated.

When we look at the world about us today, we see that man has spread to every region of the world where he can in some manner eke out an existence. Tierra del Fuego, the jungles of Brazil, the dry grasslands of North America, the tundra regions of the north, the islands of the Pacific, the oases of the Sahara, and the heights of the Tibetan plateau—no matter how remote the location or how difficult the existence, if human life can in some manner be sustained, human beings will usually be found attempting to live there.

Agriculture supports most of the people of the earth, but actually only a small fraction of the earth's surface is covered with cultivated fields. There are regions, such as the Arctic and certain heavily forested areas of the tropics, where people still live on a food-gathering basis. There are wide expanses of land which support only sparse growths of grasses and which can be used only for grazing. There are other regions which are too mountainous for crops and which can be used only for feeding domesticated animals.

Thus the population of human beings on the earth's surface is very unevenly distributed. Densities of human beings are greatest in those areas where agriculture can be carried out relatively easily and where agricultural techniques have been practiced for a long time; and they are low where intensive agriculture is impractical and life can be sustained only by hunting and fishing, or by domesticating animals and leading a nomadic existence.

Most groups of people in the world have passed through the

agricultural revolution, but only a few have passed through the
Industrial Revolution. In those regions which have not industrialized, life goes on very much as it has for many centuries. Most
people are farmers, and on the average well over 100 male agri-

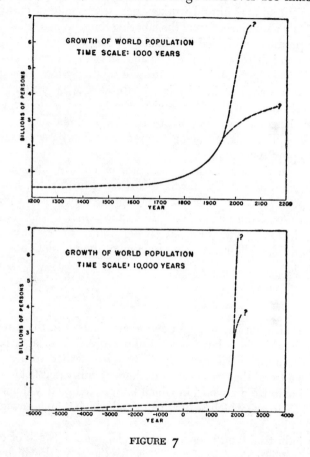

FIGURE 7

culturalists work on 1 square mile of cultivated land. Birth rates
are high—usually at the biological maximum—and until very
recently they were matched in most such areas by equally high
death rates. Populations lie close to the limit of subsistence and
are pruned constantly by slow starvation and at intervals of time
by pestilence and famine. Personal possessions are few, as there

is not the wherewithal either to manufacture or to purchase many goods. Work is done entirely with human and animal energy.

Modern industrial countries are characterized by low densities of population in agricultural areas—on the average there are only about 30 agricultural workers per square mile of cultivated land. Only a small fraction of the laboring force is engaged directly in the production of food, the balance being engaged in the production and distribution of goods and services. Nutritional levels are relatively high, and death rates are relatively low. Low death rates are nearly matched by low birth rates. A large fraction of the work, both on the farm and in the factory, is done by machines. Personal possessions are relatively abundant, for large quantities of goods are manufactured, and many people can afford to purchase them.

Between the two existing extremes of culture, characterized by extremes of nutrition levels, death rates, birth rates, and personal possessions, there are several regions which are in process of transition from one way of life to the other. Death rates are being lowered. Factories are being built. Farms are being mechanized, and an increasing fraction of the population is living in cities.

2.

Industrialization has wrought enormous changes in those regions of the world which have successfully evolved from agrarian societies into industrial ones. The factory has carried to near completion a trend that was started in the first cultivated field—it has moved man from a world in which he was completely dominated by nature to one which he dominates and which is in large measure man-made.

An industrial world consists of an elaborate network of causes and effects. In a very real sense it is like the network which exists in the universe of biological creatures—if one part of it is disturbed or modified, all parts become disturbed or modified. But whereas the universe of biological creatures possesses an over-all stability that has been achieved through no conscious directed action, but rather through the operation of natural laws which govern the behavior of biological systems, the industrial society is largely man-conceived and man-operated. Long-range stability in an industrial world cannot easily come into existence accidentally. The achievement of anything approaching stability depends first upon the extent to which man understands the causes and effects that exist within his society, and second upon his desire to create a stable situation.

The boundary which separates an agrarian society from an industrial one is fraught with major obstacles, which make a transition from one condition to the other extremely difficult. A given agrarian society might possess all the resources necessary to exist comfortably as an industrial society, yet the barrier between the two conditions might be too high to be surmounted. Indeed, it appears in retrospect that modern industrial society came into existence in the first place only as the result of a remarkable series of circumstances.

When the Industrial Revolution came to Europe, one of the early major effects was a lowering of the death rate. This apparently came about at first as the result of increased food supplies, and, to a lesser extent, as the result of improvements in public-health techniques. The increased food supplies came from several sources. New tools, and their greater general availability, permitted more rapid extension of agricultural lands. Water could be more easily drained from swamps. Trees and rocks could be more easily removed from potentially arable soil. Manufactured goods could be sold abroad in regions of agricultural surplus, and food could be imported. Higher yields could be obtained from existing agricultural lands by investing in land improvements and by applying scientific methods to agriculture.

Of course, with greatly reduced death rates, the population increased far more rapidly than it had increased in previous times. But improvements in the availability of food were able to keep pace with the rate of population expansion. In addition, emigration from Europe to the vast undeveloped lands of the Americas and Oceania provided some relief from population pressure. The emigrants and their offspring in turn were able to produce surplus foodstuffs and ship them to Europe in exchange for manufactured goods.

In addition to its fortunate situation with respect to availability of food, Europe was richly endowed with the major raw materials which are necessary for industrial expansion. Thus, once coal was linked to iron, her industries were able to expand rapidly with little danger of stoppage due to depletion of those resources.

As industry expanded, the population continued to increase rapidly, but by 1850 a new and unexpected effect was noticeable, an effect which was destined to play an enormously important role in the subsequent evolution of industrial civilization. Family sizes were decreasing, apparently in part because of a conscious desire to have fewer children and in part because of postponement of marriage—a cultural development resulting from increased social and economic pressures. The effect was most noticeable in the urban areas and in the more well-to-do classes, where children came to be looked upon more as economic and social burdens than as economic assets. With increasing urbanization, the effect of smaller families became more evident. Eventually, in spite of the decreasing death rate, the rate of population expansion ceased to climb and within a few decades began to fall noticeably. By now, the continued growth of population in Western Europe results far more from the effect of increased longevity than from an actual excessive reproduction rate. Indeed, during the period which preceded World War II, fears were expressed that the countries of Western Europe might fail to reproduce and might eventually dwindle into extinction.

The United States followed a similar pattern of evolution. There was ample arable land for expansion of food production. Iron, coal, and other mineral resources were abundant, as were also wood and waterpower. As in Europe, the population expanded at a prodigious rate. But as urbanization increased, families became smaller. By 1850 the average number of children borne by one woman had dropped from 8 to 6. By 1900 it had dropped to 4.

When we look back upon the circumstances that led to the growth of industrial civilization in Western Europe, we see that, had conditions been somewhat different, it is possible that the revolution might have been stopped short at any one of a number of points. Of course, a prerequisite was the existence of the necessary major raw materials. But beyond that, it is doubtful that industrial civilization would have arisen had the relation between the number of people and the amount of land not been so favorable, and had the potential increases in food production not been so great. The existence of America and other major colonies. which provided outlets for surplus people and reservoirs of agricultural products, was an extremely important factor. Another factor of importance was medical ignorance. Medical knowledge was increasing steadily, but it was small when compared with that which exists today. Thus, although European populations increased rapidly, the rate of growth was small when compared with rates that would have prevailed had epidemic and endemic diseases been controlled to the extent that is now possible. And finally, people learned how to limit birth rates. Had this new factor not entered the picture, it is probable that all advances industrialization made possible would have been negated.

For industrial development to be successful, it is necessary that production be increased at a rate more rapid than the rate of population increase. If production in a nation remains constant while the population grows, the people will become worse off with each succeeding year, for the same amount of goods must be distributed among a larger number of people. If production increases at the same rate as the rate of population growth, the condition of the people with respect to available goods will, of course, remain stationary.

The United States was in the fortunate position of being able to accumulate capital by producing excess agricultural products and selling them to European nations. Thus, although its industrial growth did not exceed its population growth until about 1890, it had nevertheless accumulated a sizable amount of capital by that time. Following 1890, production increased more rapidly than population, with a consequent further rapid increase of capital and greater general availability of goods. However, if the political and economic conditions had been such that the capital was not accumulated, production would have increased indefinitely at a rate far lower than the rate of population increase. Under these circumstances, the United States might have been destined to be primarily a large, overpopulated, and predominantly agricultural country.

Thus, by a sequence of events which will probably never again be repeated, industrialization came to the Western World—an area which today embraces only about one-fifth of the world's population. Once the new culture became deeply rooted, developments followed each other with incredible rapidity. Education became widespread, and illiteracy was practically eliminated. The combination of adequate nourishment and the rapid expansion of medical research and public-health techniques raised average life expectancy at birth from 50 years in 1900 to nearly 70 years in 1950. Scientists, inventors, and engineers designed an accelerated flow of new products, devised new production techniques, and greatly increased output per man-hour. Working hours were reduced, and the flow of goods per capita continued to increase rapidly. It began to appear that the combination of science, engineering, and industry might eventually transform the world into a paradise where everyone would have enough to eat, where individuals might own practically all of the material goods they might possibly desire.

However, just as the human body cannot survive on air alone, an industrial machine must be provided with energy and with raw materials if it is to survive. As industrial activity has expanded, consumption of wood, oil, coal, and a diversity of minerals has expanded proportionately. And whereas at one time industrial activity was so small that most raw materials appeared to be of infinite extent, our demands have now reached the point at which we can visualize an end to the supply of many of the basic raw materials to which we have become accustomed. At an early date wood became impracticable as a major motivating energy source in most industrial areas. A large part of the potential hydroelectric power available to most industrial areas has already been developed. The widespread demand for liquid fuels has resulted in partial dependence of some industrial areas, and total dependence of others, upon the oil resources of underdeveloped areas. Exploitation of coal in Great Britain is becoming increasingly difficult because of the great depths at which mining must be undertaken, and because of the steepness and narrowness of the coal seams. Most industrial nations must now import substantial fractions of many of the minerals which they require.

The existing situation with respect to energy sources and raw materials in the Western World raises many vital questions. How much greater will the demands for energy and raw materials become? As our mineral sources dwindle, for how long a time will we be able to import our requirements? By purchasing non-renewable raw materials from the underdeveloped areas, are we not decreasing their chances of industrializing? When we are no longer able to obtain high-grade ores either at home or abroad, will industry cease to function? When the world's supply of fossil fuels has been consumed, will society revert to an agrarian, or perhaps even to a primitive state?

3.

Approximately two-thirds of the world's population lives under conditions in which both birth rates and death rates are extremely high and the total food production is insufficient to provide adequate nourishment for everyone. The population of a given unindustrialized agrarian society such as in China or India depends first upon the total amount of food that is produced, and second upon the way in which the food is distributed. The latter factor is determined in turn by the nature of the social organization. In such societies birth rates are approximately constant, and death rates fluctuate with crop yields and social organization. Fluctuations in death rates in turn produce fluctuations in populations.

In an agrarian society at equilibrium, the natural fixed birth rate is equaled over long periods of time by the sum of the death rates from all causes: starvation, disease, accident, and old age. Such a biological system can obviously be perturbed in many ways, and we are now observing major perturbations in such societies, resulting from the influences of the industrialized areas of the world. It is important that we understand the manner in which these influences operate.

Let us assume an area on which a fixed maximum amount of food can be produced and where the population has grown to the limit that can be supported under existing conditions. Let us assume further that the average individual receives 2400 calories [1] each day, which is less than the optimum caloric intake, but nevertheless well above the starvation level. However, within the society there are some persons with a great deal of land and others with very little land, and the spectrum of wealth results in unequal distribution of food among the people. Thus, some wealthy

1. The term "calorie," as used throughout this book, is the "large calorie" (1000 small calories) used by nutritionists.

persons obtain far more than the average and live very com-·
fortably, while others in turn obtain far less than the average and
either starve to death or become sufficiently malnourished to
succumb to infections that would not otherwise have been lethal.
Under the pattern of culture which exists, the population oscillates
about an average level, and over a long period of time the deaths
resulting from all causes equal the births.

Let us assume further that the region we are discussing is composed of several areas which differ somewhat in climate, and between which communications are poor. Every so often each of the
areas is subjected to a famine resulting from a catastrophe such
as a drought, a wave of insect pests, or a hurricane. Let us assume
that each famine substantially reduces the population of an area
so efficiently that several decades are required for it to return to
its previous level. During the period of recovery there is little
starvation, and indeed there is a potential food surplus.

The recurrent famines in the areas which together make up the
region as a whole contribute substantially to the death rate of the
region and thus play an important part in determining the average
population level. Let us suppose that we now build in the region
a network of railroads linking the various areas. When a part of
the network is completed, a drought occurs in area A, but food
can now be shipped from area B, which is still recovering from a
famine of a decade previously and is thus able to produce a food
surplus. Gradually, as the network is extended, famine is eliminated and all land is kept at maximum productivity. The population climbs until a new level is reached, determined by the higher
level of average food production.

Let us suppose that the society within the region is reorganized,
and that laws placing a limit on the size of an individual's agricultural holdings are enacted and enforced. Large farms are
divided among those persons who have little or no land, thus
eliminating the situation in which one group obtains far more
and another far less than its share of food. Wealthy persons who
formerly received 3200 calories, and persons at the lower end of
the economic scale who formerly barely existed on 1500 calories,
now receive equal shares of food, averaging 2400 calories per
person. This change results in greatly reduced death rates within

the lower classes, and the population once again starts to increase. Inevitably a new group of starving individuals gradually appears, and the death rate moves upward as the result of generally lowered resistance. When the average intake drops to 2200 calories, the death rate once again equals the birth rate, and the population becomes stabilized at the new level.

Within the society with its new level of population, a substantial fraction of the deaths result from certain diseases that can be completely controlled by vaccinations and inoculations. A public-health program is started in the region, aimed at eliminating these diseases. Eventually, when several major causes of death have been eliminated in this way, the population climbs to a new level, the average caloric intake drops to 2000 calories, and starvation becomes a still more frequent cause of death.

Thus we see that although the production of food ultimately determines the number of people who can live in a given region, the number who actually exist is determined by numerous social factors. Without in any way changing the amount of arable land or the agricultural techniques, any one of a number of population equilibria can be established. But once maximum productivity from the land is achieved, all population increases result in lower caloric intake per capita, lower average vitality, and a worsened condition for the society as a whole.

We can see various factors which have been discussed thus far in operation in most unindustrialized areas of the world today. For 2000 or 3000 years prior to 1850, India probably had a stable population of somewhere between 50 and 100 million persons. Arts and crafts flourished, and India traded with the Western World, exchanging silks and other products for gold.

During the years between 1850 and 1900 the Indian population expanded rapidly, and one can see associated with this increase much improvement of internal transport, coupled with considerable effort upon the part of Great Britain to ameliorate famines. With improved transport and organized effort, grain could be taken from areas of surplus and transported to areas of food deficiency. For a while, following these improvements, there were indications that the population would again level off, but as the great epidemic diseases—smallpox, plague, and cholera—came

under control, the population took another swing upward. During
the greater part of this time the increase in food production lagged
behind that in population. Food production reached a peak in
1940, and since that time has at best remained stationary.

Since 1940 the population of the Indian sub-continent has been
increasing at a rate of about 5 million persons per year. Food
imports have been increasing, and it is estimated that at the
present time approximately 10 per cent of the Indian caloric intake has its origin outside the country. Of course, importation of
food serves to aggravate the situation still further, for, fed by
domestic food production plus imports, the population climbs to
new levels.

Over 90 per cent of the total man-hours worked in India are
devoted to the production, handling, and transportation of food.
Only 4 per cent of the people are engaged in industrial work. Thus
India is almost entirely an agricultural nation; yet it is quite clear
that the country is unable to feed itself.

In order to expand its food production appreciably, India would
have to extend the acreage which is now cultivated, or increase
the crop yields. Either of these improvements, both of which are
possible in principle, would require capital, knowledge, and
labor—the first two necessarily accumulated from the past. But,
as we have seen, whatever capital India might have had at one
time has long ago been used up. Without capital, technical
knowledge is ineffective, and unused knowledge is little better
than ignorance. India's only recourse has been to intensive
farming, so intensive it is even difficult to divert labor for the
purpose of making long-range improvements. To quote W. H.
Forbes, a recent observer:

It is almost impossible to take a million men off the land to build dams,
because if you do the food that they would have raised is not raised
and therefore food for the builders of the dam must be taken from the
farmers, who then die of starvation. The latest example of this process
was in the Bengal famine of 1943, when the Indian government provided a large number of workmen for building roads, airfields, barracks
and the like for the United States and British troops based there for
the Burma campaign. These workmen produced no food but were fed
on food bought locally, which raised the price until the farmers sold
their own food stores, believing that they could buy food later cheaper.

The price continued up and about 2 to 3 million farmers died of starvation.[1]

Mr. Forbes stresses that India was once a rich and powerful nation, and asks: "What great disaster or gross mismanagement has reduced her to permanent poverty and starvation?" And he answers: "There has been no great disaster. There has been merely the predictable operation of a natural law, a relentless rain of small disasters, 46 per thousand persons per year. . . . And to any of you who may be shocked by my referring to babies as disasters, I believe that field work in Calcutta would convince most people that when the ratio of food to population is small enough, babies are both a personal and a general disaster."

The situations in other agrarian unindustrialized areas of the world differ from the situation in India in degree rather than in kind. The population of India has probably increased more rapidly than has that of China in recent decades, primarily as the result of the greater exposure of the former to certain of the life-saving features of Western civilization. But the same types of changes can take place in all agrarian cultures, and indeed in many other areas of the world we see these processes in operation. Throughout large regions good-intentioned governments, foundations, churches, and individuals have attempted to superimpose a part of Western culture upon agrarian societies, with results that can at best be described as disastrous. Few persons can stand by and watch others suffer without attempting to do something about it. The remedial measures appear obvious at first: improved public health and improved food production. But the enormous potentials for population increase that exist in such remedies quickly undo whatever relief might have been initially obtained, and in many areas the "cure" only stimulates a worse disease.

Some of the dangers are well illustrated by a project recently undertaken in Egypt by the Rockefeller Foundation, designed to study the effect of different facilities for health improvement in five villages with a uniformly low standard of health. In less than 2 years the infant mortality dropped to less than one-third, while the birth rate remained the same. Infant mortality before the project was started was 46 per cent, and approximately 1 out of

1. W. H. Forbes, *Federation Proceedings*, Vol. II, page 667 (1952).

6 persons born reached the age of 20. The degree of health improvement made it appear likely that 5 out of 6 persons born would survive to the age of 20.

Puerto Rico is an outstanding example of an area where a great deal of effort has gone into superimposing advanced public-health techniques on a culture that is predominantly agrarian. A student of population problems describes the situation as follows:

Like a child with a bright new toy, the Americans were eager to bring the blessings of the twentieth century to this unhappy land. Schools, colleges, and experiment stations were constructed; a modest health program was instituted. . . .

Time passed, but the island's depression continued. Good intentions, and very considerable outlays of cash to implement them, brought only one major change in Puerto Rico, the population began to increase, at first gradually and then faster. Every decade since 1898 has seen a large—and accelerating—increase in numbers. The growth in population testified to the fact that modern medicine, public-health programs, sanitation, and the complex tools of the vital age were working as planned. Fewer people were dying of yellow fever, puerperal fever, and epidemics of all kinds. . . .

The medieval, essentially urban Spanish colonial culture had been supplanted almost overnight by one of the most modern and technically advanced civilizations of a new age. The new masters of the island had developed their civilization in an empty continent which set a high premium upon human life and upon human fertility. An ever-increasing population was required to populate a continent. The American philosophy could hardly conceive of a situation in which an increase in the number of people was undesirable, let alone dangerous. Nothing in the history of America suggested such an idea.[1]

In spite of the tremendous pressures in the world to increase the supplies of food, production is not increasing as rapidly as the population. The 1951 report of the Food and Agricultural Organization of the United Nations states: "Most of those who were hungry in the five prewar years are now hungrier. . . . Production in most of the undernourished areas is failing to keep pace with population growth." The 1952 report was somewhat more optimistic, for increasing food production had managed barely to keep pace with increasing population during the preceding twelve-month

1. R. C. Cook, *Human Fertility* (New York: William Sloane Associates, 1951).

period. But in some of the larger undernourished areas of the world the situation was becoming even more critical. The Government of India Planning Commission, after studying resources, plans for increasing food production, and the possibilities of support from outside India, concluded that India's population will be less well fed in 1956 than in 1951.

With every passing year the underdeveloped areas of the world perceive more clearly the enormity of their poverty, and efforts are being made to industrialize. India has launched a complex Five-Year Plan, which includes construction of heavy industry, river development, public health, decrease of illiteracy, increase of crop yields, extension of cultivated lands, and birth control. Even if the government completes the plan it has outlined for itself, it will only be placed at the beginning of a long and complicated road, traversal of which will require many decades. India's efforts can be stopped at any one of a number of points. If she is unable to remove a sufficient number of persons from the land and at the same time greatly increase food production and lower birth rates, her efforts will be doomed to failure, for population will continue to rise faster than the production of farms and industry.

It seems clear that industrialization of the underdeveloped areas cannot be accomplished overnight, nor can it be accomplished without considerable further increase of population. In view of this, it is likely that the situation will get considerably worse before it gets better. Further, we must inquire: Is betterment of the situation really within the realm of possibility? And if betterment is possible, at what level can the greatly increased numbers be supported? Lastly, are the earth's resources sufficient to meet the enhanced demand?

4.

Approximately 20 per cent of the world's population lives in regions where the cultures are intermediate, between the extremes of agrarian culture, such as that of China or India, and industrial culture, such as that of the United States or Western Europe. Machine industry is spreading in these regions, and agriculture is improving. Death rates are moderate, and birth rates, although declining, are sufficiently high to produce a substantial rate of natural increase. Death rates are declining about as fast as, or faster than birth rates, with the result that the population of these areas will probably increase considerably during the coming decades. In some of these transition countries there is evidence that productivity will increase faster than population, thus resulting in gradually improved standards of living.

Japan, a nation which is important in the group of transition countries, was the first of the Eastern cultures to embark upon a major program of industrialization and urbanization. During the eighteenth and early nineteenth centuries, prior to the opening of Japan to the West, the population of Honshu, the largest island, was about 35 million. Mortality was high, and recurrent calamities such as famines, epidemics, and natural catastrophes served to maintain a relative stability in total numbers. Abortion and infanticide were practiced to some extent, but the over-all effect was apparently small compared with the effect of calamities.

Following the opening of Japan to the West, social change took place rapidly. Feudalism was abolished, and industrialization was speeded. The science and technology which had evolved in other areas accelerated both the growth of industry and the decline in the death rate. The population increased rapidly, but by 1920 it had become clear that birth rates were declining, primarily in the newly created urban centers. Urbanization progressed so rapidly that between 1920 and 1940 the increase in the populations of Japanese cities exceeded the increase of population of the islands as a whole. By 1940 the population had reached 73 million persons, and demographers estimated that early in the twenty-first century the population would cease to rise and would reach a maximum probably between 100 and 125 million persons.

The population transition and pattern of industrialization in Japan paralleled the development in the West in many respects, although the time scale was shorter and the combination of natural resources, population density, and availability of land for expansion was less favorable. Nevertheless, Japan's resources and social structure permitted her to maintain a rate of economic development of 4 per cent per year during the period 1900 to 1940. Areas of settlement were available in Hokkaido, Karafuto, and Nanyogunto. The conquest of Taiwan, Korea, Kwantung, and

Manchuria gave access to additional food and raw materials and provided space into which some of the crowded population of the home islands could expand.

By 1939 the death rate in Japan had been reduced to 17.8 per thousand, and the birth rate had been reduced to 26.6. World War II caused a major dislocation in the downward trends of both death rate and birth rate, and during the last 5 months of 1945 the death rate climbed to 32 per thousand. Japan experienced a postwar baby boom, and by 1947 the birth rate had risen to 34.3 per thousand.

Following the war, the occupation forces worked vigorously to improve living conditions. Attention was given to increasing food production, and a new system of land tenure was introduced. Public-health techniques were vigorously applied. The death rate was reduced from 32 per thousand in late 1945 to 17.6 in 1946, to 14.6 in 1947, to 11.9 in 1948, to 11.6 in 1949. During this period the birth rate declined only slightly, to 33.2—a level considerably above the prewar rate. The net result of these changes has been that the rate of population increase has jumped from a prewar rate of less than 1 per cent per year to a rate in 1949 of well over 2 per cent per year. By 1950 the population was over 83 million, and the population density had reached 566 persons per square mile. It is now estimated that the population may well reach 100 million sometime between 1960 and 1965.

Unless drastically new techniques of agriculture are developed, there does not appear to be the remotest chance that Japan can become self-sufficient in the production of food. During the postwar period the average intake has been considerably less than 2000 calories, and there appears to be little prospect of increasing food yields to any really great extent. It has been estimated that if all known improvements, irrespective of cost, were applied to the farms, the maximum increase in return would be about 40 per cent. Even if this improvement were actually attained, it would be less than the amount required to take care of the increased population during the coming decades.

In order to feed herself, therefore, Japan must import food. In order to import food, she must export manufactured products. In order to export, she must compete on the world's markets—yet her only resource of any real consequence is cheap labor. Japanese coal reserves are of poor quality, and mining operations are not susceptible to extensive mechanization. A substantial fraction of Japan's energy requirements are met by hydroelectric power, but nearly half of the suitable waterpower sites have already been developed. It is estimated that by 1975 Japan's energy requirements will be double those of 1950.

Japan must rely, during future decades, on increased imports of coal and other raw materials. The steel industry in 1950 was running at less than one-half the prewar capacity, largely as the result of raw-material shortages. Most supplies must be imported. Prior to World War II Japan obtained more than half of her pig iron from abroad—much of this from Korea and Manchuria. Korea, together with Manchuria and other Chinese provinces, provided most of the iron ore and coking coal. These sources of supply are now cut off, with the result that Japan has had to turn to Southeast Asia for raw materials.

Japan's experience supports the thesis that industrialization and urbanization are followed by lower death rates and eventually by lower birth rates. But whether or not Japan will be able to complete the transition depends upon whether or not she is able to obtain sufficient raw materials and adequate markets for her products.

5.

Humanity is now experiencing the most rapid transition of its history—a transition that has been far more rapid than that which took place following the introduction of agriculture and the spread of urban civilization. Associated with it have been turmoil and strife, wars and social revolutions. To be sure, the basic causes of war have not changed very much since urban civilization first appeared; they still closely resemble those which brought ancient empires into armed conflict. Wars are still fought to obtain or to keep markets and supplies of raw materials, to spread economic, social, and religious creeds, to pursue power and military security, and to combat threats to power and security. But the techniques of war have changed considerably since the times of the ancient empires, largely as the result of industrialization and expanded technology. In particular, industrialization has led to the development of weapons of progressively greater range and effectiveness, with the result that wars are now much more destructive than they once were.

The development of atomic and hydrogen bombs makes it appear likely that groups of men could, if they wished or were driven to it, annihilate the greater portion of humanity. The fact that this terrible power is now in the hands of men has led many persons to believe that war is the greatest danger that mankind faces during the years ahead—and indeed this belief appears to be well founded. But it is clear that it is by no means the only danger that confronts mankind. Even without it, we are faced with the problems of producing sufficient food, of supplying ourselves with raw materials, and of supplying our machines with energy for the purpose of converting raw materials into finished products. Long-range solution of these problems is imperative if our civilization is to survive. At the same time, war cannot be divorced from these problems; although in the long run failure to solve them would lead to disintegration of Western civilization, failure would also breed war, which in turn would lead to accelerated disintegration.

We have only to look at the struggles which have taken place in the world during the last few years, and at those which are taking place today, to appreciate the enormous spectrum of situations that can lead to revolution, to war, and to willingness to die for a cause. Germany, confronted with inadequate markets, dwindling resources, and desires on the part of her leaders for power, has precipitated two wars. Japan embarked on her program of expansion in search of raw materials, food, and markets. Moslems have fought Hindus over religious beliefs and Jews over arable land. Asians and Africans have fought Westerners, fortified by the motto, "Never trust a white man." The white man has fought back in attempt to keep markets and sources of raw materials. The Soviet Union and the Western World are now locked in a struggle, the flames of which are fanned by attempts to pursue security, to combat pursuit of security, and to spread economic and political ideology.

Agrarian regions do not have the power to wage war against industrialized regions unless they are supplied with weapons that can be manufactured only by industrial societies. It is clear that the primary danger of world-wide destructive war springs largely from the one-fifth of the world which is already industrialized and from that portion of the world which has traveled a fair distance along the path of industrialization. Although many agrarian regions might be willing and even anxious to wage war in pursuit of their individual desires, they are unable to do so because they do not possess the technology or access to the technology which would enable them to pursue a war vigorously.

The problem of eliminating war and that of eliminating starvation and privation cannot be divorced from each other. We cannot speak in terms of eliminating human misery in the world unless we speak in terms of eliminating war—and conversely, we cannot speak in terms of eliminating war unless we speak in terms of alleviating human misery.

The tensions which exist in the world today are greater than at any previous period of history. At one end of the scale there is the well-fed, well-clothed, and well-housed minority, which guards jealously its present accumulation of wealth—parts of which, however, are already beginning to decay. In the middle of the scale is another minority, which, as the result of prodigious efforts, has undergone partial industrialization. The people of such regions are still poor, some are enormously overcrowded, and all are prepared to take practically any step, no matter how violent it may be, which might enable them to complete the transition. By contrast with the people of the wealthy minority, the people of the transition areas have relatively little to lose and much to gain by violent action. And at the bottom of the scale of wealth is the overwhelming majority of disease-ridden, hungry, underprivileged persons who have been exploited by the privileged minority and who cast envious eyes upon the wealth of Western nations. The people who belong to the underprivileged majority are restless, and in many regions of the world they are in active revolt. And industrialism is beginning to spread to such areas with consequences which can at present be only dimly perceived.

It is clear that the future course of history will be determined by the rates at which people breed and die, by the rapidity with which non-renewable resources are consumed, by the extent and speed with which agricultural production can be improved, by the rate at which the underdeveloped areas can industrialize, by the rapidity with which we are able to develop new resources, as well as by the extent to which we succeed in avoiding future wars. All of these factors are interlocked, but in order better to understand the ways in which each of them operates, we must consider them separately.

Chapter III

VITAL STATISTICS

Lo! as the wind is, so is mortal life,
A moan, a sigh, a sob, a storm, a strife
SIR EDWIN ARNOLD

1.

During the last 7000 years the number of human beings inhabiting the earth has increased from about 10 million to 2400 million. We have seen that this increase, large though it is, is much less than the increase which would have resulted had human populations not been checked by the limitations imposed by food supply, pestilence, physical disaster, family limitations, and, to a lesser extent, by war. Were it not for these checks, the living descendants of the 10 million persons who lived 7000 years ago would now be astronomical in number—indeed, they would weigh more than the combined weights of all of the stars in our visible universe.

We have seen, further, that the rate of increase of population during the last 7000 years has not been steady. Following the introduction of new techniques which have removed old population ceilings, there have been rapid increases in numbers of human beings. These increases have continued until new ceilings, imposed by nature and by limitations of techniques, have been reached. We are now in the middle of a population upsurge which must eventually level off at a new ceiling. Where will it be? What are the factors that will determine the population of human beings in the world during the years and centuries that lie ahead?

The period during which children can be born to a woman seldom exceeds 30 years (from age 15 to age 45). A gestation period of 9 months and a period of relative infecundity following childbirth reduce the maximum possible number of children per woman to approximately 20 if there are no multiple births. If human fecundity were fully exercised, as it is among other biological creatures, and if all women who were born lived through their fertile years, the population of the world would increase approximately tenfold each generation. But man's actual reproductive rate seldom equals his reproductive capacity. Many women die before they reach the end of the childbearing period. Others experience illnesses and disorders which prevent or lessen the chances of conception, or which give rise to miscarriages. But equally important among human beings, as distinct from other creatures, are the numerous social variables which determine the patterns of sexual behavior. It is now amply clear that the differences in reproductive rates which exist among various human groups result far more from social variables than from variations in biological characteristics.

At the time of the Revolutionary War the average American woman who successfully lived through the childbearing period could look back upon the experience of having brought eight children into the world. Some women, of course, could look back upon twenty periods of labor, and others could look back upon none. But on the average eight children were born to every woman who survived until the menopause.

By 1850 the average number of children that could be expected by a woman living through her childbearing age had dropped below 6. By 1900 an average woman could expect no more than 4 offspring. Today she can expect, on the average, no more than 3.

Thus the pattern of life in our own society has resulted in the reducing of the reproductive rate to a level which is very low compared with the reproductive capacity with which we are endowed. In some countries the average number of children expected per mother is even lower than in ours. In other countries, where the greater proportion of the world's population resides, the number of children expected per mother is considerably greater.

The large differences that exist between birth patterns become apparent when we compare the number of pregnancies to be expected by a group of women of a given age who live in one culture with the number of pregnancies to be expected by a similar

group who live in another culture. During the course of a year,
1000 Englishwomen between the ages of 15 and 20 gave birth
to about 20 children. Partially as the result of earlier marriages,
the same number of American women who belong to the same age
group give birth to four times as many children during an equal

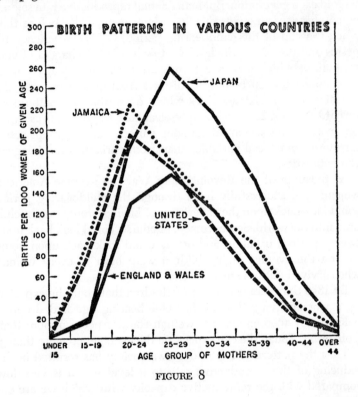

FIGURE 8

interval of time. On the tropical island of Jamaica, 1000 girls between 15 and 20 years of age give birth to 100 children during the
course of a year.

As women grow older, fertility increases until it reaches a peak
at an age which is determined in part by the culture. In both the
United States and Jamaica this occurs during the age interval
between 20 and 24 years, but in England not until considerably
later. In age groups which possess maximum fertility, birth rates
in England, the United States, and Jamaica are respectively 150,

190, and 220 births per year per thousand women. Following the period of maximum productivity, fertility declines until, following the menopause, it ceases to exist.

The birth-pattern curves of all countries are similar in the sense that they begin at zero, they pass through a peak, and they end at zero. But here the similarity ends. Just as no two countries possess identical cultures, so no two countries possess identical birth patterns. In some countries the peak is very high, in others it is relatively low. These differences result from a multiplicity of social forces.

Patterns of birth and patterns of culture are inextricably entwined. Both are causes and both are effects. In some groups marriage comes early, in others late. Some groups smile upon pregnancy out of wedlock, others frown upon it. Some groups use contraceptives, others don't. Abortion is legal in some areas, it is criminal in others. Some groups nurse their children for lengthy periods, others wean them at an early age. Some groups consider children to be economic assets, others consider them to be burdens. Some groups look upon children as symbols of virility and fertility, others see them as symbols of foolish and imprudent actions. Clearly the extent to which we can estimate future trends in birth patterns depends in large measure upon the extent to which we can estimate future trends in culture patterns.

2.

Whether or not the population of a given group of human beings is destined to increase, decrease, or remain stationary depends ultimately upon the birth and death patterns of women. To be sure, men are necessary for fertilization, but birth rates are far less sensitive to male population fluctuations than to female.

In a given culture where birth and death patterns remain approximately constant, a population will be stable if 1000 girls born at the same time produce, during the course of their lifetimes, a total of 1000 female babies to replace them. If the original girls were to give birth to 1100 replacements during their lifetimes, the population as a whole would double every 7.2 generations, or approximately every 200 years. On the other hand, if the number of girl replacements was decreased to 900, the population would be decreased by one-half every 180 years. (This, of course, takes into account the fact that some of the original girls will die before reaching breeding age, and that some will produce more than one girl each.)

The number of replacements that will be born to such a group of 1000 girls depends upon the number of girls who reach breeding age, upon the number who survive the years in which reproduction is possible, and upon the birth pattern for the group of survivors. These factors vary widely from culture to culture, but generally speaking, those areas which have been least influenced by Western culture have the highest birth rates for a given age and the highest female death rates to and through the fertile period. However, there are notable exceptions to this generalization, for Western public-health techniques have spread more rapidly than most other aspects of Western culture. Thus there are several areas in the world where death rates have been greatly lowered, but where the birth patterns have been altered very little. It is in such areas that populations are increasing at an unprecedented rate.

It is instructive to compare the patterns of births and deaths in widely differing cultures. For this purpose England and her agricultural colony Jamaica provide two convenient examples where adequate statistics are available. Let us compare the expected history of 1000 newborn English girls with that of an equal number of newborn Jamaican girls.

During the first year following birth, approximately 30 of the English girls will die. In Jamaica, where the available food supply per capita is considerably less than in England, and where medical services are less extensive, nearly 90 girls will have died by the end of the first year. By the time the girls reach their fifteenth birthdays and are able to reproduce, approximately 960 of the original 1000 English girls will still be alive, but only 840 of the Jamaican girls will have survived.

Between the fifteenth and twentieth years of age the social patterns are such that the survivors of the group of English girls engage in relatively little sexual intercourse—at least unprotected intercourse—with the result that only 80 children are born during this period. Jamaican girls, on the other hand, are introduced to sexual intercourse at an early age. Frequent early intercourse and a general acceptance of the view that childbirth out of wedlock is not shameful result in the birth of 400 children to the survivors of the original group by the time the twentieth birthday is reached. As there are not many more than 800 survivors, this means that on the average in a group of Jamaican girls who are 20 years of age, there will be 1 child for every 2 girls.

By the twenty-fifth year, the English girls will have given birth to a total of 680 offspring and the Jamaican girls will have given birth to 1300. By the thirtieth year, the totals will be 1400 and 1970 children respectively. By the time 45 years have passed, the group of 1000 English girls will be represented by 906 survivors and will have given birth to a total of 2340 children. Since approximately 48.5 per cent of newborn children are girls, the original group of 1000 English girls will have been replaced by 1130 new girls starting life by the time their mothers are 45 years of age.

By contrast, only 695 of the original 1000 Jamaican girls will still be alive at the age of 45, but a total of 1330 girls will have been born. If breeding were to stop at this point, and if the age-specific death and birth rates were to remain constant, the Jamaican population would double every 2.4 generations, or every 70 years. On the other hand, the doubling time for the English population would be 5.7 generations or 160 years.

The number of female children which the average newborn girl can be expected to have during the course of her lifetime is often called the net reproduction rate—a figure which is in many ways the most satisfactory index of the degree of instability of a population. However, it must be emphasized that few groups of girls born during the last century have experienced the net reproduction rates calculated for them at birth. Mortality rates have changed greatly, and birth patterns have shifted rapidly in the span of a single generation—so much so that girls born in the era of one pattern of births and deaths live to breed in another. The net reproduction rate tells us how rapidly a population can be expected to increase or decrease only if birth and death patterns remain constant.

Mortality rates have decreased considerably during the course of the last few decades. As is discussed in another part of this chapter, we can expect them to decrease in the future to the point at which death prior to and during the breeding period will have but small effect upon the reproductive rates of populations. In

view of this fact, the *gross reproduction rate* is a convenient index
which tells us how rapidly a population would increase or decrease
if the birth pattern at the time were maintained and if mortality
were zero until the breeding period had passed. The gross reproduction rate is the number of female children which an average
newborn girl could be expected to have during the course of her
lifetime if she were to live through the entire period of fertility.

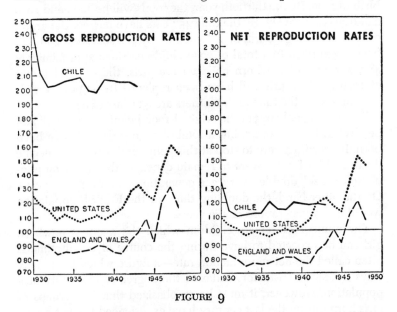

FIGURE 9

Figure 9 shows a comparison between the net and the gross reproduction rates of England, the United States, and Chile over
a period of several years. Chile, where the birth patterns are typical
of those in many areas of the world, has a high gross reproduction
rate. The net reproduction rate is considerably lower than the
gross rate, due to the fact that mortality is high both prior to and
during the breeding period. (Between 15 and 20 per cent of newborn Chilean children die during the first year following birth.)

The differences between the net and the gross reproduction
rates of the United States and England are not very large, since
mortality has been reduced to a point so low that it has but small
effect upon the reproduction rates.

It is noteworthy that the net reproduction rate of the United States remained below unity (1.00) for several years during the great depression. The net reproduction rate of England and Wales dropped below unity in 1923 and remained there for a quarter of a century—until the postwar boom in birth rate shifted the figure to well above unity. There are indications, however, that the net reproduction rate is again returning to a level of unity or slightly below. If the reproduction rates characteristic of the 25 years prior to the Second World War were maintained, the English population would dwindle away in about 800 years.

It may seem paradoxical that, according to the reproduction rate, the British population has been "dwindling away," while the population as a whole clearly has been increasing rapidly. However, the increases in the English population since 1923 have resulted not from an increased number of births, but from the fact that more people are living to reach old age, a phenomenon which, of course, produces a purely temporary population increase.

3.

Two thousand years ago the average baby born in the heavily populated city of Rome had a life expectancy of little more than 20 years. His contemporaries who were born in the provinces of Hispania and Lusitania, away from the unhealthy congestion of the capital of the empire, could expect to live for a considerably longer time—girls had a life expectancy of about 35 years, and boys, of about 40 years. In Roman Africa the chances of survival were even greater. Girls could expect to live about 45 years, and boys had nearly a 50-year life expectancy.

Life expectancy did not rise appreciably above those levels until very recent times. In 1850 the life expectancy at birth of a girl born in Massachusetts was little more than 40 years—only a little greater than that in ancient Hispania and Lusitania. In England, at the same time, the life expectancy at birth was very nearly the same as in the United States. Between 1850 and 1900 some decrease in mortality was achieved, and female life expectancy at birth rose to 47 years in England and to 50 years in the United States. Nevertheless, the life-expectancy figures at the turn of the

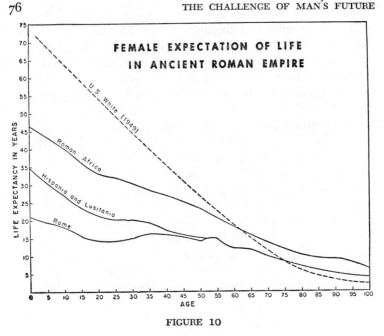

FIGURE 10

century were not far removed from those which had existed in
Roman Africa.

During the first half of the twentieth century enormous reductions were made in mortality rates in the United States, particularly
in the younger age groups. Female infant mortality decreased from
approximately 110 deaths per thousand births in 1900 to 26 per
thousand in 1946. In 1900 only 80 per cent of the girls who were
born could be expected to reach the age of 15. In 1953 over 96 per
cent of all white girls born were expected to reach the onset of the
breeding period. In 1900 only 65 per cent of newborn girls could
be expected to survive until the end of the breeding period. In
1953 over 90 per cent of all white girls born in the United States
could expect to reach their forty-fifth birthdays. The most important single factor associated with the enormous decrease in mortality during the past 50 years has been the increase in knowledge,
which permits us to control many epidemic and endemic infections which are themselves associated with the existence of civilization—diseases which were practically unknown in primitive so·

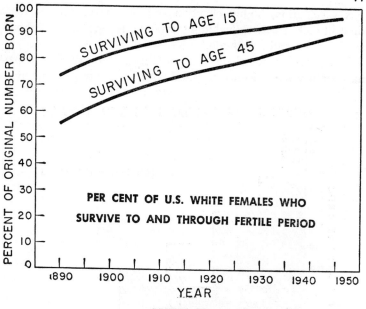

FIGURE 11

cieties. As we have seen, civilization has resulted in the crowding of many people into small areas. This, in turn, has created conditions for rapid incubation and spread of disease.

Since the time of Pasteur we have accumulated a vast amount of knowledge concerning the nature of various infections and the ways in which they are spread. Our knowledge permits us to control infections by blocking the routes by which germs enter the body, by inducing immunity to diseases through inoculation, and by reducing the mortality of diseases, once contracted, through the use of drugs and proper hospital care.

A classic example of the application of the principles of immunology has been inoculation against smallpox, which was practiced irregularly long before the time of Pasteur. Prior to the introduction of vaccination, few people in Europe escaped having smallpox—and usually 1 out of 12 infected persons died. Today, by contrast, smallpox is a medical curiosity in the Western World. Following Pasteur's work, the principles of immunology have been extended to the point where we have today, in addition to small-

pox vaccination, highly effective and preventive serums for a
diversity of diseases, including typhoid fever, tetanus, rabies,
scarlet fever, and diphtheria.

The most dramatic changes in mortality patterns during the past
half-century have been connected with the control of infections

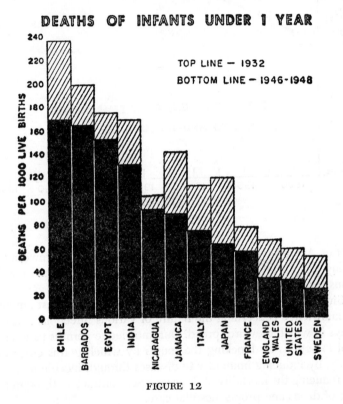

FIGURE 12

in children. The pasteurization of milk alone has been largely
responsible for the drop in the frequency of diarrheal diseases in
children under 5 years of age—a drop which has resulted in a
decrease from 40 deaths per thousand children from this cause
alone to a negligible number. During the early part of this century diarrhea and enteritis ranked as the chief causes of death of
children under 1 year of age. Today these diseases rank fifth in
importance as causes of death.

Death rates due to other diseases of childhood have likewise declined steadily through the years—some rapidly, others more gradually. The introduction of diphtheria antitoxin treatment in 1895 has led to a reduction of deaths resulting from that disease to a negligible proportion. Deaths resulting from scarlet fever, measles, and whooping cough have likewise decreased to levels which are low compared to those which existed at the turn of the century. We have now reached the point at which death rates among infants are determined, in the main, by causes other than infection—premature births, congenital malformations, and injury at birth. But the main causes of death during the second year of life are still diseases over which we have some, but not complete, control—bronchitis, pneumonia, measles, whooping cough, diarrhea, and enteritis.

In the Western World there is a clear relationship between mortality rates for the diseases of childhood, and economic class or "standard of living." For example, the infant death rate in England resulting from bronchitis and pneumonia in families of the poorest economic group was found recently to be seven times greater than that in families belonging to the professional class. Similarly, the ratio of deaths resulting from measles and whooping cough in the two groups were in the ratio of 15 to 1 and 7 to 1 respectively.

It seems likely that with further increased general medical care and further elevations of standards of living, death rates among children will be reduced to even lower levels than those which prevail today. Whereas at the present time we can expect approximately 96 per cent of the girls who are born to survive to the age of 15, it is not unlikely that two or three decades from now 98 per cent of the girls who are born will reach maturity. With further advances in the techniques of caring for prematurely born infants, a 99-per-cent survival to the age of 15 might be possible. Further reductions of infant and child mortality will be difficult, however, because of the limits imposed by congenital malformations and by congenital debility.

The principal reductions in mortality during the years from age 15 to age 40 have likewise been brought about by the control of infectious diseases. Perhaps the most outstanding achievement in this connection has been the virtual elimination of typhoid

fever as a cause of death in the United States. Mortality from typhoid fever was highest in adolescence and early adult life, and
its elimination has therefore substantially increased the proportion
of persons who live through the breeding period.

During the latter part of the last century deaths from typhoid
fever in Chicago were approximately 50 to 100 per year per 100,000
inhabitants. During occasional major outbreaks, mortality rose
to even higher levels. Following the installation of filters in the
water system in 1906, the inauguration of water chlorination in
1913, and the introduction of pasteurized milk, the number of
typhoid deaths dropped precipitously to extremely low levels. In
the United States as a whole, the further protection given by typhoid inoculations has reduced the annual mortality from the disease to less than 1 death per 200,000 persons.

Tuberculosis still remains one of the greatest of all threats to the
lives of young adults, yet the decrease in mortality during the last
50 years has been dramatic. In the United States in 1900 nearly 200
out of every 100,000 persons were killed each year by the disease.
With the spread of increased facilities for treating the disease, and
improved methods of early diagnosis, mortality has been lowered
to one-sixth the former number.

It is likely that mortality from tuberculosis will be decreased
still further in the future, for we know that the death rate depends
greatly upon the environment. Recently, for example, the tuberculosis mortality rate in the poorest class in England was found to be
greater than twice the mortality rate in the wealthiest class.

It seems likely that with continued improvement of living conditions, coupled with continued increase in the general availability
of adequate nutrition and medical care, death rates resulting from
diseases such as tuberculosis, bronchial and lobar pneumonia,
and rheumatic fever will be decreased to levels much lower than
those which exist today, even if no really specific cures for the diseases are found. When this point is reached, the main barriers
to further decreases in mortality will be deaths from such phenomena as childbirth, accidents, virus diseases such as influenza
and poliomyelitis, cancer, and "degenerative" diseases such as
hypertensive vascular disease. It is quite possible that further research on the nature of virus diseases will disclose more effective
controls than those which exist today. Further, it seems likely that

death rates resulting from childbirth will be reduced to a level considerably lower than that now prevailing. In addition, growing awareness of the considerable incidence of accidental death has resulted in the establishment of accident-prevention programs of increasing scope and effectiveness.

When we take all of these factors into consideration, it is probable that the adult mortality curve of a century from now will be determined in the main by such diseases as cancer, nephritis, heart disease, cerebral hemorrhage, and diseases of the arteries. When that time arrives, we can expect approximately 96 per cent of all girls born to reach their forty-fifth birthdays.

Beyond the age of 45 a high percentage of deaths results from degenerative diseases. The human body, like other highly organized living structures, will apparently serve for only a limited period of time before certain processes start which we are helpless to combat—at least at the present time. A part of our helplessness results from our lack of understanding of the nature and the causes of the processes associated with aging. Nevertheless, a good case can be made for the view that although medical science is making it possible for ever-increasing numbers of people to live out their natural life span, the ultimate "limit" of the human life span is not being increased appreciably.

It seems likely that every human being is genetically endowed at conception with a certain "life potential"—a natural life span which could be fulfilled in the absence of physical or biological accidents, and which seems to vary greatly from individual to individual. At one end of the scale are those babies who are born with biological weaknesses that terminate their lives within a few minutes or hours. At the other end of the scale are those relatively few individuals who live to pass the century mark. The bodies of most individuals are of intermediate stability and appear to be sufficiently well constructed to permit them to function for at least 75 years (barring physical or biological accidents) before degenerative processes bring about death.

The record of decreasing mortality during the last half-century attests to the difficulty of increasing the life expectancy of the aged. Since 1900 we have lowered the mortality rates of infants, children, and young adults to one-fifth the previous number, but our success in reducing mortality rates in older age groups has been

82 THE CHALLENGE OF MAN'S FUTURE

less spectacular. The probability of an 80-year-old woman dying during the course of a year is only 20 per cent less today than it was 50 years ago. In spite of our greatly increased medical knowledge and our improved facilities for the care of the aged, the decrease

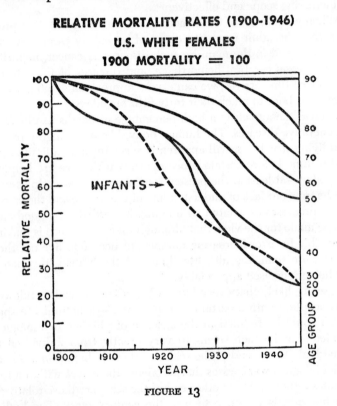

RELATIVE MORTALITY RATES (1900-1946)

U.S. WHITE FEMALES

1900 MORTALITY = 100

FIGURE 13

in mortality rate for 90-year-old persons is so slight as to be only barely observable.

It seems clear that the primary reductions in the mortality rates of older persons have resulted from the same developments which lowered the death rates of young people. But with older persons the probability of death due to degeneration and resultant stoppage of any one of the innumerable functioning components of the body is large compared with the probability of death due to infectious diseases. Consequently, although the deaths due to disease have been reduced considerably, the decreases have had but small effect upon the over-all death rates of older groups.

It is unlikely that the general situation with respect to the degenerative causes of death will change very rapidly in the future. Some progress has been made in the treatment of certain types

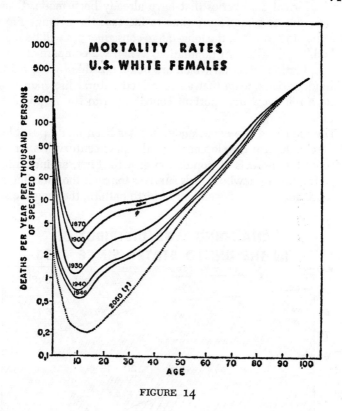

FIGURE 14

of cancer and heart disease, but the over-all demographic effect has been small. When the body grows old, there are many possibilities of failure. An older man might be saved one day from death from cancer, but he might die soon afterward of nephritis or heart failure.

Our knowledge of the processes of aging and degeneration must be considerably greater than it is today if the human life span is to be increased much beyond that which exists at present. And even when we understand the processes of aging, it may well turn out that there is little that can be done about it. However, in the unlikely event that new biochemical discoveries result in our attaining greatly increased life spans, the demographic consequences will be small when compared with the consequences of the biological discoveries that have already been made. Even if we are able at some future time to increase the average life expectancy to 150 years, the long-range consequences will be merely a doubling of Western population. When we compare this with the population increases which are made possible by our existing techniques, it appears that an increased natural life span would make a relatively unimportant contribution to future population changes.

The increased life expectancy that has been made possible by the technological developments of the past century has strongly affected two aspects of population growth. First, an increasingly large fraction of newborn girls survives to reach the breeding age. Second, and quite independent of birth pattern, the long life span

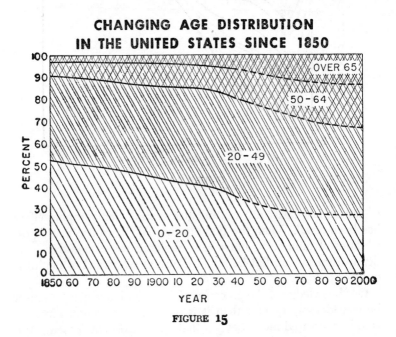

CHANGING AGE DISTRIBUTION
IN THE UNITED STATES SINCE 1850

FIGURE 15

has resulted in increased population solely because more people are living longer. The latter effect has produced, in addition to its contribution to population increase, a marked change in the composition of the population.

One hundred years ago over 50 per cent of all persons living in the United States were under the age of 20, a mere 2.6 per cent were over the age of 65, and the median age of the population was only 18.8 years. By 1900 the median age had risen to 22.9. During the last 50 years the proportion of persons in the United States under 20 years of age has dropped to 34 per cent, the proportion of persons over 65 has increased to approximately 7 per cent, and the median age of the population has risen to 30.1. These changes are still under way, and during the course of the next few decades we can expect the proportion of persons over 65 years of age to increase further and approach 15 per cent.

One hundred years ago the population age distribution in the United States and in the rest of the Western World was very much the same as it is in the Far East and in many other areas of the world today. Even in the United States and in England we can expect further population increases, solely on the basis of increas-

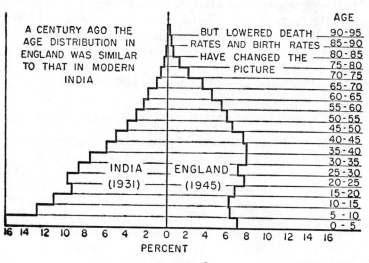

FIGURE 16

ing the average life span, even if the net reproduction rates should drop again to the neighborhood of unity and remain there. However, these expected increases are small when compared with the increases that would result from this effect alone in India and China if the mortality rates in those areas were lowered to the rates which we now know are medically possible. Given adequate food and medical care, the populations of those countries would double even if birth rates were drastically lowered to the levels prevailing in the West.

4.

In view of the fact that populations cannot increase without limit, the birth rate must eventually equal the death rate. All too often we lose sight of this fact, living as we do in a period of rapid population transition. But under what circumstances can we expect the two rates to become equal? Clearly equalization might take place in a variety of ways. We could have low birth rates and low death rates, or high birth rates and high death rates; or we could have any of the gradations between the two extremes.

If we extrapolate (i.e., calculate a future trend on the basis of past experience) the mortality rates prevailing in Western culture to the limits which might be achieved in the foreseeable future, the death rate for the population at equilibrium will be between 13 and 14 per 1000 persons. If intercourse took place freely in such a population, and if no protective measures were taken, the annual birth rate would be extremely high—over 40 per 1000. In order for it to be as low as 14 per 1000, the population must condone or urge one or more of several possible practices:

1. Restriction of sexual intercourse, either through postponement of marriage coupled with strong condemnation of intercourse prior to marriage, or through the establishment of culture patterns which severely restrict intercourse frequency after marriage. Included in this category would be restriction of intercourse resulting from reliance upon the "rhythm" or "safe-period" technique of family limitation.
2. Abortion.
3. Sterilization.
4. Fertility control, either through the practice of coitus interruptus or

through the use of chemicals or devices designed to prevent conception.

In the absence of restraint, abortion, sterilization, coitus interruptus, or artificial fertility control, the resultant high birth rate would have to be matched at equilibrium by an equally high death rate. A major contribution to the high death rate could be infanticide, as has been the situation in cultures of the past. More likely, the high death rate would result from debility arising from insufficient food supply, poor living conditions, and inadequate medical care. If the population is limited primarily by food supply, medical care can never be adequate. No numbers of doctors and hospitals, or quantities of medicine, can lower mortality rates if there is insufficient food to support the population.

Two conditions must be fulfilled for successful family limitation. First, there must be readily available means for limitation which are reasonably effective and which can be easily utilized without conflicting seriously with the desires of the individual or the culture patterns of his society. Second, the individual must have the desire to avoid producing excess children or to engage in practices which, perhaps without his realizing it, result in lower birth rates.

In principle the practice of two of the oldest techniques of family limitation, coitus interruptus and infanticide, could long ago have resulted in population stabilization in the world. But coitus interruptus conflicts with desires concerning sexual gratification, and infanticide conflicts with the instinct of parents to protect their children. Thus the desire for smaller families had to be very strong before these particular techniques had significant effect. In similar manner the effectiveness of any family-limitation technique is determined by the social, psychological, and economic pressures which govern the actions of individuals.

Although at least some members of practically all societies have engaged in practices that have had the direct or indirect effect of limiting family sizes, the rise of cities, and, associated with it, the struggle for the acquisition of material possessions, were largely responsible for the spread of such practices. During the last 150 years birth rates in the Western World have declined greatly. There is ample evidence that widespread increase in the use of chemical and mechanical preventatives to conception, instead of the less reliable ancient method of coitus interruptus, has played a major part in this decline. To the results of these practices may be added those of delayed marriages and abortions.

Throughout a large part of human history recipes aimed at permitting intercourse without penalty of pregnancy have been available in most cultures. Some of the recipes have probably been helpful, but many have been of the nature of old wives' tales or magicians' formulas and have been of dubious effectiveness. In the former category were pessaries made of crocodile dung, and medicated lint tampons, used by the ancient Egyptians, as well as condoms made from goats' bladders, used by the Romans and later widely used in Southern and Western Europe. In the latter category were numerous potions, rituals, and incantations passed from mother to daughter for generation after generation.

The development of the technology of rubber made possible the mass production of thin but reliable condoms at a price so low that a substantial fraction of the male population could afford to purchase them in quantity. Techniques for the mass production of rubber goods at low cost also made possible the large-scale production of removable rubber diaphragms and of douche bags. Advances in pharmaceutical technology resulted in the development of solutions, jellies, and creams with the power of killing sperm, or of decreasing sperm mobility.

Although modern contraceptive techniques are relatively inexpensive and effective, it is an undeniable fact that they are inconvenient and unesthetic. But in the United States these considerations are overbalanced by the combination of strong social forces and inexpensiveness. However, there are many families in the United States where children are both wanted and unwanted—where inborn desires for children are mixed with thoughts of economic and social penalties. In such cases, in the overwhelming euphoria and passion accompanying sexual intercourse, the inconvenience and unesthetic qualities associated with existing contraceptive techniques often result in either abandonment or unsystematic use of control measures, with a consequent increase in the probability of conception. It is highly likely that if contraceptive measures were of such a nature that their effectiveness was independent of moods during and immediately following periods of passion, the birth rate in the United States would be far lower than it is today.

Contraceptive techniques will be widely used in a society only if there are social and economic pressures which increase the desirability of small families. The advantages gained by having fewer children must be clearly perceptible to the individual, so that he or she will take strong measures to avoid conception. Control methods that are inexpensive, effective, and preferably convenient and not unesthetic to use must be available. Ideally the method should be of such a nature that the natural sequence of emotional events associated with coitus is uninterrupted.

Most of the conditions for widespread use of contraceptive measures exist in the Western World. But in many heavily populated areas of the world the favorable factors are by no means present. Frequently the desire for small families is absent. Children, although they may in reality be economic burdens, are looked upon as economic assets, for they can work, earn money, and eventually support the parents in their old age. Frequently personal ego promotes large families, for children are often looked upon as symbols of virility.

Nevertheless, in many of these regions old patterns of life are changing, and desires for less frequent conception are increasing. But there is little available in the way of techniques that can be used on a widespread basis. Existing devices such as condoms, diaphragms, and douche bags are far too expensive. The factor of inconvenience in such regions is enormous, for facilities which we take for granted in our Western culture—such as hot water, bathrooms, and privacy—are usually nonexistent. The net result is that the inconvenience and expense associated with existing control measures are far too great to permit widespread use. In the light of this situation it seems likely that effective practice of contraceptive techniques in less developed areas must await either marked economic development in those regions or the invention and dissemination of drastically new techniques of contraception which eliminate many of the existing difficulties.

Research aimed at developing markedly new methods of conception control has not been carried out very intensively. Indeed, in the United States far less money has been spent on research on human reproduction than has been spent on research on either bovine or plant reproduction. Nevertheless, there are marked indications that possibly within the next decade, and almost certainly within the next quarter-century, new techniques will be available—techniques far less expensive and more convenient than existing ones.

Conception and birth involve a complicated chain of events. The secretion of hormones in the pituitary gland stimulates production of spermatozoa in the male and the development and release of ova (approximately 1 every 28 days) from the ovaries of the female. If mobile spermatozoa are discharged into the vagina of the female at a time when a released ovum is ready for fertilization, at least one of the many million discharged spermatozoa moves through the uterus of the female into one of the two Fallopian tubes, where it unites with the ovum. The joined ovum and spermatozoon descend into the uterus and become attached to the uterine lining as an embryo. The embryo develops for approximately 9 months, through the fetal stage, into an infant.

Up to the present time a number of techniques have been used to prevent these processes. Coitus interruptus and such devices as condoms, when successful, prevent the spermatozoa from entering the vagina. Diaphragms and pessaries, when successful, prevent the passage of the spermatozoa from the vagina into the uterus. Vaginal douches wash the spermatozoa out of the vagina. Spermicidal jellies and liquids, when placed in the vagina, destroy the vitality of the spermatozoa or render them immobile. Such intra-uterine devices as buttons and rings irritate the lining of the uterus and prevent the joined ovum and spermatozoon from becoming attached to the uterine lining. Coitus can be avoided at the time in the monthly cycle when ovulation takes place—if the approximate time can be discovered. The fetus can be aborted after conception takes place. But, theoretically at least, there are points other than those toward which these methods are directed, at which the process can be stopped.

The biochemical processes that lead to the development of the spermatozoa and the discharge of the ovum may be interrupted by the administration of the hormone estrogen. Experiments have shown the method to be effective. But available hormones are still scarce and expensive, and there are numerous side effects which seem to be unfavorable and which have yet to be more fully explored.

Certain American Indians have used an infusion made from the desert plant *Lithosperum ruderle,* which, when taken orally by a woman, once daily during periods when it is desirable to avoid conception, apparently acts on the pituitary gland in such a way that ovulation is prevented. Experiments on animals seem to indicate that the substance lowers conception incidence, and that when the dosage is discontinued there is an immediate return to normal reproduction. But again, the side effects have yet to be thoroughly studied before it may be considered safe.

Another attempt is being made in experiments with a substance known as phosphorylated hesperidin, which, when taken orally by both the male and female, seems to prevent the spermatozoa from piercing the jelly-like coating of the ovum. In experiments with rats fertility seems to have been lowered by this dosage, and a quick return to normal was observed when the substance was discontinued; and there is no evidence so far of serious side effects.

Other approaches include the injection into female rats of a protein from the umbilical cord which seems to produce sterility for from 2 to 6 months; and small doses immediately after conception of a chemical known as aminopterin, which results in the death of the fetus, followed by its absorption or discharge.

Although there remains much work to be done before the "perfect" contraceptive can be said to be a reality, the probability that it will be in existence within the next few years appears to be very high. However, before its use can really become widespread there will have to be much clinical testing, with particular emphasis upon side effects and possible long-range damage to the human system. It might well be that the material eventually used will be quite different in nature from the substances discussed briefly here. But the flow of developments is in the direction of our being able to turn fertility on and off at will, simply, with safety, inexpensively, and without offense to esthetic sensitiveness.

The long-range implications of the development of the perfect contraceptive can, of course, be enormous. It will offer man the opportunity to enjoy the fruits of public health and at the same time to create a stable population. It will give the less-developed areas of the world a chance to lower rates of population growth to levels commensurate with feasible rates of industrial growth and expansion of food-production facilities. At the same time, however, it will have to be used with caution. Indiscriminate use could create grave dangers in other directions.

We have seen that the net reproduction rate in England remained below unity for a quarter of a century, and rose above that point during the "baby boom" that followed World War II. During the period preceding the increase in birth rate there were dire prophecies to the effect that the population of England was doomed to extinction. There have also been innumerable such prophecies about France and other nations of the Western World.

It is impossible to estimate the extent to which birth rates in England, France, and other Western countries would have been further lowered had the perfect contraceptive been in existence during the last 50 years. It seems likely that they would have been lower, particularly in view of the fact that a substantial fraction of the births in these countries appear to be unplanned.

Nevertheless, the postwar boom in babies in the Western World has resulted from increased birth rates in those groups that have had greatest economic and educational access to contraceptive techniques. This development makes it appear likely that, given the perfect contraceptive, Western populations will not disappear. Instead, we can expect far greater oscillations in birth rate than have ever been observed previously, the oscillations being reflections of fluctuations in over-all economic and social well-being. Whereas 150 years ago the death rate fluctuated with the economy, and the birth rate remained relatively constant, in the Western society of the next century the reverse will be true. Death rates will remain relatively constant, but birth rates will be extremely sensitive barometers of economic and social progress.

The development of the perfect contraceptive will not lower birth rates in the less-developed areas of the world overnight. A satisfactory contraceptive is a necessary but by no means sufficient prerequisite for population stabilization in a culture that possesses low death rates. Other factors must operate simultaneously: knowledge of the techniques must be diffused through the culture; the techniques must be accepted philosophically; and these factors must be accompanied by a desire to have fewer children and an understanding that limitation of birth rate will result in individual economic and social betterment. The fulfillment of the latter prerequisite will take much time and enormous effort.

The severe requirements nature imposes upon us—either to balance low death rates with low birth rates or to permit high birth rates to be balanced inevitably by high death rates—have created major philosophical problems in a number of sections of the world's population. The Catholic Church, for example, condemns vigorously all artificial means of preventing conception, including coitus interruptus. The "rhythm" method of fertility control is not condemned by the Church but it is by no means enthusiastically recommended. Abortion and sterilization are strictly forbidden. Official church doctrine states, in effect, that a man and a woman should not engage in intercourse unless they are willing to receive a child into their household. Pius XI, in his encyclical on *Christian Marriage*, stated: "Any use whatsoever of matrimony exercised in such a way that the act is deliberately frustrated in its natural power to generate life is an offense against the law of God and nature, and those who indulge in such are branded with the guilt of grave sin."

Pius XI specifically approved of periodic continence and intercourse during the "safe" period—a family-limitation method that requires careful calculation and planning, places heavy burdens on individual powers of restraint, and is by no means infallible. Although the method can, in principle, from a statistical point of view, contribute significantly to population stabilization, individual effectiveness is not completely predictable. Any biological or emotional disturbance may upset the menstrual cycle sufficiently to make adequate calculation impossible.

Church officialdom feels compelled to advocate large families and to condemn artificial means for the prevention of conception. At the same time, in common with members of other Christian denominations and in common with most human beings, irrespective of religion, Catholics believe that pain and suffering should be relieved and lives should be saved wherever possible. Indeed, large numbers of selfless priests and nuns dedicate their lives to the task of helping the underprivileged by providing medical care, nourishment, clothing, and education.

The horns of the dilemma that confronts many devout Catholics whose lives are guided by Church law are sharp in the extreme. Is it less sinful to bring into the world a child who is doomed to die of malnutrition at an early age than to prevent the conception of the child in the first place? The Church answers by saying that children should not be brought into the world unless they can be cared for properly, and that superfluous numbers of children need not be brought into the world—couples who believe that they cannot provide for additional children have only to restrain their sexual activities. But sexual activities are difficult to restrain —so difficult, in fact, that many otherwise devout Catholics use birth-control techniques, thus committing sin in the eyes of the Church, rather than risk having children who cannot be provided for adequately. We have but to examine the rapidly declining birth rates in two predominantly Catholic countries, France and Italy, to see evidence of increased conception control in spite of Church opposition, and in spite of the fact that sale of contraceptives is strictly illegal. It is doubtful in the extreme that sexual restraint has played a significant role in lowering the birth rate in either country.

In the past, religious laws have been molded in part by public attitudes and cultural pressures. We have seen, for example, that the attitudes of the writers of Hebrew law toward birth control changed with time as social forces changed. Christian attitudes are likewise changing. It is probable that, in the face of existing public attitudes, Catholic law will be modified during the years to come, particularly in the light of the new techniques for family limitation that will probably be available in the near future. But we cannot expect those changes to come rapidly.

Although Catholic doctrine had little effect on slowing the decline in birth rate in Catholic countries of Western Europe, the effect upon areas such as Mexico and Central and South America has been enormous. Western Europeans possessed wide knowledge of contraceptive techniques and practices long before the pronouncement of Pius XI in 1930. But the pronouncement has effectively hampered widespread education concerning family-limitation techniques in areas which are now in desperate need of such information. During the last half-century modern public-health methods have been applied with increasing vigor in Mexico and in the countries of Central and South America. In a short span of time, the death rates in many of those areas have dropped considerably. But birth rates have remained at high levels. For example, in Mexico the death rate dropped from 26 per 1000 in 1932 to 17 per 1000 in 1948. During the entire period, however, the birth rate has remained in the neighborhood of 45 per 1000. Thus the rate of population increase has jumped during those few years from 1.7 per cent per year to 2.8 per cent per year.

Catholic attitudes at present also effectively prevent widespread activity upon the part of Western nations to help many non-Catholic areas of the world start vigorous public birth-control programs of their own. Although the government of India is instituting a major family-limitation movement, it dares not ask the government of the United States for help in the matter, nor would the government of the United States give help were it asked, at the present time, for its leaders would fear the political turmoil that would ensue.

The Catholic attitude toward birth control is discussed here at some length for the reason that, although Church law will have a negligible effect upon future population trends in areas of greatest existing Church economic power—notably Western and Southern Europe and North America—it will have enormous effect upon population trends in other areas of the world, both Catholic and non-Catholic. If Church resistance to family limitation should suddenly end, the course of population growth in many parts of the world might be drastically altered.

5.

A number of nations, which altogether are inhabited by approximately one-fifth of the world's population, have now traversed the long pathway leading from high birth rates and high death rates to low birth rates and low death rates. These areas, which include Northern and Western Europe, the greater part of Southern and Central Europe, and the United States, have reached the point at which net reproduction rates are now very close to unity.

Populations are still rising, but the present rise is due in the main to the fact that increasing numbers of people are living to reach old age. It seems probable that equilibrium for the present cycle of growth will be reached when the population of those areas increases another 20 to 30 per cent.[1] It now appears that equilibrium may be closely approached by the time another 50 years have passed.

At the other end of the spectrum are those areas where birth rates are essentially at the biological maximum, and the death rates, although somewhat smaller, lie very close to the birth rates. These areas embrace over 30 per cent of the world's population and include China and a majority of the Moslem areas.

In India, Indonesia, most of South and Central America, and the greater part of Africa, birth rates are still very close to the biological maximum, but the introduction of modern techniques of sanitation and medicine have lowered death rates in varying degrees. Generally speaking, populations are increasing more rapidly in those areas than in other regions of the world.

Another 20 to 25 per cent of the world's population is now in a transition stage which is characterized by falling birth rates and relatively low death rates, but in which the population is still increasing rapidly. This group includes the populations of Japan, most of Eastern Europe, and Oceania.

One-third of humanity, therefore, has yet to start the transition from one extreme of the pattern of births and deaths to the other. A second third is lowering mortality rates, but family-limitation techniques have not yet been introduced on an appreciable scale. The remaining third of the population is approaching stability, but the equilibrium level in the present cycle will be considerably higher than the existing population.

The population level of the world a century from now will be determined in the main by the rapidity with which sanitary, medical, and family-limitation techniques are introduced and incorporated into the cultures of areas with high growth potentials. A glance at past history shows us that this is a slow process requiring

1. The term "present cycle of growth" refers to the growth which is taking place within the framework of our existing methods of agricultural and industrial production and our existing material wants. As we will see in later chapters, further cycles of growth, leading to still higher populations in the Western World, are possible.

at least a generation for deep-rooted assimilation. Even in areas such as Japan, where transition has been rapid, people have not changed their ways of life overnight. Adults have difficulty in changing their patterns of life under any circumstances, with the result that changes usually arise through the exposure of the young to new concepts. As the first generation of young is still strongly influenced by parental conditioning, the new way of life frequently does not become truly widespread until the second generation reaches maturity.

Thus we can expect that, should intensive programs be started aimed at reducing mortality in those areas that now possess high birth rates and high death rates, about 25 to 50 years would be required for death rates to decline to the levels now prevailing in Western cultures. On the other hand, there has been in the past a lag between decline in death rate and decline in birth rate. Techniques which enable individuals to live longer are more readily appreciated and more quickly adopted than those which enable individuals to have fewer children.

However, once birth rates start declining they fall about as rapidly as do death rates. Here again, the diffusion of knowledge and the assimilation of new techniques into the culture require a generation or two.

The time lag between declining death rates and declining birth rates leads to high rates of population increase such as now exist in Africa, South Central Asia, Latin America, Japan, and Eastern Europe. In the last two regions, it is possible that stability will be approached within the next 30 years. How long it will take to achieve the same result in Africa, South Central Asia, and Latin America will be determined in part by the rapidity with which family-limitation techniques are introduced into the cultures and in part by the rapidity with which the desire for smaller families is diffused through the culture. In Latin America, this might require a considerable period of time in view of existing strong Church opposition. In India, where a major family-limitation program backed by the government is now under way, reduction in birth rates may come more rapidly.

The new methods of contraception which may become available during the course of the next decade may shorten the time lag between decreasing death rates and decreasing birth rates and thus make it possible for an area such as China to lower death rates and birth rates in unison, avoiding rapid population increase during the transition stage. However, although the new techniques will diminish resistance to contraception by eliminating inconveniences and great expense, they will not eliminate that component of resistance which arises from general social forces. Thus, even with drastically new contraceptive techniques available, it seems likely that a generation or more will be required for the methods to be generally accepted.

Thus far we have discussed only *rates* at which populations are increasing at present and at which they might increase in the future. Existing growth rates tell us little about the equilibrium population levels which might be reached eventually. Except for the relatively brief periods of transition from one cultural level to another, the size of the world population at a given time will be determined primarily by such factors as agricultural development, general technological development, and the wants and needs of the people. A study of rates of growth tells us only how rapidly equilibrium levels might be reached.

It is dangerous to attempt to extend human population growth curves into the future on the basis of past and present trends. In a period of changing birth and death rates the slopes of population curves can change quickly. In a transition period such as that which we are now experiencing, such an extension for a time 100 years hence could well be greatly in error. A direct extension based upon the existing rate of increase leads to an estimate that population at the end of another century will be roughly 2.5 to 3 times larger than that which now exists. On the other hand, it is conceivable that increasing desires for small families, coupled with the introduction of new family-limitation techniques and new methods of mass propaganda, might prevent a rise of more than an additional 50 per cent. However, one can equally well imagine a situation in which the introduction of drastically new methods of food production, coupled with the prohibition of contraceptive techniques, might lead to a tenfold or even a fifteenfold increase in population during the course of the coming century.

Estimates for a period of a generation or less, based on past and present experience, are reasonably safe and are fairly reliable if we are not interested in meticulous accuracy. It seems probable that the population of the world will increase no less than 25 per cent and no more than 50 per cent in the coming 25 years. In order to extrapolate further than 25 years, we must make some assumptions concerning future birth and death patterns.

On the basis of past experience, the following assumptions might be considered plausible: 1. The population of Europe (excluding Eastern Europe) and North America will cease to increase appreciably after another quarter-century. 2. The rates of population increase of Japan, Eastern Europe, and Oceania will decrease during the next 25 years to present Western levels. In an additional 25 years, the population will become stabilized. 3. Africa, South Central Asia, and most of Latin America will require 75 years to complete this process. 4. A full century will be required for most of China and the Near East to pass through the transition.

When we apply these assumptions (which, we must remember, are little better than guesses), we find that the growth of world population would be as follows during the course of the next century:

	BILLIONS
1950	2.4
1975	3.4
2000	4.8
2025	6.0
2050	6.7

It is difficult to visualize any reasonable combination of circumstances not involving catastrophe which could lead to a population increase of less than twofold during the next century. It seems far more likely that we can expect the world to be populated by at least 5 billion persons and perhaps 10 billion persons by the time another 100 years have passed. But before we can estimate the level at which the population might stabilize, we must analyze the various factors that determine how many persons can be supported by the resources of the earth.

6.

When man lived in a completely natural environment, rather than one which he had modified greatly, many selective forces were in operation which permitted the survival, in the main, of only those persons best equipped for life under the conditions then prevailing. We cannot imagine persons with badly crippled arms or legs or poor eyesight surviving for long in a food-gathering society in the absence of special protective social mechanisms— nor can we imagine persons surviving in such a society who could not learn quickly the habits of the animals and the properties of the various forms of vegetation upon which their lives depended.

Humanity survived, during the days of pre-history, because individuals were endowed with three extremely powerful instincts or drives. The fear of death caused man to protect himself from attack and to go to great lengths to obtain food when he was hungry. The sexual drive caused him to engage in coitus frequently. The parental instinct caused him to protect the children who resulted from his sexual acts.

Of the many children born, perhaps only one-half survived to reach breeding age, and of those who managed to reach maturity, only a tiny fraction survived the entire breeding period. Those who managed to survive to reproduce were, on the average, those individuals who were best fitted for life under the conditions then prevailing—they were perhaps the stronger, the fleeter of foot, the more disease-resistant, and, above all, they perhaps were able to learn more rapidly than their brothers and sisters who perished during childhood. Thus the relatively unfit were constantly being pruned from the human race.

Modern civilization has drastically changed the whole pattern of operation of natural selection in human society, with consequences which today can be only dimly perceived. The major change has been the elimination of large numbers of selective forces that previously operated upon uncivilized men. But, in addition, new forces of selection have come into existence, which, over long periods of time, will probably modify man's nature.

All about us we can see age-old forces of selection being eliminated from our society. Whereas once a man who was born with poor eyesight often stood a worse chance than average of surviving, the invention of spectacles drastically decreased the handicap, with the result that increasing numbers of men and women with poor eyesight survive to breed. Indeed, blindness itself is no longer the major survival handicap that it once was, for the blind are generally watched over and nurtured by their fellow men.

Natural resistance to the lethal effects of certain diseases is no longer necessary in the Western World. Whereas smallpox once exerted a strong selection effect on people in the Western World, and the majority of persons who lived to breed were the most resistant to the lethal effects of the disease, the invention of vaccination has completely eliminated smallpox as a selection force in civilized society. And thus it is with numerous other diseases we have learned to control. We have only to look at the plight of the Westerner who travels to the Far East to appreciate the change that has taken place in but a few generations. Before he leaves he must be inoculated against a variety of diseases. While he is there he must live in special quarters and be meticulous in his choice of foods. If he does not take these precautions, the chances of his surviving will be small. And even with all the precautions, it is rare that an individual traveling in the Orient does not suffer from some minor or major illness that is foreign to his experience. Yet he sees about him when he travels multitudes of people who live without benefit of the protection he requires.

Cases are well known of isolated groups of people who have lived for generations unexposed to certain diseases that exist elsewhere in the world. Since they had not been exposed to a particular disease—as, for example, measles—selection effects did not operate. But once the disease was brought from the outside, mortality rates were extremely high. In the same way, by isolating ourselves from the effects of specific diseases, we make ourselves all the more vulnerable to their effects if for any reason our ability to isolate ourselves should end.

In our Western society we use a multiplicity of medical and surgical techniques to correct or compensate for the physical defects that endanger our survival and the survival of our offspring. A young child in the United States will survive the experience of a ruptured appendix, while his counterpart in China will almost certainly die. Premature babies can be saved in the West, but they usually die in the East. Mothers who, for a variety of reasons, cannot give birth to children naturally with safety to both mother and child, now resort to Caesarean section. Persons whose natural fertilities are lessened by defects in body biochemistry and who want children now go through elaborate procedures involving hormone injections, temperature-taking, and either precise timing of coitus or artificial insemination. For many such persons, who would have been incapable of bearing children in earlier times, our more detailed knowledge of the mechanism of conception now makes childbearing possible. Persons born with a wide range of defects which formerly meant certain death can now be saved. And to the extent to which these and other defects, or susceptibility to defects, result from specific gene combinations, they will be transmitted to posterity.

The primary consequence of our removal of the forces of natural selection which have operated for so many generations will be that civilized man will become increasingly dependent on an artificial environment for his survival. As time goes on, he will become less and less able to recover from any major perturbation in civilization which might prevent the smooth functioning of his elaborate network of medical facilities. It is not at all unlikely that in future generations the majority of children born will have to be repaired in one way or another, and ever greater numbers of people will have to adjust their biochemical functioning throughout their lives with diverse pills and injections.

In the past there has been considerable selection in favor of intelligence characteristics involving abilities to learn, to solve problems, and to transmit experience to offspring. In recent decades this pattern of selection has been completely reversed. Whereas in former times high intelligence increased the probability that many of an individual's characteristics would be reproduced and would spread throughout the population, today a high intelligence actually decreases this probability. The present situation has arisen as a result of the uneven adoption of birth-control techniques by differing social and economic groups in the Western World.

As modern contraceptive techniques have come into existence, they have first been used extensively by the wealthier and better-educated members of society. The techniques have been adopted only very gradually by the poorer and less-educated groups, with the result that these groups have been breeding much more rapidly than have the wealthier and better-educated ones. Although all of us have known intelligent people who are neither rich nor well educated, and we have known rather stupid people who are both rich and well educated, it is likely that on the average the more well-to-do and better-educated persons in our society have higher intelligence than the others. Although there are admittedly numerous individual fluctuations, it does appear that the feeble-minded, the morons, the dull and backward, and the lower-than-average persons in our society are outbreeding the superior ones at the present time. Indeed, it has been estimated that the average Intelligence Quotient of Western population as a whole is probably decreasing significantly with each succeeding generation.[1]

Fortunately there are indications that this trend may well be of a temporary nature. It is likely to be but a symptom of the transition period in which we are now living, where fertility control has been only partially accepted. Recent trends in the Western World, and particularly the recent developments in Sweden, indicate that within a few decades we may actually achieve a birth pattern according to which parents least able to provide for children will have small families; and as the ability to provide—both economically and intellectually—increases, family size will increase proportionately.

Practically all of the recent changes in selection forces which we can imagine are of a negative nature. We can easily conceive of changes that may lead eventually to a lessened effectiveness of the human machine, but it is difficult to visualize forces that are leading to human betterment from the point of view of survival values. Nevertheless, a few slow changes which might or might not, in the long run, play important roles can be imagined. Traffic accidents tend to remove the reckless, the inattentive, and persons unable to judge time and distance at high speeds. Among children as well as adults, accidents of all types tend to remove from society persons who cannot obey instructions or heed warnings. General pressures of living tend to select in favor of persons who can adjust themselves to city and to factory life. Among the laboring groups, selection effects favor those who can work with groups and who can follow instructions meticulously.

1. See, for example, the studies of Intelligence Quotients in England by R. B. Cattell (*Eugenics Review*, Vol. 28, p. 181, 1936) and the discussion of other studies in *Human Fertility* by R. C. Cook (New York: William Sloane Associates, 1951).

Another selection force involves standards of beauty and other standards which are sought after in mates. Girls who are deemed to be most desirable marry, on the average, earlier, and as a consequence bear more children. This type of effect has had enormous consequences in the past and is dramatically illustrated by groups who lived during the fifteenth century in regions of Europe where iodine was deficient in the diet. Goiters were prevalent and came to be considered a mark of feminine beauty—a fact which is well illustrated by paintings of the time, in which madonnas and angels alike were portrayed as having marked thyroid swellings. Once the goiter became a mark of beauty, it is possible that those women who possessed the greatest susceptibility to goiter, and showed symptoms of it at an early age, married earlier and had more children, so that the weakness spread rapidly throughout their society.[1]

In years to come, as childbearing becomes increasingly a voluntary matter, a selection force which until recent times has had but a small effect upon society will in all likelihood come into existence. It will result largely from the removal of conception as a necessary consequence of coitus. Whereas in earlier times childbearing came about entirely as a consequence of the sexual drive, we are approaching the time when it must result in the main from an urge to have children. We see about us today a wide range of desires concerning children—some persons truly want many of them, while others want none. As time goes on, those persons who really want children will, on the average, outbreed those who do not want children. The net result might well be a gradual growth of a population dominated in large measure by a desire for childbearing.

Is there anything that can be done to prevent the long-range degeneration of human stock? Unfortunately, at the present time there is little, other than to prevent breeding in persons who present glaring deficiencies clearly dangerous to society and which are known to be of a hereditary nature. Thus we could sterilize or in other ways discourage the mating of the feeble-minded. We could go further and systematically attempt to prune from society, by prohibiting them from breeding, persons suffering from serious inheritable forms of physical defects, such as congenital deafness,

1. I am indebted to Professor G. E. Hutchinson for bringing this illustration to my attention.

dumbness, blindness, or absence of limbs. But all these steps would be negligible when compared with the ruthless pruning of man that was done by nature prior to the rise of civilization.

Unfortunately man's knowledge of human genetics is too meager at the present time to permit him to be a really successful pruner. The science of human genetics is not very old, and reliable facts and figures which enable one to differentiate satisfactorily between genetic effects and environmental effects are few and far between. Nevertheless, there is at present sufficient information to permit man to make a start toward pruning, however small it may be. And it is quite possible that by the time another ten or fifteen generations have passed, understanding of human genetics will be sufficient to permit man to do a respectable job of slowing down the deterioration of the species.

This can be accomplished in two ways. First, man can discourage unfit persons from breeding. Second, he can encourage breeding by those persons who are judged fit on the basis of physical and mental testing and examinations of the records of their ancestors. A small start has been made in this direction in the cases of childless couples where the male is sterile and artificial insemination is utilized to impregnate the female. It is quite likely that artificial insemination will be used with increasing frequency during the coming decades, and increasing care will be taken to insure the genetic soundness of the sperm.

If civilization survives, it is likely that in the long run we will be able to slow down and perhaps even to halt deterioration of the species. The methods that will be employed would probably not be palatable to many of us who are alive today. Nevertheless, the human animal is a flexible creature and has thus far been able to adjust his outlook to his needs with remarkable agility.

Although man may eventually succeed in halting the deterioration of the species, it is doubtful that he will be able successfully to improve upon the species by selective breeding for specific qualities. We know to some extent what we don't want in the human machine and can eliminate those particular features. But when it comes to our carrying out a planned evolution during the course of a few thousand years, we are far more seriously handicapped. We can carry out selection processes satisfactorily with sheep, cows, horses, and dogs, for in all cases we are able to examine the animals objectively and decide upon desirable qualities. But when we examine ourselves we are unable to do so objectively. We cannot hope to carry out a planned evolution of our species for the simple reason that we haven't the slightest idea of what we want, and no mechanism is available that will permit us to determine what we want. A "super-race" of men or a panel of gods could examine us objectively and plan a wise pattern. But in the absence of either, we will probably remain pretty much as we are for hundreds of thousands of years.

Chapter IV:

FOOD

> *Let us never forget that the cultivation of the earth is the most important labor of man. When tillage begins, other arts follow. The farmers, therefore, are the founders of civilization.*
>
> DANIEL WEBSTER

1.

All living things require energy if they are to survive. Most animals, including man, obtain their energy by ingesting other living things and burning the organic matter with oxygen:

$$\text{Organic matter} + \text{oxygen} \longrightarrow \text{carbon dioxide} + \text{energy}$$

In the case of higher animals, such as man, organic matter is eaten, oxygen is taken in through the lungs, the oxygen reacts with organic matter in the body, carbon dioxide is expelled, and the energy is used by the body for various activities such as breathing, circulating the blood, digesting food, and performing external work.

A man lying in bed and performing no external work requires a certain minimum energy intake. This basic quantity of energy needed to maintain life depends upon sex, age, body weight, and certain other biological characteristics, but averages about 1700 calories per day for an adult. If we superimpose upon this requirement the energy required for approximately 16 hours of light physical activity, such as slow walking, light housework, or office activity, the total energy requirement becomes about 2800 calories per day.

A man who weighs 125 pounds and who is engaged in moderate activity requires about 2600 calories per day, while a man weighing 200 pounds requires 3700 calories per day. A man who weighs 165 pounds requires about 2800 calories per day if he is engaged in light work, about 3300 calories if he is engaged in moderate work, and as many as 4500 calories per day if he is engaged in heavy physical labor.

The main sources of food energy are carbohydrates, the most important of which are starches (the main constituents of potatoes and cereals) and sugar. If energy intake constituted the only nutritional requirement of human beings, the average person could live adequately by consuming each day 1.5 pounds of sugar, 1.7 pounds of rice or wheat flour, or 7.5 pounds of potatoes.

A second important source of energy is fat, which provides about twice as much energy per pound as do carbohydrates. A person could obtain his full quota of energy by consuming daily between three-quarters of a pound and one pound of lard, butter, or margarine.

We know from experience, however, that a person who consumes a diet consisting only of carbohydrates or fats will soon perish. For proper functioning, the body must be furnished with a number of substances whose functions are other than that of providing energy. Important among those substances are the proteins and amino acids, the vitamins and minerals, such as calcium, phosphorus, salt, iron, and iodine.

Protein is the principal constituent of the cells which make up the human body, and a liberal supply is needed in food throughout life for growth and repair. Like carbohydrates, protein contains carbon, hydrogen, and oxygen. But in addition all protein contains nitrogen to an extent of 15 to 20 per cent. Most proteins also contain sulphur, and a few contain phosphorus and iron.

The animal digestive system breaks proteins down into components which are known as amino acids. These, of which there are many (but not all are essential to an adequate diet), in turn are the building blocks from which body proteins are formed. The human body has the power of synthesizing certain amino acids from others. Those which cannot be synthesized in the body at a rate required for normal growth are known as essential amino acids and must be present in adequate amounts in the diet if the body is to function satisfactorily. Existing evidence indicates that proper functioning of the human body requires eleven of these, the necessary proportions of which in an adequate human diet vary with the composition of the body proteins being formed. As foods differ one from the other in protein composition, they differ in effectiveness in providing for growth and maintenance of the body. Foods which provide all of the needed amino acids in proportions most nearly like those in which they exist in the protein to be formed are of the highest quality and can be utilized most efficiently. Foods which are deficient in one or more of these will not provide adequate protein nutrition no matter how much is eaten. However, amino acids which are unused in the formation of body protein are not wasted, for they are burned much as are carbohydrates and fats.

Vegetable proteins frequently have amino-acid distributions which differ from those of animal proteins, with the result that persons who live solely on a vegetable diet stand a greater chance of suffering from a protein deficiency than do those persons who have a steady ration of animal protein in their diet. For example, a person who consumes about one-half pound of dry skimmed milk a day will obtain adequate amounts of each of the essential amino acids. Soybean meal contains about the same amount of protein as an equivalent amount of dry skimmed milk, but it contains less methionine, one of the essential amino acids. Unless this substance is added to soybean meal, it would be necessary to consume three times as much soybean meal as dry skimmed milk in order to obtain equal quantities of methionine. Similarly, corn meal contains approximately one-third the protein content of dry skimmed milk. Thus, if one were to consume $1\frac{1}{2}$ pounds of corn meal each day, the total protein intake would be adequate. But corn meal is likewise deficient in methionine, with the result that a corn-meal consumption of 3.6 pounds per day would be necessary for the maintenance of protein balance in the body. This would lead to excessive caloric intake (over 6000 calories per day).

Generally speaking, the adult human body will be adequately served if the daily food ration includes about 70 grams of protein per day, provided that about one-half the protein is of animal origin. If all the protein is of vegetable origin, considerably larger daily protein rations are usually necessary for the maintenance of good health.

Bone consists largely of calcium and phosphorus (as phosphate), so these elements are both required in substantial quantities, particularly during pregnancy, lactation, and growth. Calcium deficiency is widespread in the world and exists even in countries where nutrition is otherwise adequate. For example, lack of adequate calcium intake is the most serious nutritional deficiency in Britain today.

A number of elements are necessary in minute amounts for proper body functioning. Lack of iron in the diet causes one type of anemia. Iodine is necessary for proper thyroid functioning. Sodium chloride (salt), the source of hydrochloric acid in the stomach, is lost in sweat, particularly in warm climates, and must be replenished.

Even if a person receives adequate rations of carbohydrates, proteins, and minerals, he still may not survive. Other substances essential for life, known as vitamins, are needed in small amounts. Most important among them are vitamins A and D, the vitamins of the B Complex, and vitamin C.

Vitamin-deficiency diseases are common in most heavily populated areas of the world. Vitamin B_1 deficiency results in beriberi, a disease characterized by muscular spasms, heart damage, and eventually, if unchecked, death. Vitamin A deficiency results in eye disease, which is a common cause of blindness. Lack of vitamin C results in scurvy, so common at one time in England during winter months that it was called "the London Disease." Deficiency of vitamin D results in rickets, which occurs most frequently in northern climates.

Recently, following extensive investigations, the Committee on Foods of the National Research Council drew up a recommended daily allowance for specific nutrients, including carbohydrates, proteins, calcium, iron, and vitamins. The recommendations for an adult whose average caloric needs are 2800 calories per day are shown in Table 1. The allowances listed will be used as a basis for discussing future world food requirements.

2.

Since World War II the average American has consumed annually about 250 quarts of milk, 360 eggs, 170 pounds of meat, poultry, and fish, 190 pounds of grain, 130 pounds of potatoes, 65 pounds of fats and oils (including butter), 120 pounds of citrus fruit and tomatoes, 360 pounds of other vegetables and fruits, 110 pounds of sugar, 20 pounds of beans, peas, and nuts, and 20

TABLE 1

RECOMMENDED DAILY FOOD ALLOWANCES
(For adults whose caloric needs are 2800 calories per day)

Protein (about one-half containing animal protein factor)	66 grams	Yielding 300–400 calories
Fat and Carbohydrate }		Yielding 2400–2500 calories
Calcium	0.9 grams	
Iron	12 milligrams	
Vitamin A	4700 International Units	
Riboflavin	2.3 milligrams	
Thiamine	1.6 milligrams	
Ascorbic Acid	70 milligrams	
Niacin	16 milligrams	

pounds of chocolate, coffee, and tea. The total food intake comes to about 1300 pounds per person, not counting the water in the milk, and provides each person with over 3200 calories per day and a daily ration of 88 grams of proteins, a large part of which is of animal origin.

By contrast, prior to the war, the average resident of Java consumed each year a negligible quantity of milk, 270 pounds of cereals (mainly rice), 315 pounds of roots and tubers, 130 pounds of fruits and vegetables, 55 pounds of peas and beans, 16 pounds of meat and fish, 10 pounds of sugar, and 5 pounds of fats and oils. The total yearly food intake of the average Javan was about 800 pounds, in contrast to the 1300 pounds consumed by the average American. The average daily energy intake per person in Java was about 2000 calories, half of which was provided by cereals. The total protein intake of 43 grams per day was found to be the lowest in all the 70 countries surveyed by the Food and Agricultural Organization of the United Nations. The greater part of the protein intake was of vegetable origin; animal-protein consumption was found to average only 4 grams per person per day.

The diets of the United States and Java represent two extremes of the patterns of human food consumption. At one extreme, approximately 30 per cent of the population of the world has an average per capita caloric intake of more than 2750 calories per

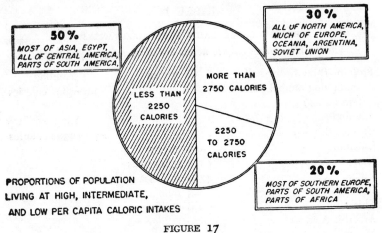

50%
MOST OF ASIA, EGYPT,
ALL OF CENTRAL AMERICA,
PARTS OF SOUTH AMERICA.

30%
ALL OF NORTH AMERICA,
MUCH OF EUROPE,
OCEANIA, ARGENTINA,
SOVIET UNION

MORE THAN
2750 CALORIES

LESS THAN
2250
CALORIES

2250
TO 2750
CALORIES

PROPORTIONS OF POPULATION
LIVING AT HIGH, INTERMEDIATE,
AND LOW PER CAPITA CALORIC INTAKES

20%
MOST OF SOUTHERN EUROPE,
PARTS OF SOUTH AMERICA,
PARTS OF AFRICA

FIGURE 17

day. These high-caloric areas embrace most of the Western World —all of North America, much of Europe, Oceania, Argentina, and the Soviet Union. About 20 per cent of the population, embracing most of Central Europe and parts of South America and Africa, has a per capita caloric intake of between 2250 and 2750 calories per day.

But, at the low extreme, over 50 per cent of the world's population, including most of Asia, Egypt, all of Central America, and some parts of South America, consumes on the average fewer than 2250 calories per day per person—in other words, the energy intake is barely sufficient to maintain life.

Averages do not, of course, tell the whole story. Even in the wealthier nations malnutrition is not unknown; some people consume far more than the average, and others consume far less. In a country such as Java, which has an average daily intake of only 2000 calories per person, many receive far less than this because some fortunate persons receive more.

It can be argued that the areas of low per capita caloric consumption are not quite as badly off as the figures indicate. In the first place, most such areas are in the relatively warm regions of the world, where, because of high temperatures, food requirements are less than in colder climates. In the second place, most such areas, not having passed through the demographic transition, have a relatively high proportion of children, each of whom requires fewer calories than does an adult. Thirdly, the average weight of adults in such areas is considerably less than the average weight of adults in the better-nourished regions. In view of the fact that caloric requirements increase with increasing body weight, the average Western European adult, who weighs 155 pounds, requires more calories than does the average adult in Southeastern Asia, who weighs 110 pounds. On the basis of these factors—temperature, age distribution, and weight—it is generally believed that the per capita caloric requirements of Western Europeans are perhaps as much as 50 per cent greater than those of Southeastern Asians.

However, the differences in stature between Asians and Western Europeans do not appear to be primarily of genetic origin. It is well known that the children of Asian immigrants in the United States are generally considerably taller than the children of corresponding age in their home land. For boys 15 years of age, the difference is about 4 inches and appears to result largely from improved diet.

The effects of diet upon stature and well-being are well illustrated by experiments in which two widely differing Indian diets were fed to rats. The inhabitants of the Pathan area are tall and healthy; rats fed the Pathan diet become large and healthy and had large litters. However, when rats were fed the average diet of the Madrassis, who are physically inferior to the Pathans, they remained small, had poor coats, and disease incidence was high.

Even if the population of the world should increase no further, an increase of total caloric production of at least 20 per cent would be necessary to bring the average world consumption up to minimum standards, and an increase of about 35 per cent would be required to bring the world average up to the Western average. When we take into account the substantial population increases which probably lie ahead of us, even in the absence of further increases in food production, we see that the task of providing adequate nourishment for the greater part of humanity is indeed a formidable one.

In 1946 an estimate was made by the United Nations Food and Agricultural Organization of the increased annual food production required in India in order to meet the minimum nutritional requirements of its growing population by 1960. It was estimated that production of fruits and vegetables, meat, fish, and eggs would have to be tripled; production of roots and tubers, fats and oils, and pulses and nuts would have to be doubled; milk production would have to be increased by 60 per cent; cereal production would have to be increased by 40 per cent.

When we examine the food production of the world as a whole, we find that over 85 per cent of the human race secures the greater part of its nourishment from cereals such as wheat, rice, corn, and oats, and relatively inexpensive starchy foods such as potatoes and cassava. Nearly two-thirds of humanity derives over 80 per cent of its nutritional energy from these sources. Both cane and beet sugar are important energy sources for much of the Western World, accounting for about 15 to 20 per cent of the daily caloric intake. But in Asia and other heavily populated areas sugar contributes but a tiny fraction of the total energy intake.

Perhaps the most important change in the food habits of people since the beginnings of agriculture has been the decreasing proportion of animal products in the average human diet. The fraction of the population which today consumes over 100 pounds of meat, fish, and poultry per person each year is very small and seems destined to decrease in years to come. By contrast, animal products undoubtedly made up a substantial part of the diet of our preagricultural ancestors who specialized in hunting and fishing.

We do not have to search far to find the reason for this change. More people can be fed on an acre of land by growing plants which are directly consumed by human beings than by transforming the foodstuffs into meat before they are consumed. Approximately seven original calories derived from vegetation are required to supply one derived calorie in the form of meat.

In regions of the world where population densities are relatively low, and where food production per acre is high, the people can afford to convert plant calories into meat calories. In America, prior to World War II, for instance, about 2200 calories from foods that were directly of plant origin were consumed daily per person. In addition, 870 calories were obtained from animal products. As each of these derived calories required approximately 7 original plant calories, the energy actually consumed by the meat animals before they were eaten by human beings was about

6100 calories. When we add this to the energy intake directly from plants, we see that the food intake of each American required the production of 8300 original calories.

When we consider protein production we find a similar situation. On farms operating under good management soybeans will yield 450 pounds of protein per acre per year, and wheat will yield 220 pounds per acre. By contrast, milk derived from cows fed on grass, silage, and alfalfa yields but 120 pounds of protein per acre per year, and only 50 pounds of protein per year can be derived from beef grown on the same land.

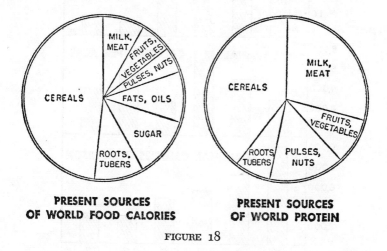

**PRESENT SOURCES
OF WORLD FOOD CALORIES**

**PRESENT SOURCES
OF WORLD PROTEIN**

FIGURE 18

A considerable part of the animal products consumed in the world does not, however, decrease the vegetable calories and protein available to man. Animals grown in most of the low-calorie areas of the world are usually fed on waste that is unfit for human consumption. Such areas usually have few cows but fair numbers of hogs, goats, and chickens, which are seldom given the opportunity of consuming plant food which, as such, is useful to man.

The present distribution of food production in the major regions of the world is illustrated in Figure 19. It can be seen that North America has by far the largest number of cultivated acres per person—eight times greater than the cultivated acreage per capita in Eastern Asia. But in calorie yields per acre we are far behind

Western Europe, which leads the world in this regard, and even Eastern Asia, where the per-acre calorie yield is over twice that in North America.

It is clear that the high per capita calorie intake and the high

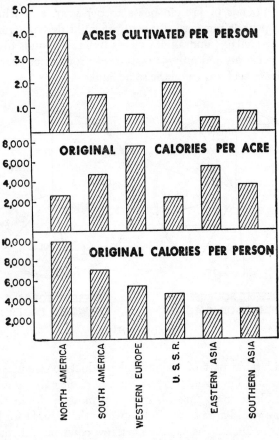

FIGURE 19

animal-protein intake in North America result far more from low population density than from high crop yields. Conversely, the low levels of nutrition in Asia result far more from high population densities than from low crop yields. If North Americans obtained the caloric yield per acre characteristic of Eastern Asia, a population of 350 million persons could be supported at our present nutritional standards, or 670 million persons could be fed at standards now characteristic of Western Europe. If we lowered our per capita caloric intake to that characteristic of Asia, the North American continent, with maximum calorie yields per acre, might well support a population of 1,300,000,000 persons without increasing the acreage of our crop lands.

3.

The total land area of the world amounts to about 36 billion acres. If we could obtain from this area crop yields such as are now obtained in Western Europe, the earth could support 35 billion persons living on American levels of food consumption, or 90 billion persons living at the nutritional level which now exists in Eastern Asia. If we based our considerations of population limitations solely upon the availability of land, it would appear that human populations have barely started the climb to the levels which might ultimately exist.

But nature is not uniformly generous in her blessings. It is easier to obtain high crop yields in France than in Lapland. Wheat planted in the Nile valley will flourish—but wheat planted in the dryness of the Sahara will die.

During the course of human history, man has invariably done the easiest things first as far as feeding himself goes. Agriculture started in the river valleys and only gradually radiated outward into the areas more difficult to cultivate. Heavily forested areas where cultivation can be carried out only after much preliminary effort were among the last regions to be transformed by men into farm land. By now man has taken over most of the relatively easy arable land, together with a large amount of land less favorable to cultivation. But the total area he has conquered represents but a tiny fraction of the earth's surface—no more than 10 per cent of the land area of the world. Of this cultivated area, less than half is utilized directly for production of human food; a substantial fraction is devoted to the production of food for work animals and to the growing of fibers such as cotton, flax, and silk.

By far the most important crops cultivated by man are the cereals, varieties of which form the basis of the diet of the great majority of mankind. Among these, wheat is consumed in the greatest quantity—greater even than the quantities of rice eaten by the huge populations of Southeast Asia. Approximately 400 million acres of the world's lands are devoted to wheat cultivation, and because of the varieties developed during the course of human history, its cultivation is possible as far north as southern Finland and as far south as central India. Altogether, nearly 180 million tons of wheat are harvested each year—approximately 150 pounds for every person in the world. Although wheat is usually thought of as the food of the white race, one of whose main staples it is, its production is being extended ever farther into the tropics, and today increasing quantities are being consumed by people who are traditionally rice eaters. The cultivation of wheat, like the cultivation of any crop, is conditioned by climatic conditions, by the nature of the soil, and by the terrain. A cool, moist climate is required during the growing season, followed by hot, dry weather during the period of ripening. When we examine the land areas of the world, including the regions of perpetual ice and snow, we find that temperature conditions limit wheat production to about 80 per cent of the available land. The fact that there must be neither too much nor too little rainfall reduces the amount of land to 20 per cent, and the need for fairly level and fertile soil still further cuts it to about 10 per cent of the earth's surface, or 3.4 billion acres. Actually less than one-ninth of the suitable land is used for wheat, largely because of the competition of other crops such as corn, oats, and alfalfa, and partly because a substantial fraction of it is still uncultivated grassland utilized primarily for grazing.

Rice is the characteristic crop of the wetter regions of Southeastern Asia and probably feeds more people than any of the cereals. High summer temperatures are required for ripening, and extraordinary amounts of moisture are necessary for growth. As rice requires water on top of the soil as well as in it, cultivation is limited to level land that possesses an impervious substratum. Thus, in general, its culture is confined to the flat bottoms of river valleys and to coastal plains in the tropic and subtropic regions.

The regions in which rice can be easily grown have considerably less area than do the potential wheat-growing regions of the world. But the average rice-yields per acre are about 70 per cent greater than wheat-yields, with the result that although world rice acreage is only half as large as wheat acreage, the total production is nearly the same.

In terms of both acreage and total production, corn or maize ranks equally with rice as one of the main cereals. But the ultimate consumer uses of the two products are quite different. Whereas less than 10 per cent of the rice production is diverted to animal feed and industrial uses, by far the greater part of the corn production of the world is diverted to produce "secondary calories" in the form of animal products. The United States produces over half of the corn grown in the world, but the greater part of the production reaches the consumer in the form of animal products. Only in a few areas, such as Mexico, South Africa, Italy, and Rumania, is it consumed to any great extent directly as food for human beings.

In many regions of the world oats, barley, and rye are important cereals. Oats flourish in the cooler and damper parts of the intermediate wheat lands and have become the principal cereal **in**

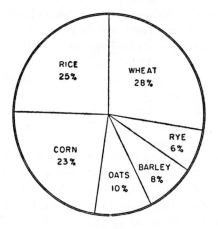

WORLD CEREAL PRODUCTION

TOTAL ANNUAL PRODUCTION: 650 MILLION TONS
TOTAL WORLD CEREAL ACREAGE: 1,200 MILLION ACRES

FIGURE 20

Scotland, Ireland, and Scandinavia, where they are consumed directly by human beings. In most other regions, however, this cereal is used primarily as animal fodder. Rye forms the staple foodstuff of the peasants of Eastern Europe, where it is cultivated extensively for the reason that it can be grown in relatively poor soil and in cool, damp climates. Barley is much more adaptable to variations in both climate and soil than is wheat, with the result that it is a major foodstuff in cold, northern Scandinavia and parts of Northwest Africa. However, in regions where wheat forms the basic foodstuff, barley is grown primarily for the production of fermentation products such as beer and whisky, and for animal feed.

In terms of actual weight, potatoes constitute the world's largest food crop. But the actual energy value of the crops is considerably smaller than the weight would imply, for over 60 per cent of a potato is water, and an additional 20 per cent is refuse. Nevertheless, potatoes, together with other starch-yielding plants such as yams, plantains, bananas, and cassavas, contribute substantially to the world's supply of food energy.

Although the common white potato is a native of America, by far the greater part of the annual crop is grown in the USSR, Germany, and Poland. A large portion of the crop is consumed directly by human beings, the remainder being used for hog feed and the industrial production of alcohol and starch. In terms of energy production per acre, potato culture results in high yields. During the period from 1935 to 1939, the German potato crop yielded 3.5 times as many calories per acre as did the United States wheat crops, and nearly twice as many calories per acre as were produced by United States corn crops.

Until recent times sugar contributed but a small fraction of our food energy. But today it is considered a necessity in almost every country in the world, particularly in the Western World, where it contributes substantially to our total caloric consumption, supplying as it does between 15 and 20 per cent of the caloric intake in Denmark, Sweden, Switzerland, the United Kingdom, the United States, Australia, and New Zealand.

If all the sugar produced each year were to be distributed evenly among the people of the world, every person would receive a yearly allotment of about 30 pounds, which would provide approximately 150 calories per day. But the actual consumption varies greatly from locality to locality. The per capita consumption in Denmark, for example, is four times the world average, while in China, where the average person obtains considerably less than 1 per cent of his daily caloric ration from sugar, it is less than one-half the world average.

Sugar is produced from cane grown in the tropics and subtropics, and from beets grown in the temperate regions of the world. From the point of view of conversion of solar energy into food energy, the cane and the beet are the most efficient plants known. On some plantations in the Hawaiian Islands as many as 20 tons of cane sugar per acre have been obtained in a year. In terms of calories, this is thirty times greater than the average obtained from the United States corn crop per acre. On some California farms yields of sugar from beets have been obtained ranging as high as 8 tons per acre. Such yields are, of course, exceptional. But in general the per-acre caloric yields from sugar beets are considerably greater than those obtained from cereals. In continental Europe caloric yields per acre exceed even those obtained from potato culture.

Sugar cane is a type of grass which attains considerable height. Growing seasons are frequently twelve months or longer, during which period there must be no frost. The plant requires abundant moisture and continuous hot sunny weather. Thus cultivation is limited to a belt around the equator in which the mean annual temperatures do not fall below 68 degrees Fahrenheit. Outside of this belt cane cultivation is possible, but frost damage can be severe. An annual precipitation of 60 inches, or its equivalent in irrigation, is required, but during the time of ripening there must not be excessive moisture. Thus a climate which is perpetually wet, such as that in the basins of the Amazon and the Congo, is unsuitable for cane cultivation.

Sugar beets thrive in a temperate climate where there is ample rain during certain periods of growth, particularly when the seed is germinating and when the beets are forming. During the later stages of growth moisture must not be excessive.

The combination of cereals, potatoes, other starchy roots and tubers, and sugar accounts directly for about 70 per cent of the caloric intake of the world's population. An additional 8 per cent of the calories are provided by meat and milk. These secondary foodstuffs are produced by feed cereals, roots and tubers, grasses such as alfalfa which are cultivated by man, and natural grasses which grow in uncultivated regions. The balance of food calories, amounting to something over 20 per cent, is provided by fats, such as animal fat and butter, by oil derived from such sources as peanuts, coconuts, olives, soybeans, and cottonseed, by fruits and vegetables, and by a variety of nuts and legumes.

4.

For the entire time during which man has existed on the earth he has competed with other animals for food. Primitive man interfered with the conditions of his environment relatively little, but since the beginnings of agriculture man has displaced animals from their natural habitats through the processes of taking over natural animal environments such as forests and grasslands for his own purposes and destroying those animals which interfered either with his agriculture or with his animal domestication. Today, although most large animals not useful to man have been removed from the regions he cultivates, he is still battling species which threaten the productivity of his land—varieties of rodents, insects, and bacteria. It is probable that the battle will continue for as long a time as human beings exist.

With increasing use of non-animal energy sources, the population of work animals in the world is destined to decrease, eventually to the vanishing point (if industrial civilization survives), leaving those which produce meat and milk as the only major large non-human animal residents of the land areas of the earth. The effect of farm mechanization upon this trend is well illustrated by the change in the population of horses and mules in the United States; since 1910 it has decreased from 24 million to 9 million, indicating a fall from a level of 1 animal for every 4 persons to a level of 1 for every 17 persons.

The world population of cattle, sheep, and swine is about 1800 million—not much less than the population of human beings. But the caloric value of the food consumed by them is roughly about three times that of the food consumed by human beings.

Although, as we have seen, many swine, goats, and chickens

are nourished by refuse unfit for human consumption, the great majority of animals are nourished by food which is grown on land that otherwise could be utilized for the direct production of food for man. Thus, in effect, man's own domestic animals compete with him for food. If men were to exist solely on a vegetable diet, the present crop and grazing land of the world could support far more people than now exist.

For this reason, in areas of high population density such as China, the people live primarily upon a vegetable diet—they can little afford the luxury of spending 7 vegetable calories to obtain 1 meat calorie. By contrast, we have seen that in regions where the population densities are low, relative to the carrying capacity of the land, calories can be "wasted" and meat consumption is high.

Among the regions which consume large quantities of animal foodstuffs, Europe ranks first as producer of both meat and dairy products. Prior to the destruction caused by World War II, over 40 per cent of the meat production and over 50 per cent of the milk production of the Western World were centered in Europe west of the USSR. Even so, production was not equal to the demand, and nearly 15 per cent of the meat eaten in Europe was imported. The United Kingdom is by far the largest importer, buying heavily from Australia, New Zealand, and Argentina.

The meat and dairy products involved in international trade are produced either in areas of relatively low population density where there are grasslands which have not yet been taken over for cultivation, or in regions where the inhabitants specialize in the production of highly finished animal foodstuffs, often by importing a substantial portion of the feed. The former areas include Argentina (which has become the foremost supplier of meat for the rest of the world), New Zealand, and Australia. The latter, or elaborating, areas embrace Denmark, Holland, Switzerland, and Ireland, all of which export quantities of dairy products and high-grade meats.

From the point of view of converting vegetable matter into animal protein, the production of dairy foods is considerably more efficient than the production of beef. On an acre of farmland under good management, about 300 pounds of beef containing about 50 pounds of protein can be grown annually, with the use of grass, alfalfa, and corn as fodder. On the other hand, dairy cattle, fed the same food, will produce annually about 3000 pounds of milk containing 120 pounds of protein. For this reason, over most of agricultural Europe dairy farming forms an integral part of a mixed agricultural economy. The raising of cattle for meat alone is seldom attempted.

In Asia, where the per capita intake of animal protein is extremely low, patterns of consumption vary, determined in part by the availability and nature of the land, by the proximity to the sea, and by religious and social restrictions. Moslems, Hindus, and Jews are forbidden to eat pork. The cow is a sacred animal to the Hindus, and although consumption of milk is permitted, slaughter is forbidden by law. The Chinese do not consider milk fit for human consumption, but raise immense numbers of pigs. In Japan fish is the primary source of animal protein.

In both China and India cattle are used primarily as draft animals. There are perhaps 200 million cattle on the Indian subcontinent—by far the largest number in any region of comparable size in the world—and they probably consume about three times as many calories as are consumed by the human population. But, paradoxically, only about one-third of them are working cattle; the number falls far short of the need for draft power. In most Indian provinces useless and uneconomical stock, protected by religious conviction and by sentiment, forms the largest proportion of the cattle population. There is thus a colossal waste of food energy in India, and, in view of the religious restrictions, the waste can be remedied only by limitation and careful control of breeding, by more efficient use of grazing land, and, eventually, by mechanization of the farms so that the population of work animals can be decreased. As trucks and tractors replace cattle, increasing quantities of land can be diverted to the production of food for human consumption.

In both India and China beef is eaten only by Moslems, and even the more well-to-do Moslem cultivators are unable to consume meat more frequently than once a month. It is only during the Id Festival that the Moslems of India use mutton and beef liberally. In China so great is the need for subsistence crops that there are no grazing grounds. Although milk is almost never used, the Chinese peasantry consumes quantities of pork, mutton, eggs, and poultry—quantities which are small but nevertheless larger than those consumed in India.

In heavy meat-producing areas fish contribute but a small fraction of the animal protein intake. In the United States, for example, only about 7 per cent of our animal protein consumption is obtained from fish. Nevertheless, when we consider the world as a whole, fish contribute substantially to the animal protein supply. Indeed, in certain areas such as Japan, where high population densities, relative to the capacity of the land, prohibit an appreciable production of either milk or meat, the availability of fish is an indispensable asset to national well-being.

The oceans cover over 70 per cent of the surface of the earth. From this vast expanse man extracts annually nearly 20 million tons of fish and shellfish, or about 280 pounds for every mile of surface water. However, fish are by no means uniformly distributed in the oceans. They are dependent upon the growth of marine plants for their food, and marine vegetation varies in quantity in different localities of an ocean. Like terrestrial vegetation, it requires nutrients such as nitrogen and phosphorus, and the availability of these substances depends upon ocean circulation patterns and upon the proximity of a given area of water to the continents from which supplies of phosphorus and other substances are carried by rivers into the ocean. In addition, plants must have light for growth, and the depth to which light penetrates in the ocean depends upon the turbidity and the absorption of light in the sea water. The zone in which light intensity is sufficient for photosynthesis extends from the surface to an average depth of about 250 feet, but there are enormous variations.

Thus the yield of fish which is obtained from a given area depends first upon the intensity of the fishing and second upon the rate of growth of marine vegetation. In addition, the yield of fish depends considerably upon the depth at which fishing operations are conducted. Recent studies indicate that appreciable increases in yield can be obtained by extending operations to great depths.

Approximately 98 per cent of the annual world fish catch is derived from the Northern Hemisphere. The extremely small contribution of the Southern Hemisphere probably results more from lack of intensive fishing operations than from any inherent deficiency in biological productivity. The highly industrialized countries which border the waters of the northern Pacific and Atlantic Oceans conduct far more intensive fishing operations than do the countries to the south.

Under special circumstances, both fish and shellfish can be cultivated. It is well known that the addition of phosphates to freshwater lakes will increase the production of vegetation and, as a result, the production of fish. This method has been applied to some extent in various parts of the world.

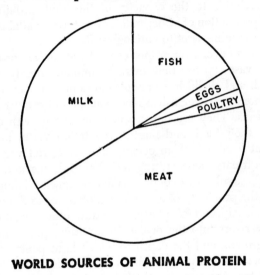

WORLD SOURCES OF ANIMAL PROTEIN

FIGURE 21

Oysters, mussels, and clams can be cultivated, and, under favorable conditions, the annual crops may exceed the yield of meat obtainable from the best agricultural land. Good oyster bottoms, for example, are capable of yielding as much as 750 pounds of oyster meat per acre. Yields of mussels are even larger. However, grounds suitable for shellfish culture are limited to inshore waters, and, in view of this, it is doubtful that such marine life will ever contribute more than a small percentage to the world's supply of seafood.

To sum up, the annual world production of foods containing animal protein amounts to about 200 million tons of milk, 45 million tons of meat, 20 million tons of fish, 1.5 million tons of poultry, and 100 billion eggs. If this food were to be divided evenly among all the inhabitants of the earth, each person would receive weekly less than 2 quarts of milk, 1 pound of meat, fish, and poultry, and less than 1 egg. But, as we have seen, averages do not tell the whole story. If some people receive more than the average, others must receive less. The average person in the United States consumes 2.7 times the average quota of milk, 3 times the average quota of meat, fish, and poultry, and 8 times the average quota of eggs.

5.

The land areas of the world provide man with his food, but they provide him, in addition, with a multiplicity of products which enable him to clothe and shelter himself and to produce a variety of goods which increase the comfort of his daily life. Important among these products are natural fibers such as cotton, jute, flax, and hemp, and tree crops, the most important of which is wood.

The cultivated area devoted to the production of vegetable fibers is small when compared with that devoted to cereal production— about 80 million acres as compared with 1200 million acres. Altogether, approximately 5 per cent of the world's better crop land is devoted to the culture of vegetable fibers, and between 30 and 40 per cent of the grazing land is occupied by sheep and goats, which provide the greater part of the animal fibers.

The annual per capita consumption of fibers is about 10 pounds, approximately 7 pounds of which are used for apparel and for general household purposes. However, the range of consumption is far greater than the range of food consumption. The average American, for example, consumes more than 40 pounds of fibers annually, while the average Chinese consumes but 3.5 pounds annually. The consumption in Europe lies somewhere between these two extremes. France has a normal yearly consumption of about 20 pounds of fibers per person.

Cotton is by far the largest of the fiber crops, accounting as it does for nearly 60 per cent of the world fiber production and nearly 75 per cent of the area devoted to fiber cultivation. Next in importance is jute, which is used primarily for industrial purposes; it is followed closely by wool, flax, and hemp. Synthetic fibers

such as rayon and nylon now account for more than 10 per cent
of the total world fiber production, and the relative importance
of such products is increasing rapidly.

By far the largest crop harvested by man is wood, obtained from
the forests which cover nearly 10 billion acres of the earth's surface. Each year about 1300 million tons of wood are consumed by
the peoples of the world, approximately one-half being used for
fuel, and the balance for construction, the production of paper,
and a variety of industrial purposes.

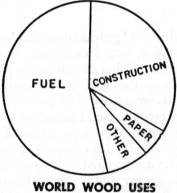

WORLD WOOD USES
TOTAL ANNUAL PRODUCTION:
1300 MILLION TONS
TOTAL WORLD FOREST ACREAGE:
10 BILLION ACRES

FIGURE 22

At one time forests covered nearly 15 billion acres of land.
But men have consumed and destroyed trees far more rapidly than
the trees have been replaced by nature, with the result that approximately one-third of the original forests have disappeared.
In most industrial countries wood is still being consumed more
rapidly than it is being replaced by new growth—in Europe and
North America, at a rate between 10 and 15 per cent faster than
the rate of replacement.

Three centuries ago, approximately 830 million acres of the
United States and Alaska were covered with dense forests. So

rapidly have the trees been cut that today there are left only 450 million acres. Of this area, only about one-third is suitable for cutting, the balance being cut-over forest, some of which is now growing, and some dying.

Approximately two-thirds of the forested areas of the world, or 6.5 billion acres, are classed as being of such a nature that they lend themselves to sustained-yield management; approximately half of these are classed as accessible on the basis of existing transportation facilities and existing techniques of forestry. The balance of 3.5 billion acres is of a submarginal nature, and sustained-yield management would not be warranted.

Per capita wood consumption, like food consumption, varies throughout the world. Approximately 1000 pounds of wood are consumed each year for every person living, but the patterns vary from those of desert tribes where consumption is very small to countries such as the United States where 1700 pounds of wood are consumed per person per year.

Although trees do not contribute greatly to the world's food supply, they influence it in many ways. First, they occupy a large area of the earth, some of which might be utilized for the production of food crops. Second, they are important instruments in the prevention of land erosion and excessive water run-off. These factors, which must be balanced against the relative needs for food and wood during the years to come, are discussed in more detail in later sections of this book.

6.

The food production of the world can be increased in a variety of ways. Clearly we have not yet reached the limit of our land resources, and an obvious approach to increased production would be to place under cultivation lands which at the present time are either forest, uncultivated grassland, or waterless desert. A second approach would be to increase the amount of food produced from each acre of land. Experience has shown that this can be done by careful breeding and selection of plants, by proper cultivation, and by application of fertilizers, insecticides, and other chemicals such as plant hormones. A third approach would be to make increased use of the living resources of the oceans. We have already seen that the Southern Hemisphere is practically virgin territory for the fishing industry, and the yields of fish might be greatly increased by devising means for fishing at greater depths. A fourth approach would be to devise new methods, other than the traditional agricultural ones, for the efficient production of food.

We must now ask ourselves: What are the fundamental limits to each of these approaches? What would be the cost in terms of our other resources of a greatly increased world food production? How many people might eventually be supported comfortably by the potential food production of the world?

As we have seen, in discussing specific crops, successful cultivation by conventional agricultural techniques requires that the climate must not be excessively cold, that there must be adequate moisture, that the terrain must not be too rugged, and that the soil must be sufficiently fertile and deep to permit cultivation. In a given area inadequacy with respect to any one of these factors can prevent the cultivation of crops.

Approximately 10 per cent of the world's 36 billion acres of land area is covered with perpetual snow and ice. Another 4 per cent of the land is situated in such high latitudes that only sparse growths of tundra vegetation, consisting largely of rugged grasses, mosses, and lichens, can survive. Desert regions where precipitation is so low that at most only scanty growths of shrubs and desert grasses can be supported occupy another 20 per cent of the land area. When we add to this the regions of mountain tundra, mountain deserts and steppes, and other regions of sparse and sporadic rainfall, we find that nearly one-half of the land area of the world is excluded from agricultural use by the restrictions of severe cold or excessive dryness. Of the remaining half of the world's lands only about 15 per cent is cultivated, an area amounting to between 2.5 and 3 billion acres. For reasons including unfavorable terrain, excessive rainfall, the presence of poor soil, or the presence of forests, the remaining 15 billion acres of land which are cultivable from the climatic point of view remain uncultivated.

In addition to the cultivated areas, approximately 6 billion acres of pasture land are in use, drawn from lands which are less favorable climatically or which are more rugged or less fertile than the cultivated lands. Thus, altogether man draws his food and related materials from an area of about 9 billion acres, which represent approximately one-quarter of the land area of the earth.

Areas which can be classified as "good" or "fair" on the agricultural scale are already in the main under cultivation. In order further to extend the area of agricultural activity, it will be necessary to place under cultivation lands which are less fertile than those in the major regions where crops are now being grown. But cultivation of relatively unfertile land is fraught with difficulty and frequently leads to disaster.

Prior to the advent of man as a geologic force, the land areas of the earth were covered with natural vegetation the local nature of which was determined by climatic conditions and terrain. Forests were supported in the wetter regions of the world and merged into grasslands in regions of less rainfall. The grasslands in turn merged into deserts in dry regions and into tundra in regions of intense cold.

The grasses and the trees derived their mineral nutrients from the soil, but in the balance of nature the greater part of the nutrients were returned to the soil by way of decaying vegetation, animal excreta, and animal remains. Each year a small fraction of the mineral nutrients was leached from the soil and carried by the rivers into the oceans, but this process was balanced by the slow introduction of new mineral nutrients from weathered rocks.

When man first came on the scene the picture was not altered. He, like other animals about him, ate vegetation and meat, but the minerals were eventually returned to the soil by way of his excreta while he lived and his body when he died.

With the evolution of urban culture, the pattern began to change. When men began to ship vegetation and animals to cities, where the mineral nutrients were expelled into the rivers rather than being returned to the soil, trouble began. As the availability of mineral nutrients diminished, crop yields lessened, and eventually the land had to be abandoned. The residents of the Nile valley were particularly fortunate in this respect, for the seasonal floods returned nutrients to the soil. But in other regions empirical procedures had to be devised to permit continued cropping of the land. Thus there slowly evolved the practices of permitting land to lie fallow, of crop rotation, and of both organic and inorganic fertilization of the soil. In a large part of Asia a balance came into

existence whereby practically all human excrement was returned
to the soil. In much of the Western World crop rotation and artificial fertilizer are used extensively, but in a large part of the world
the nutrients are being removed from the soil more rapidly than
nature replenishes them.

If soil is of good quality and sufficiently deep, many crops can
be removed before a decrease in fertility becomes noticeable. But
if the soil is thin and relatively unfertile, it may become unproductive after only one or two crops. Thus, much farm land, which
under proper management could have been productive, has been
cleared, cultivated, and after a few years abandoned because
the land became unproductive. With the natural protective covering of vegetation gone, the soil was then exposed to the elements,
and frequently it was washed away, leaving behind barren rock
where formerly there had been a layer of top soil which was thin
but nevertheless usable with proper management.

In many areas, particularly in the tropics, where soils are relatively thin and of poor fertility, it is a common practice to burn
out an area of vegetation, plant a crop, harvest it, and then move
elsewhere to repeat the process.

Overgrazing has resulted in similar losses of useful soil. Seldom
are fertilizers applied to grazing land, and the steady shipment
of sheep and cattle away from the land depletes the soil of its nutrient minerals. Eventually grass can no longer grow, the protective
cover is lost, and the soil can be washed away.

The removal of trees and other vegetation accelerates the process of erosion still further by diminishing the ability of the land to
retain water. Practiced in excess and in the absence of other control measures, removal of vegetation frequently results in floods
which remove soil that otherwise would not have been washed
away.

Dr. Hugh H. Bennett, former chief of the Soil Conservation Service of the U.S. Department of Agriculture, has estimated that during the short life of the United States approximately 280 million
acres of crop and range land have been essentially destroyed, and
that about 100 million acres have been so badly damaged by erosion that they cannot be restored. Altogether it is estimated that
of the original average 9 inches of top soil in existence when the
nation was founded, approximately one-third has been washed

away. If the process is left to nature, every inch thus lost can be replaced only by many centuries of geologic and biologic activity.

When we survey the extent to which soil has been abused in various parts of the world, we are forced to the conclusion that the areas of potential crop production are decreasing. It is a well-known fact that the processes of deterioration can be stopped by sound land management, and this is being done in a few restricted areas such as in the Scandinavian countries. But when we think of expanding the areas of agriculture for the greater part of the world, we must also think in terms of measures to stop the contraction that is taking place at the present time, and to prevent the loss of soil in the new areas that have been opened.

The greater part of the world's agricultural production comes from regions which were originally prairies, steppes, and broad-leaf forests under which a fairly thick layer of organic material had accumulated. Most of these areas are now under cultivation, where the terrain permits, and we cannot look forward to any major expansion of agriculture in such regions.

Such expansion in the future must be largely in regions where the soils are of types that have not been cultivated to any great extent heretofore. These regions embrace the areas where soils have evolved mainly under coniferous forests in relatively cool climates, and the areas of reddish and yellowish soils in the regions of the tropics. The former soils, known as "podsols," dominate in the northern forested lands of North America, Europe, and Asia, and consist of a thin layer of organic matter lying upon a shallow layer of coarse-grained, whitish, heavily leached material. The natural fertility of such soils is low. The red or "lateric" soils of the tropics likewise consist of a thin layer of organic material overlying a layer of heavily leached material, but in such soils the layer of leached material is usually of considerable thickness. The lateric soils cover large regions of South America, Africa, southeastern North America, Southern Asia, and Oceania. Throughout all such areas the small accumulation of humus and the intensity of the leaching have generally resulted in soils of low fertility.

The podsols cover approximately 9 per cent of the land area of the earth, and the red soils cover an additional 19 per cent. Although most areas of red soils in southeastern Asia and southeastern North America are now in use, it is likely that less than 1 per cent of the sum of all podsols and laterites is now under cultivation.

Agriculture will probably be extended into the podsol areas of the north and into the vast areas of red soils of South America and Africa. But, for the reasons indicated, the difficulties will be enormous. In particular, in rainy tropical climates improvements in soils that are naturally very low in organic material and mineral nutrients do not have a lasting effect. The problem of insuring stability and fertility in tropical soils has yet to be solved.

Nevertheless, the problems involved in cultivating podsols in the north and lateric soils in the south are by no means insurmountable. The crops of Finland are grown almost entirely in podsols, and the agriculture of the Philippine Islands is carried out under conditions of both soil and climate similar to those in the large lateric regions of Africa and South America.

The areas of podsols and laterites add up to approximately 10 billion acres. If all of this acreage were put under cultivation, the agricultural lands of the world would be four times more extensive than they are today. But for a number of rather obvious reasons a substantial fraction of these areas cannot or should not be cleared for agricultural purposes. Large parts of the regions are now covered with forests which either are productive at present or can be made productive in the future. Unfavorable topography and stoniness will further eliminate a large proportion of the land. Taking these factors into consideration, a number of persons who have studied the problem believe that approximately 300 million acres of northern soil and 1 billion acres of tropical soil could be placed under cultivation.[1] Such a move would require prodigious effort and capital investment, and the problems of maintaining land stability would be far greater than those which exist in the major agricultural regions of the world today. Nevertheless such a development would by no means be impossible, and, barring a major world catastrophe followed by technological regression, we can expect major efforts in this direction during the course of the decades ahead.

The increase in food production that might be expected should 1.3 billion acres of tropic and northern soils be placed under

1. See R. M. Salter, in *Science*, May 23, 1947; H. R. Tolley, F. A. O. Release, February 19, 1949.

cultivation has been estimated by Salter,[1] using the experience in Finland as the basis for estimating crop yields in northern regions, and the experience in the Philippine Islands as the basis for estimating yields in the tropics. These estimates are given in Table 2, from which it can be seen that, when compared with exist-

TABLE 2

ESTIMATED ATTAINABLE FOOD PRODUCTION WITH EXISTING TECHNIQUES [*]

From 1000 Million New Acres of Tropic Lands and 300 Million New Acres of Northern Lands

	MILLIONS OF METRIC TONS			
	PRESENT WORLD PRODUCTION	NORTHERN LANDS	TROPICS	TOTAL NEW PRODUCTION	PER CENT OF INCREASE
Cereals [†]	300	36	358	394	130
Roots and Tubers	150	66	240	306	200
Sugar	30	0.6	143	144	480
Fats and Oils	15	1.4	52	53	350
Pulses and Nuts	35	0.8	12	13	37
Fruits and Vegetables	155	0.0	259	259	170
Meat	65	7.5	11	19	29
Milk	150	134	9	143	95

[*] See R. M. Salter, loc. cit.
[†] Total cereal production is actually greater than this, but a substantial fraction is used for animal feed.

ing production, the potential production of food calories from the new areas is spectacular. The potential increase in protein production, although less spectacular, is nevertheless substantial.

When all factors are taken into consideration, it can be seen that an increase in food production, such as is outlined in Table 2, would permit doubling of world population. Further, it should be emphasized that the increased production from the extension of agricultural land would have little effect upon the large undernourished areas of Asia, as the greater part of the increased production would be in the northern regions and in Africa and South America.

1. R. M. Salter, loc. cit.

7.

Low crop yields can result from any one of a number of causes. For optimum development, a plant of a given species must grow in an environment which possesses the proper light intensity and temperature; the soil must be of a specified quality and must contain the proper ecological balance of micro-organisms; the proper mineral nutrients, including trace elements, must be available. As the plant grows it is subject to a variety of diseases which hinder growth or cause death. The plant may be devoured by insects and rodents. Too much or too little moisture during certain stages of growth can result in low yields or even in complete destruction.

During the last half-century basic research by plant breeders, plant pathologists, agricultural biochemists, and soil chemists has resulted in enormous increases in acreage yields of many crops. In the United States in recent years yields of corn, wheat, oats, and barley have increased from 10 to 25 per cent per acre—even in some areas where soil fertility has been decreasing. More recently, yields of potatoes, sugar beets, and other vegetable crops have been increased greatly.

A large part of the increased yields has resulted from careful breeding and selection. Today plants can be bred for optimum growth under particular climatic and soil conditions, for resistance to specific diseases, and for resistance to insects. The development of varieties of hybrid corn has increased corn production in the United States by 20 per cent, and there are indications that by planting hybrid seeds yields in certain other countries can be increased several fold. Breeding and selection have increased the sugar content of sugar beets from 5 per cent to as high as 20 per cent. Breeding for resistance against scourges such as wheat rust and potato blight may eventually eliminate losses from these diseases, whereas today losses of from 10 to 25 per cent are not uncommon. Yields have been further increased by the development of varieties of insecticides coupled with the use of proper cropping sequences.

On the husbandry side, we in the United States are now raising 12 per cent more pigs per litter than we were a quarter of a century ago, and their body weights have been increased about 25 per cent without increasing the feed. The body weights of beef cattle have been increased by 15 per cent without increasing feed. The use of antibiotics has reduced mortality of chicks and has promoted more rapid growth. An understanding of balanced rations for chickens has resulted in many more eggs per hen per year.

The increases in crop yield in the United States have been dramatic, but we still have far to go before we attain the agricultural level that prevails in Europe. The production of grain in the United States amounts to 18.6 bushels per acre as compared with yields in Germany and the United Kingdom of about 30 bushels per acre, and yields in Denmark, the Netherlands, and Belgium which approach 40 bushels per acre. The United States produces 110 bushels of potatoes per acre, as compared with 320 bushels per acre in Belgium. In a group of nineteen European countries only one has an average potato yield of less than 150 bushels per acre. However, it will be some time before crop yields such as are obtained in Western Europe become economic necessities for the United States.

When we compare existing average crop yields with the maximum yields that have been achieved under favorable conditions, we can obtain some idea of possible future increases in soil productivity. While the present yield of potatoes in the United States is 110 bushels per acre, yields of 1000 bushels per acre have been reported. Our average corn yield is 35 bushels per acre; yields of 150 bushels per acre have been obtained. Our average flax yield of 10 bushels per acre is dwarfed by reported yields of 60 bushels per acre.

High crop yields require adequate supplies of moisture and constant replacement of the mineral nutrients that are consumed by the plants and leached from the soil. In a number of areas irrigation is used, both to permit cultivation where it was previously impossible, and to increase crop yields in regions where rainfall is not dependable. In the world as a whole approximately 200 million acres are now under irrigation, and it is estimated that an additional 200 million acres of deserts and near-deserts could be irrigated, given sufficient effort. In addition, approximately 1 billion acres of humid and sub-humid land could benefit from supplemental irrigation. This area, which is now being cropped at less than optimum intensity because of moisture deficiency, could give considerably higher crop yields than are now being obtained. In some areas two crops could be grown per season where only one is being grown at the present time. In other regions, where rainfall is adequate only two or three years out of five, irrigation could be used to provide moisture during years of drought.

Supplemental irrigation of 1 billion acres of land now being cultivated and complete irrigation of an additional 200 million acres of desert land could be expected to double the present world food production. Such a development would be enormously expensive in terms of both labor and investment, but physically the irrigation of such large areas is possible. The average annual discharge of the world's 80 major rivers, which would have to be diverted for this purpose, is approximately 12 billion acre-feet— more than enough to provide the necessary water. Obviously, however, in many regions the water would have to be transported enormous distances. Further, such a development would be virtually impossible within the framework of existing national sovereignties. Few of the great river basins lie within the sole jurisdiction of a single nation—a fact which causes the political difficulty to overshadow the physical one.

When crop yields are at high levels, mineral nutrients are removed at rates much more rapid than the rates of replacement by nature. Because of this fact, such elements as phosphorus, nitrogen, potassium, calcium, and magnesium, together with a variety of trace elements, must be added as fertilizer at rates approximately equal to the rates of removal by cropping and by leaching. Frequently atmospheric nitrogen is fixed by the nitrogen-fixing bacteria of the soil at a sufficient rate to permit steady cropping, but the elements which are obtained from rocks—in particular, phosphorus and potassium—must be added continuously if a rapid growth rate is to be maintained.

When plants are cropped, those portions which are inedible are frequently returned to the soil. The edible portions are eaten by man. Usually animal excreta, together with the inedible portions of the animal, such as the bones, are returned to the soil. But in societies such as that which exists in the United States, the mineral content of food that reaches the market is lost. Man's excreta and garbage are expelled into rivers,[1] and his bones and flesh are interred in cemeteries.

At the present time, even in the United States, where per capita consumption of phosphate fertilizers is higher than in any other country, phosphorus is being removed from the soil, both by erosion and by cropping, more rapidly than it is being replaced. Thus, in the world as a whole, greatly increased use of fertilizers will be necessary even to maintain crop production at existing levels on a stable basis. And if we are to increase food production to any noticeable extent, the increased production of fertilizer must be very great indeed. This production is, in turn, essentially a problem of energy. Using existing techniques and existing phosphate deposits, it requires the energy equivalent to the burning of three tons of coal to produce a ton of phosphorus in a form suitable to put into the soil. The consequences of this energy requirement are discussed in detail in a later section of this book.

TABLE 3

ATTAINABLE PRODUCTION OF FOOD FROM EXISTING CULTIVATED LANDS *

		MILLIONS OF METRIC TONS						
	CEREALS	ROOTS, TUBERS	SUGAR	FATS, OILS	PULSES, NUTS	FRUITS, VEGETABLES	MEAT	MILK
Present production	300	150	30	15	35	155	65	150
Attainable production	360	230	34.5	18	43	211	79	180

* R. M. Salter, loc. cit.

It is clear that, given conscientious efforts to prevent further land erosion, more widespread use of fertilizer, coupled with the application of those principles of plant breeding and agricultural biochemistry which are already known, world production of food can be increased appreciably without the development of a single acre of new land and without increasing the amount of irrigated land. Table 3 shows a reasonable estimate of the pro-

1. Steps to eliminate this waste have been taken in some cities of the United States. In Oakland, California, for instance, the municipal garbage-disposal plant processes the city garbage and returns it to the soil as agricultural fertilizer. In Milwaukee, Wisconsin, city sewage is processed and shipped to points as far distant as the West Coast, as high-grade fertilizer.

duction obtainable from existing cultivated land. In general, a
12-per-cent increase of food production appears to be obtainable
with existing techniques.

8.

Plants can be limited in their growth rates by a variety of factors.
Mineral nutrients must diffuse through the soil to the elaborate
root structure, and from there they must be transported through
the body of the plant. Carbon dioxide must be taken into the leaves.
Light must fall upon the plant with sufficient intensity to give
rise to a rate of photosynthesis greater than the rate of consumption of energy by plant metabolism.

It is now known, as the result of a variety of plant studies, that
growth rates can be greatly increased by cultivating plants in
manmade environments where the limiting factors to growth are
minimized. Perhaps the greenhouse is the best-known example
of a means for increasing growth rates under generally adverse
conditions. By providing an enclosure of glass or plastic which
permits light to enter, and by controlling the temperature within
the enclosure, plants can be grown in northern climates during
winter months when they would normally be either dead or dor-
mant. It is known further that soil is not necessary for plant growth.
If the roots are immersed in a solution containing the necessary
mineral nutrients, and satisfactory mechanical support is given,
the plant will grow, provided, of course, that the other environmental conditions for growth are fulfilled. Indeed, in view of the
fact that the necessary nutrients can be diffused more readily
through a solution than through soil, plants which are nurtured
by this method (known as hydroponics) can grow considerably
more rapidly than can their soil-grown counterparts.

Once the unavailability of mineral nutrients is eliminated as a
major limitation to plant growth, the rates become limited, under
normal conditions, by the concentration of carbon dioxide in the
air. The earth's atmosphere contains only a minute concentration
—about 0.03 per cent—of this substance, and in the absence of
winds and breezes the air can become depleted locally of carbon
dioxide, and the growth rate is lessened. It has been demonstrated

that a tripling of carbon-dioxide concentration in the air will approximately double the growth rates of tomatoes, alfalfa, and sugar beets. A point is eventually reached, however, where no further increase in growth rates can be achieved by further increasing the concentration of carbon dioxide. The plant is then limited in growth rate either by light intensity or by the fundamental physiological make-up of the organism.

When a plant is removed from darkness, photosynthesis begins, the rate depending upon the light intensity. As the intensity is increased, the growth rate increases. But a point is eventually reached where further increase of light intensity ceases to increase the rate of growth. The "saturation" level of light intensity is determined by the extent to which growth is limited by other factors. If mineral nutrients and carbon dioxide are readily available, the light saturation point is determined entirely by the general physiological make-up of the plant. Maximum photosynthesis in a normally exposed leaf of corn appears to be reached at about one-fourth full Iowa summer sunlight. By contrast, light saturation for certain species of algae appears to be reached with only 2 or 3 per cent of full sunlight.

To what extent might man be able to control the various factors that limit plant growth? Can we expect the future food supply of the world to be increased significantly by the use of soilless culture, controlled atmospheres enriched in carbon dioxide, and perhaps even by the use of artificial light to increase the length of the growth period? Clearly, in principle, all of these things could be done. Enormous greenhouses could be built, within which plants could be grown in nutrient solutions. In northern regions artificial light could be supplied during winter months. In all regions carbon dioxide could be added to the air. But the cost would be prodigious both in terms of capital investment and operation.

During the recent war, and immediately thereafter, the techniques of hydroponics were tested on a large scale. At present prices the capital investment necessary is approximately 10,000 dollars per acre—far greater than that involved in the most expensive land-reclamation project. Operating experience shows that only the higher-priced luxury vegetables can be grown economically in this way at the present time. It is highly unlikely that the present major sources of nourishment in the world—wheat, rice, corn, sugar beets, sugar cane, and potatoes—will ever be obtained in appreciable quantities from soilless culture. As we shall see later, other radically different methods of food production are on the horizon, which are potentially far more efficient and far less expensive than hydroponics.

To return to more conventional agricultural procedures, a major possibility exists for increasing yields of specific crops beyond those already obtainable in open field culture. Special chemicals can be applied to plants for the purpose of accelerating germination and ripening. Other chemicals can prevent premature dropping of leaves from fruit trees. Still others can be used to kill, selectively, weeds that interfere with crop growth. These developments will undoubtedly lead to larger yields of crops.

We have seen that plants grow more rapidly in an atmosphere that is rich in carbon dioxide. It would perhaps be easier to adopt methods which would increase the carbon-dioxide concentration in the atmosphere as a whole than to attempt to build elaborate greenhouses to confine the enriched air. If, in some manner, the carbon-dioxide content of the atmosphere could be increased threefold, world food production might be doubled. One can visualize, on a world scale, huge carbon-dioxide generators pouring the gas into the atmosphere. But here we are faced with several serious limitations. First, the oceans would absorb the excess carbon dioxide at an appreciable rate. Second, the "capital investment" in carbon dioxide would be enormous. There are between 18 and 20 tons of carbon dioxide over every acre of the earth's surface. In order to double the amount in the atmosphere, at least 500 billion tons of coal would have to be burned—an amount six times greater than that which has been consumed during all of human history. In the absence of coal, the equivalent in energy would have to be provided from some other source so that the carbon dioxide could be produced by heating limestone.

In general the most likely prospects for increasing world food yields, utilizing conventional agricultural methods, appear to lie in the direction of breeding plants for specific environments, more widespread use of fertilizer, the use of supplemental irrigation, increased protection against insects and disease, and the use of special chemicals to control the life cycle of the plant. Hydroponics, the construction of vast greenhouses, or the use of carbon-dioxide-enriched air all appear to be too expensive to compete success-fully with other methods in the foreseeable future.

We have seen that it is possible to grow land plants without soil in a manmade environment. A further and far more important step in soilless food cultivation would be the domestication of marine plants such as unicellular algae. Land plants with their elaborate systems of roots, stems, and leaves are cumbersome or-ganisms. Marine plants, by contrast, evolved in an environment where there was little need for roots or supporting structure. Under optimum conditions they are able to grow far more rapidly than their more complex terrestrial relatives.

There are hundreds of species of unicellular algae. Some, such as the red and brown algae, are ocean species which provide much of the food for zooplankton and larger animals of the sea. Others, such as the green and blue-green varieties, predominate in fresh-water ponds. The tiny organisms photosynthesize much as do terrestrial plants, and after a certain stage is reached in growth, they divide. Under favorable conditions algae will double their numbers in the course of but a few hours.

It is known that varieties of marine plants can be eaten by human beings. The Japanese have for many years consumed quantities of certain species of algae, and studies during World War II showed that the mixture of marine plants and micro-animals found in the open sea can be strained from the water and used to support human life.

It is possible, in principle, to construct shallow ponds, add neces-sary mineral nutrients, inoculate the solutions with a suitable species of alga, and harvest the "crops" continuously as they grow. Harvesting could be done mechanically by filtration or centrifuga-tion, and, after harvesting, the nutrient solutions could be re-plenished with minerals and returned to the ponds to be re-used.

The advantage of algae culture over hydroponics is obvious. Supporting structures for the plants would not be necessary. Yields would be high, for algae grow in depth, making extremely effi-cient use of the incident light, and they have no elaborate roots and stems through which nutrients must be diffused. Neither "planting" nor "harvesting" would require an appreciable amount of human labor—both could be done mechanically, using techniques already developed by the chemical industry. The large-scale cultivation of algae would inaugurate a new age of agriculture, in which the producing units would resemble modern chemical plants more than farms.

A particular species of single-celled alga, known as *Chlorella,* has been studied in some detail from the point of view of cultivation on a large scale, and although there is still much to be learned, it is apparent that algae culture offers considerable promise. It has been demonstrated that *Chlorella,* over 50 per cent of which is protein, can be supplemented with methionine and used as adequate chicken feed. Forms suitably processed can perhaps be consumed directly by human beings. Other forms could be cultivated to be used as raw material in the organic chemistry industry. As we will see later, some even offer promise as sources of fuel.

But human consumption of algae on a large scale would require rather drastic changes in eating habits. As a result, incorporation of algae-based foods into culture patterns would probably come slowly except in areas such as Japan, where they would be no novelty. Yet in spite of this, it seems likely that algae culture is destined to occupy an important place in world food production during the decades ahead—particularly in view of the large yields of food per acre which are obtainable. Modern food technology makes possible the transformation of dried algae into a variety of foodstuffs possessing widely differing flavors and textures.

Existing evidence indicates that algae farms in the tropics might yield 20 tons (dry weight) of food per acre per year. If air that is enriched with carbon dioxide could be used, even higher yields might be obtainable, but we have seen that operating costs, and in particular energy costs, become very large if carbon dioxide must be manufactured.

Capital costs for an algae farm would be considerable—approaching the capital investment per acre required for a hydroponics farm. Land would have to be leveled and covered with a coating of thin plastic to contain the water. Piping and pumping facilities, together with a central harvesting plant, would have to be erected. Altogether, a 1000-acre farm containing a central harvesting plant might cost close to 10 million dollars. But once the plant was built, operating costs would be very small. A crew of 20 men could probably handle the entire operation, including all

FOOD

seeding, maintenance, and continuous harvesting of the 20,000-ton dry-weight annual crop. Amortizing the capital over a 10-year period would permit the algae to be produced at a cost of about 10 dollars per ton.

The potentialities inherent in algae culture as a source of food can be appreciated when we realize that, should 50 million acres of tropical land be devoted to it, the food supply of the world could be more than doubled. However, it should be emphasized again that a large amount of research and development will be necessary before the existing possibilities can be transformed into reality.

Algae farms are ideally suited for regions possessing ample water and sunshine but poor soil. In regions where soil is adequate for cultivation of sugar cane, further possibilities exist for augmenting the world's food supply. Varieties of micro-organisms can be cultured in solutions of sugar and mineral nutrients. As of this writing, a pilot plant is in operation on the island of Jamaica which produces on a large scale a variety of edible yeast, 40 per cent of which is protein of good quality. Although the protein is somewhat deficient in methionine, it has a high vitamin content, and nutritional experiments have shown it to be very useful as a food supplement.

The potential sugar-producing regions of the world are vast. By coupling sugar plantations with yeast factories, it seems likely that large quantities of proteins and even fats can be produced. Yeast animals are far more efficient than cows or chickens. A plantation that produces 5 tons of sugar annually per acre would yield 2½ tons of yeast per acre, or over 1 ton of protein per acre. Beef cattle on well-managed farms yield about 50 pounds of protein per acre per year. It seems likely that the greater part of the protein needs of the present world population could be adequately met by the yeast production from sugar grown on about 70 million acres of tropical land.

9.

In the one-half of the world which is badly undernourished, an increase in food production of approximately 50 per cent is necessary if the people are to have adequate nutrition. Thus, for the world as a whole at the existing population level, an increase in food production of approximately 25 per cent is necessary. But we have seen that in the years to come the population of the world probably will increase considerably above the existing level —possibly reaching 4.8 billion in another 50 years and 6.7 billion in another century. Thus in another 50 years food production might have to be two and one-half times greater than it is today, and by the year 2050, production might have to be multiplied three and one-half times.

Such increases are clearly possible in principle. If we designate existing world food production by unity (1.0), we can summarize the foreseeable potentiality on the earth's surface as follows:

Existing food production	1.0
Production possible from existing land, using known conventional agricultural techniques	1.1
Production possible from existing cultivated land plus 1.3 billion new acres of tropic and northern soils	2.0
Production possible from existing land, using supplemental irrigation of 1 billion acres now under cultivation and complete irrigation of 200 million acres of desert and near-desert land	2.0
Production possible from all above sources	3.0
Production possible from above sources plus increased yields due to improved plant-breeding and selection and foreseeable improvements in agricultural techniques	6.0
Production possible from 100 million acres of algae farms	2.0
Production possible from all sources, including 1 billion acres of algae farms	25.0

Thus we see that when we consider population limitation solely on the basis of potential food supply, enormous increases of numbers of human beings are possible in principle. Given adequate raw materials for the production of plant nutrients, the necessary capital with which to undertake major irrigation, land-reclamation, and soil-conservation projects, and capital to construct algae farms and yeast-food plants, a population of several billion persons could clearly be supported at adequate nutritional levels. Indeed, if food habits were to change sufficiently so that the people of the world were content to derive their main nourishment from the products of algae farms and yeast factories, a world population of 50 billion persons could eventually be supported comfortably from the point of view of nutritional requirements.

However, it must be emphasized that an enormous food-production potential is no guarantee against starvation. Throughout most of human history a substantial fraction of the population has existed on a near-starvation diet, and there appears to be little likelihood that starvation can be eliminated in the world for many decades to come. Development of new lands, irrigation, increase of productivity of old land, soil conservation, and the construction of new facilities such as algae farms and yeast factories require enormous expenditures of labor and of manufactured goods. Expressed in terms of money, on an average, an expenditure of about 50 dollars in labor and material is required to develop an acre of new land and bring it to a high level of productivity. An investment of about 20 dollars is required to bring an acre of old land to a level of high productivity. Thus, in the undernourished half of the world which exists on the cultivation of about 1.6 billion acres, an investment of about 30 billion dollars would be required to bring productivity to the high levels which are possible in principle. The development of 1.3 billion acres of new northern and tropic lands would require an investment of about 60 billion dollars. Necessary erosion-control projects to protect land already cultivated would cost an additional 10 billion dollars. Thus altogether a capital investment of approximately 100 billion dollars would be required to double world food production.

In the undernourished half of the world, most people are farmers barely able to produce sufficient food for their own needs. Practically all effort goes into food production—there is little surplus for the production of the capital goods necessary for the rapid extension of food-production facilities. In order to increase food production, tools, machines, and fertilizers are needed. In turn, the production of tools, machines, and fertilizers requires factories. Fuel is required to run the factories. Men are required to produce the fuel and raw materials and to build and operate the factories. The men must come from the farms—yet they cannot be spared from the farms until mechanization and increased crop yields permit the same amount of food to be produced by fewer farmers. All of these developments—mechanization of farms and industrialization and development of resources—require far more capital than that required solely for improvement and development of land.

At the present time there is insufficient food production to provide adequate nourishment for the people of the world, and the population is rising rapidly. If the rate of increase of food production in the underdeveloped areas continues to be less than the rate of population increase, ever-increasing numbers of people will starve. If there is to be an improvement in the situation, capital investment must be made in land development, resource development, and industrialization at a rate which is greater than the rate of population increase.

The underdeveloped areas are in the position, however, of being unable to provide new capital at the necessary rate. If left to themselves, they are destined to live at a starvation level for at least another century, and probably for a much longer period of time. To be sure, they might develop more land, they might improve their yields, and they might slowly industrialize; but it will be extremely difficult to do so by themselves at a rate greater than their rate of population growth. The rapidity with which starvation is diminished in the world depends, in short, upon the extent to which those nations which are already industrialized help those which are not. The industrialized areas of the world possess the capital necessary to break the vicious circle. Indeed, the United States alone could, in principle, provide sufficient capital, without appreciably lowering its own standard of living, to permit the underdeveloped areas to industrialize and increase food production at a rate sufficient to eliminate starvation in the course of about 50 years.

Thus far we have seen that increased food production in the world requires increased industrialization. Increased industrialization in turn requires increased consumption of the earth's resources—coal, oil, iron, phosphate rock, and a variety of other substances. It is important that we now examine the extent to which limitations in the availability of these substances might further affect human development.

Chapter **V**:

ENERGY

One of the most difficult of intellectual tasks is to maintain a sense of proportion. When we hear a large number or a superlative adjective, we cannot help being vaguely impressed. Trillions of tons of coal, hundreds of billions of barrels of oil and tar, mountains of oil shale, many tens of thousands of square miles of peat bogs—what does it all mean? Can we sit back comfortably with a sense of abundance of natural resources? Can we regard seriously the optimistic pronouncements of all the energy we shall need for thousands of years?
EUGENE AYRES AND CHARLES A. SCARLOTT

1.

We have seen that the daily energy intake, in the form of food, required to support a human being adequately is approximately 3000 calories. For countless thousands of years men lived at or below this level of energy consumption. But following the discovery of fire and the domestication of animals, the total daily energy consumption, for all purposes, counting the wood which was burned for fuel and the food which was consumed by domesticated animals, rose to about 10,000 calories per person. As time went on and an increasing variety of material goods came to be considered necessities rather than luxuries, the daily consumption of energy per person rose to increasingly high levels.

Wood was the first fuel to be used in large quantities, and even today it is still an important fuel. In Brazil, where coal resources are poor, wood supplies about 85 per cent of the non-food energy consumed, and the per capita energy consumption in that country is about one-third of that of the United States. In the world as a whole, wood satisfies over 7 per cent of the non-food energy requirements.

The ancients consumed large quantities of wood for the production of brick, lime, and metal. With the development of iron metallurgy, wood consumption increased rapidly, and, as we have seen, the techniques of converting coal into metallurgical coke arrived on the scene just in time to prevent the British forest reserves from disappearing completely. Great Britain quickly shifted to a coal economy, but wood remained the major fuel in the United States until about 1880.

In 1800 the world-wide per capita production of energy from coal amounted to little more than 300 calories per day. This rose to about 10,000 calories by 1900. By 1940 approximately 22,000 calories of energy from the combustion of coal and petroleum were being produced each day for each human being living on the earth. We can obtain some idea of the eventual energy consumption by human society when we realize that the present total rate in the United States is approaching 160,000 calories per person per day—an amount eighty times greater than that required for bare subsistence and fifteen times greater than that required for a primitive agrarian existence.

From the beginnings of the machine age coal has been our most important source of energy. By 1950 approximately 80 billion tons had been removed from the earth's mines, of which 50 per cent had been removed and consumed since 1920, and 75 per cent since 1900. In 1948 coal was being mined throughout the world at a rate of 1.6 billion tons per year.

Petroleum came into widespread use as an energy source at a considerably later date than did coal. But with the developments of the internal-combustion engine, the automobile, the airplane, and Diesel-electric power, approximately one-half as much energy is now being obtained in the world from petroleum as is being obtained from coal. By 1949, petroleum was being produced at the rate of over 3.4 billion barrels a year. By 1950, over 70 billion barrels of oil had been removed from the earth, almost all of it since 1900.

The trends of relative importance of coal, petroleum, natural gas, and waterpower as sources of energy in the United States

can be seen in Figure 23. In 1949 the distribution in the United
States was about as follows:

Coal	37·7%
Petroleum	35·6%
Natural gas	18.4%
Waterpower	4.6%
Wood fuel	3·7%

In the United States, the energy released from utilization of
coal, petroleum, natural gas, and waterpower is equivalent to that
which would be obtained if we burned 50 pounds of coal each
day for every person in the nation. In other words, in the absence
of other fuels, it would be necessary for us to consume nearly 9
tons of coal each year per person in order to maintain our present

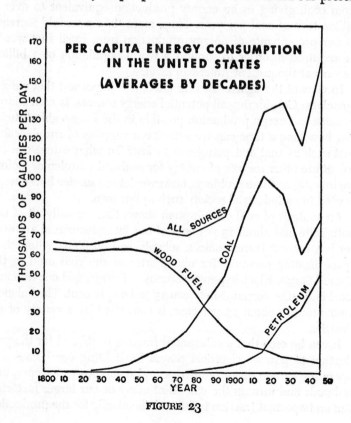

FIGURE 23

mode of life. As we will see later, there is good reason for believing that this per capita rate of energy consumption will increase in the years ahead. But even if the consumption necessary to maintain our present per capita industrial capacity does not increase, when we think in terms of a world that might eventually become industrialized to the present United States level, we encounter some formidable figures. A world containing 3 billion individuals and producing goods at a per capita rate equivalent to the present production rate in the United States would consume energy at a rate equivalent to the burning of nearly 30 billion tons of coal per year. As we know, the present world-wide rate of coal production, large as it is, amounts to only 1.6 billion tons per year. The energy we obtain from petroleum amounts to about one-half that obtained from coal, giving us an energy production equivalent to over a billion tons of coal per year. Thus, more than a tenfold increase in our present rate of energy production from fossil fuel would be required in order to support a world population of 3 billion persons at the present American level.

In view of the figures thus far cited, it is important that we ask ourselves: Considering all potential energy sources, is such a large increase in energy production possible in the foreseeable future? For how long a time can we expect our supplies of irreplaceable fuel such as coal and petroleum to last? To what extent can we substitute other sources of energy for coal and petroleum? Before we investigate these problems, however, let us examine how energy is used in an industrial society such as our own.

An analysis of coal consumption shows that virtually all of our anthracite and about 15 per cent of our bituminous coal are used for heating our homes, offices, schools, and hospitals. Altogether, space heating accounts for one-quarter of the coal used in the United States. Electric-power stations, railroads, and our iron and steel industries consume between 15 and 20 per cent. The balance, amounting to about 25 per cent, is consumed by a variety of industries.

It can be seen that a substantial fraction is utilized for the production of power—electrical power for lighting our homes and operating certain major industries, and steam power for operating railroads and turning the wheels of many of our larger factories. But an important fraction is utilized chemically for the production ot metals and the production of a diversity of important industrial chemicals. The iron and steel industry is a major example of this utilization of coal.

Iron-ore deposits consist of iron chemically combined with oxygen. In order to obtain metallic iron, it is necessary to remove the oxygen, and this is done commercially by heating the iron oxide with carbon:

iron oxide + carbon $\longrightarrow$ metallic iron + carbon dioxide.

Nearly 20 per cent of all the coal produced in the United States is converted to coke, with an average yield of 0.7 pounds of coke per pound of coal treated. The iron and steel industry is by far the largest consumer of coke. Approximately 1 ton of coke, made from 1.4 tons of coal, is required for the production of 1 ton of steel. For each ton of steel additional sources of energy are used, equivalent to the burning of 0.4 tons of coal per ton of steel. Thus, in effect, the production of 1 ton of steel requires the energy obtained from burning almost 2 tons of coal.

A variety of industries utilize coke in fairly large quantity. In addition, the by-products of coke manufacture have considerable usefulness. Among these, the most important is coke-oven gas, which is piped to neighboring industries and through city gas mains. Others are ammonia, oils of various sorts, and coal tar. Altogether, the by-products of the coke industry have a monetary value equivalent to about one-third the value of the coke which is produced.

Almost 50 per cent of our petroleum is used in transportation— in automobiles and trucks, which consume by far the largest proportion, and also in Diesel-electric power units, which railroads are using in rapidly increasing numbers. Second in importance is space heating; 10 per cent of the petroleum output of the United States is burned to heat our buildings. Only 4 per cent is used to generate electric power. The balance, amounting to about 40 per cent, is used to provide energy for a variety of industrial operations.

The use of natural gas, which occurs in intimate association with petroleum deposits, is increasing rapidly as pipelines make it available at ever greater distances from the sources. At the present time it provides nearly 20 per cent of our total energy, and its use is bound to increase during the course of the next few years. Approximately 25 per cent of the output is now being used for space heating, 8 per cent for the generation of electric power, and the balance to provide energy for diverse industrial operations.

Waterpower contributes only 5 per cent of our total energy production, but, as we shall see later, we should not let this small figure cause us to underestimate its eventual importance to the economy of the world. Virtually all of the waterpower now being used is converted to electrical power.

**CONSUMPTION OF ENERGY IN
THE UNITED STATES (1948)**

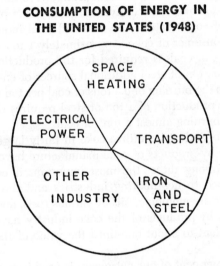

FIGURE 24

The pattern of energy utilization in the United States is illustrated in Figure 24. When we total the contributions of energy from each of the primary sources to each of the major consumers, we find that the distribution can be illustrated as shown in Figure 25.

2.

Ordinarily, when a tree or some other plant dies, oxidation processes take place which convert the carbon of the plant to carbon dioxide. The process may be actual burning, as in the case of a forest fire, or the much slower process whereby bacteria or higher animals consume the plant for food and by their metabolic processes return the carbon to the air as carbon dioxide. There are certain special circumstances, however, in which plants may not be destroyed by oxidation when they die. If they grow in fairly still water, when they die and become waterlogged they sink to the bottom. Before they actually reach the bottom, much of the vegetable tissue is decomposed, but complete decomposition is prevented by subsequent layers of vegetable matter which are

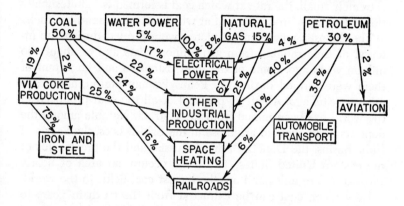

DIRECT UTILIZATION OF ENERGY RESOURCES
IN THE UNITED STATES (1948)

FIGURE 25

deposited and thus shield the matter still further from the action of the air. Under the pressure of the water and subsequent layers of vegetation, the mass of partially decomposed vegetation becomes compressed, water is squeezed out to some extent, and partial cabonization takes place. The material which results, and is found and utilized in a number of limited areas of the world, is known as peat. Peat bogs vary from about 5 feet to 30 feet in thickness.

If, due to sinking of the land, a peat deposit is overlaid by sand and mud of considerable thickness, the additional weight compresses the decomposed material enormously. The extent to which water is removed from the vegetation and carbonization takes place depends upon the pressures and temperatures to which the matter is later subjected. The end result of such a process is coal, which, depending upon the conditions and the length of time involved, may be lignite, containing about 50 per cent carbon, or bituminous, containing 80 per cent carbon, or anthracite, containing as much as 95 per cent carbon.

We can see, then, that coal is formed only under rather special circumstances. Since the fraction of the plant life on the earth which becomes trapped by sediments and reappears as coal is extremely small, the rate at which coal is formed is infinitesimally slow when compared with that at which man consumes the fuel.

The deposits now being depleted were formed during the interval of time ranging from 360 million years ago to about 100 million years ago. Some of the most extensive and important of them were formed during the Pennsylvanian period, about 250 million years ago. About 80 per cent of all the coal produced in the world has been mined from these strata. Notable among the deposits being worked are those in the British Isles, the Saar and Ruhr Basins, the Donetz Basin of Russia, and the great fields of the eastern United States. The latter occupy an area of nearly 250,000 square miles and are the largest coal fields in the world.

How much coal can be extracted from the earth in years to come? In an attempt to answer this question, the International Geological Congress, which met in Canada in 1913, made an estimate of the world's coal resources based upon knowledge of the frequency of appearance of coal seams, sedimentary deposits of various types, and the general distribution of sedimentary deposits over the surface of the earth. For the purposes of its estimate, the Congress took 1 foot as the minimum workable thickness of seams down to a depth of 4000 feet from the surface, and 2 feet as the minimum at depths greater than 4000 feet. A depth of 6000 feet was regarded as the maximum workable depth for any seam. With these limitations, the Geological Congress arrived at the estimate shown in Table 4 of world coal reserves by continents. In 1938, some adjustments were made in the original estimates, in which the total was essentially unaltered but the reserves in the United States were revised downward, while those in Asia were revised upward.

Although both the 1913 and 1938 estimates are little more than informed guesses, they probably indicate closely the upper limit of the amount of coal that can be removed from the earth's crust. As a matter of fact, the estimate has been criticized in recent years by mining engineers, who say that while the amount of coal estimated by the Congress may actually be present, only a small fraction of the total can be recovered by practical mining operations. The fraction may easily be as small as 10 per cent of the total coal available.

TABLE 4

ESTIMATES OF WORLD COAL RESOURCES

CONTINENT	RESERVES IN BILLIONS OF METRIC TONS	
	1913 ESTIMATE	1938 ESTIMATE
Europe	800	800
Asia	1300	2000
North and South America	5100	4300
Oceania and Africa	200	200
Total	7400	7300

Oil, like coal, was formed slowly over long periods of time from living matter that became trapped in sediments. The question of the exact mode of origin of our petroleum deposits is still the subject of lively debate in geological circles. But the evidence strongly supports the theory that marine organisms living in shallow coastal waters were the basic stuff from which most petroleum deposits evolved. It is believed that dead organisms carried into the oceans by rivers and streams were, along with the mud of the ocean floor, subsequently compacted into shale. Later the folding of mountain ranges elevated the shale, and the organic material, in the liquid form of petroleum, flowed, under the influence of gravitation, gas pressure, and the circulation of water, into pools or pockets. Thus the locations of oil deposits are determined by the locations of ancient shorelines, mountain upheavals, and overlying rocks suitable for the trapping of pools of displaced oil.

Although we do not know the mechanism of oil formation in detail, we do know empirically the kinds of locations where oil is found, and the kinds where it is not. Knowing the oil-production history of a large area that has been well explored, such as the

United States, and knowing the general extent of likely oil-producing localities, we can make an estimate of the oil-production potential of the world as a whole.

Estimates of oil reserves have come to be looked upon with suspicion, and rightly so, for time and time again our petroleum companies in the United States have produced more oil in a given decade than extensive preliminary study had indicated as a possibility. In 1908 our reserves were estimated to be 8 billion barrels. Within a few years the total production exceeded this figure. In 1935 experts were predicting a serious oil famine by 1945, but when that year arrived oil production was greater than it had been before, and the *proved* domestic reserves totaled 20 billion barrels —more than double the estimated reserve in 1908.

We need not search far for the reasons underlying these discrepancies. Research has given rise to techniques undreamed of a few decades ago. Wells can now be drilled to depths of 4 miles or more. Modern engineering techniques have enormously increased the efficiency with which oil can be extracted—even fields which were once abandoned have been made to yield the precious fluid once again. Most important, however, new and vastly improved methods of exploration unknown to the geologists of 1908 have come into existence.

By the trial-and-error approach we have learned a great deal about oil deposits and their occurrence. In particular, it appears that the *oil content of the crust of the earth is considerably smaller than the coal content.* How much smaller? Here we must resort to estimates of petroleum geologists. Comprehensive studies by Weeks [1] indicate that ultimate production of oil from the land areas of the world may total about 600 billion barrels. We have already consumed about 10 per cent of this, leaving a potential reserve of something over 500 billion barrels. He estimates that in the underwater sediments on the Continental Shelves the potential reserves might amount to 400 billion barrels, giving a total potential production of about 1000 billion barrels. These figures have been criticized on the one hand as being somewhat pessimistic and on the other hand as being greatly optimistic. But, as we shall

1. L. G. Weeks, "Concerning Estimates of Potential Oil Reserves," in *Bulletin of the American Association of Petroleum Geologists,* Volume 34, No. 10, October 1950.

see, even if this estimate should prove to be ten times too large or ten times too small, the over-all world picture of energy resources would not be changed greatly.

To our inventory of fossil fuels, then, we can add about 1000 billion barrels of oil that might be extractable from oil shales which exist abundantly in various regions of the world. We can add, further, a quantity of tar, estimated roughly at perhaps 1000 million barrels, which might be utilized. To this we should add the available natural gas, which is genetically related to the petroleum and frequently occurs in close association with it.

In the United States about 400 cubic feet of natural gas are produced for every cubic foot of petroleum. It is reasonable to suppose that this ratio of available natural gas to available petroleum is valid for the world as a whole, at least so far as our land petroleum resources are concerned. Since 1000 cubic feet of natural gas will produce about as much energy as 1 cubic foot of petroleum, when we assess the total energy content potentially available from petroleum reserves, we can add approximately 40 per cent for the natural gas associated with the petroleum in the land areas of the world.

We can now add together our various estimates and guesses of fossil-fuel resources, and arrive at the results shown in Table 5.

TABLE 5

ESTIMATES OF WORLD RESOURCES OF FOSSIL FUELS
(*Equivalent Tons of Bituminous Coal*)

	BILLIONS OF METRIC TONS	
SOURCE	OPTIMISTIC ESTIMATE	PESSIMISTIC ESTIMATE
Coal	7300	730
Liquid Petroleum	200	30
Natural Gas	80	12
Oil Shale	200	10
Tar	200	—
Total	7980	782

No great accuracy can be claimed for the figures, but, as we shall discover, that is relatively unimportant. If we are very fortunate, we have available in the earth fossil-fuel energy equivalent to that in perhaps 8000 billion tons of coal. If we are unfortunate, we may have available the energy equivalent only to that in 800 billion tons of coal.

3.

In 1950 energy was expended in the world at a rate equivalent to burning 2.7 billion metric tons of coal per year. Over 60 per cent of the energy was actually obtained from coal; about 30 per cent was obtained from petroleum; wood fuel accounted for about 7 per cent; and waterpower for about 1 per cent. The world-wide energy expenditure per capita was equivalent to burning slightly over 1 ton of coal per person per year. But regions of the world

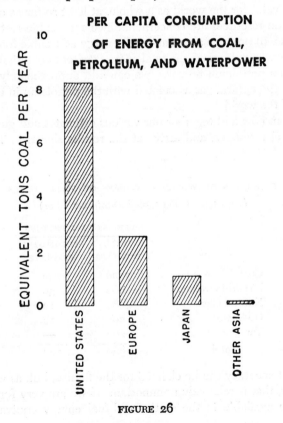

FIGURE 26

differed widely in their per capita energy consumptions. The United States, which consumed close to 60 per cent of the world's petroleum production, and over 25 per cent of the coal production, and which possesses nearly 30 per cent of the world's harnessed waterpower, consumed the energy equivalent to that derived from burning over 8 metric tons of coal per person. Europe, exclusive of the USSR, consumed the equivalent of about 2.5 tons of coal per person, and Japan consumed the equivalent of slightly over 1 ton per person. By contrast, the rest of Asia, where nearly one-half of the world population resides, consumed energy from coal, petroleum, and waterpower at a rate equivalent to burning slightly over 100 pounds of coal per person per year. This is about the amount that is consumed in the United States per person in 2 days.

Even in the United States, which is already highly industrialized, per capita energy consumption is increasing. It seems likely that by 1960 it will probably be 25 per cent above the 1950 level, and

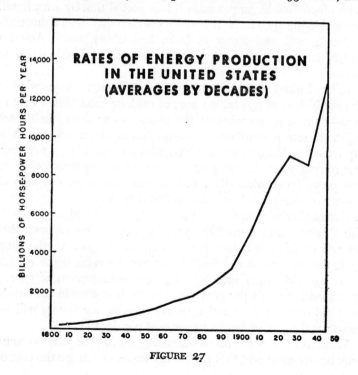

FIGURE 27

by 1975 the increase might well amount to 60 per cent. Taking into account the indicated population increase, this would mean that the total energy expenditure in the United States might increase by one-third by 1960 and be nearly doubled by 1975. By that year we might well be consuming energy at a rate equivalent to burning 2.3 billion tons of coal per year—nearly the present rate of consumption for the whole world.

The rate of increase of energy consumption for the rest of the world will probably be far greater than this, particularly if major efforts are made to industrialize the underdeveloped areas. We can see from the experiences of transition countries such as Japan and the Soviet Union that it is possible for energy consumption to rise with enormous rapidity. In the Soviet Union coal production has been doubling approximately once in 5 years and it is possible that by 1960 the country will produce as much energy as the United States. Between 1930 and 1939 energy consumption in Japan increased by 70 per cent; it is expected that by 1975 it will be double the 1950 level. It is quite possible that once industrialization is well under way in India and China, South America and Africa, fuel consumption in those areas will double every 10 years.

In the United States we have fossil-fuel resources amounting to the equivalent of 250 billion tons of coal, or 2200 billion tons of coal—depending on whether the pessimists or the optimists are right. At our present rate of consumption of energy, which is equivalent to the consumption of 1.2 billion tons of coal per year, our resources would last perhaps 1800 years (optimistically) or 200 years (pessimistically). But, as we have seen, our rate of energy consumption is still increasing rapidly.

Economists vary in their estimates of the demand for goods in the United States during the years to come. One suggests that we will double our output between 1950 and 1960. Another suggests that by 2050 our scale of living may be eight times as high as in 1950. Between 1900 and 1950 our consumption of energy increased nearly 20 per cent per decade. If it rises in the future as it did between 1940 and 1950, our demand for energy will increase at the rate of nearly 50 per cent per decade.

Whatever the real demand for energy during the years to come may be, we must add to it the energy losses which are the cost of processing the source materials from which energy is obtained. As the demand for liquid fuel increases, and the underground supply of petroleum decreases, we shall manufacture petroleum from coal—a costly process in terms of energy. As the demand for electricity increases, we shall generate more electricity from coal —again a process which is costly in terms of lost energy.

Eugene Ayres and Charles Scarlott,[1] in their recent discussion of energy sources, predict a possible energy-consumption pattern for the United States based upon a series of conservative assumptions. They assume that: 1. the demand for energy in the United States will increase by 50 per cent every 50 years; 2. by the end of another 20 years the demand for electricity will be four times that of the present, and will rise to ten times the present demand by the time 100 years have passed; 3. the demand for liquid fuels will rise to the point where they contribute 60 per cent of the total energy consumed. This point will be reached in two decades.

On the basis of these assumptions, the demand for energy would be equivalent to 1.6 billion tons of coal by 1970, 3 billion tons by 2050, and 6 billion tons by 2150. To this we must add the losses associated with converting coal into liquid fuels and into electricity.

Demand for liquid fuels will probably continue to rise. But we have already reached the point where domestic production cannot keep pace with the demand. An analysis of the oil situation in the United States indicates that by 1960 we may have passed our peak of domestic oil production. By 1970 we may well have to import or manufacture from coal more than 2 billion barrels annually. Production from the Continental Shelf may postpone the peak for a few years, but once we have passed it and countries such as Venezuela and Canada can no longer supply the demand for petroleum, the United States will be forced into the production of liquid fuels from shales and from coal.

When we add the conversion losses inherent in producing oil from shales and coal, and the losses involved in converting coal into electricity, to the estimated energy demand, we find that our over-all energy needs may approach the equivalent of 2.4 billion tons of coal annually by 1970, 7 billion tons by 2050, and 13 billion

1. Eugene Ayres and Charles Scarlott, *Energy Sources* (New York: The McGraw-Hill Book Company, 1952).

tons by 2150. Comparing these estimates of over-all demand with our estimated resources of fossil fuel, we find that if the pessimistic estimate is correct our fossil-fuel reserves may last no longer than another 75 years. If the optimistic estimate is correct, they may last another 250 years.

It should be emphasized at this point that precise estimates of the longevity of fossil-fuel resources are impossible. The above estimates and guesses have been given in an attempt to demonstrate that, under the prevailing philosophy of an expanding economy, the fossil-fuel resources of the United States may easily fall short of demand by the time another century has passed. But the exact time at which the United States passes the peak of coal production cannot be predicted with any certainty; far too many variables are involved. It is possible, for example, that industrial production and resultant demand for energy may increase more rapidly than 50 per cent every 50 years. If this should be true, our reserves would be depleted more rapidly than estimated.

On the other hand, one can conceive of a number of developments which might increase the life span of our fossil fuels. Desire for material goods may cease to increase after a few years. A major depression would lower the rate of energy consumption. Important improvements may be made in the efficiency with which energy is converted from one form to another. Existing estimates of fossil-fuel reserves may prove to be far too low. Useful energy may be derived from other sources in sufficient quantity to operate industrial machinery. But barring a war or other catastrophe which destroys humanity, the fossil-fuel deposits of the United States will one day be exhausted.

4.

With respect to coal resources, the people of the United States are far better off than are the people of other areas of the world. Speaking optimistically, we have a potential supply amounting to about 15,000 tons per person, compared with reserves in the United Kingdom of about 3400 tons per person, reserves in China amounting to 2200 tons per person, or reserves in India and Japan amounting to about 200 tons per person. This does not necessarily mean that the coal in the United States will last for a longer period of time than will the coal of China or India, for our per capita energy consumption is very much larger than that in any other country, and it is still rising rapidly.

The life of the world's coal resources will be determined in part by the extent to which other nations attempt to emulate the United

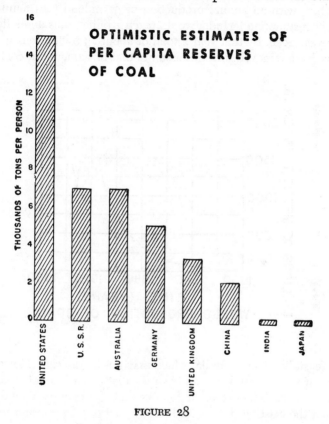

OPTIMISTIC ESTIMATES OF PER CAPITA RESERVES OF COAL

FIGURE 28

States in producing and consuming large quantities of goods. To what extent can we expect such items as automobiles, refrigerators, telephones, radio and television sets—which are now considered to be "necessities" in the United States and are luxuries in most parts of the world—to become "necessities" in the world as a whole?

As an example of what may happen, let us suppose that India

starts a major industrialization program aimed at creating a society
within which per capita consumption of goods would be as high
as that at the present time in the United States. We have seen
from the experience of Japan and the Soviet Union that it is possible for coal production to be doubled every 10 years. At this rate,
starting with an annual production of 32 million tons annually,
coal consumption in India would reach 1 billion tons annually by
the year 2000. By that year a total of about 15 billion tons would
have been removed. But this assumes that this amount of coal can

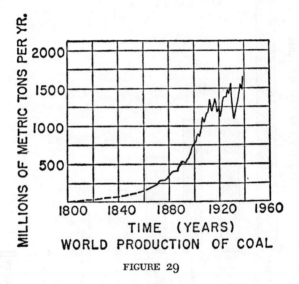

WORLD PRODUCTION OF COAL

FIGURE 29

be feasibly mined in India, which may not be the case. However,
even if we are optimistic and assume that India has potential reserves of 60 billion tons, it follows that the country would not
reach the existing per capita level of energy consumption in the
United States until about 2020—making due allowance for population increase during the intervening years. By that time, however, India's coal resources would be depleted.

Thus we see that it would be impossible for India to achieve
a high degree of industrialization based upon coal as the primary
energy source. China, however, with reserves that may total more
than 1000 billion tons, is in a somewhat different position. A major
industrialization program, leading to a doubling of production

every 10 years, could lead, by 2050, to a per capita production rate equal to that of the United States at the present time. According to an optimistic view, China could continue to produce at this rate for an additional 50 years. On the other hand, if its per capita production continued to rise as it is rising in the United States, reserves might be exhausted within an additional two decades.

When we take all the obvious factors into consideration, it seems highly likely that by the time another 100 years have passed, world production of fossil fuels will be approaching its peak.

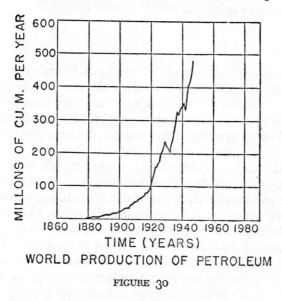

WORLD PRODUCTION OF PETROLEUM

FIGURE 30

Shortly thereafter, depletion of resources will probably become so serious that fossil-fuel production will necessarily decline. When the decline starts, either the difference between production and demand must be made up from other sources of energy, or the level of consumption must decline. The latter events would in turn lead to declines in the production of many things that are necessary to support a large population. Adequate sanitation, high levels of food production, and advanced medical technology require the support of an advanced industrial technology. If our energy resources dwindle, our industrial technology will dwindle, and life expectancy and population will slowly dwindle with it.

Consumption of the earth's stores of fossil fuels has barely started; yet already we can see the end. In a length of time which is extremely short when compared with the span of human history, and insignificant when compared with the length of time during which man has inhabited the earth, fossil fuels will have been discovered, utilized, and completely consumed. The "age of fossil fuels" will be over, not to be repeated for perhaps another 100 million years. Will its passing mark the end of civilization and perhaps the beginning of the downward path to man's extinction? Or can we expect other sources of energy to fulfill the need?

5.

Approximately 30 per cent of the energy which reaches the surface of the earth from the sun is used for the evaporation of water. Each year 400,000 billion tons of water are lifted from the oceans and the land areas of the world and fall again as rain. Each year, on the average, over 1 pound of water in the form of rain or snow falls on every square inch of the earth's surface.

Over the land areas of the world, more water falls to the ground than evaporates, and the difference is carried back into the oceans by rivers and streams. Each year about 40,000 billion tons of water flow down our rivers and streams into the ocean. Flowing water can be harnessed to perform work—a fact that was appreciated by the ancients who constructed the first water wheels. To what extent can these thousands of billions of tons of flowing water be harnessed so that the energy can replace the energy we now derive from fossil fuels? Waterpower, unlike fossil fuels, will be available for use as long as the sun continues to radiate energy. As distinct from coal and oil, our rivers and streams constitute a "permanent fuel" which will always be available for tapping.

In modern establishments for the utilization of waterpower, water is dropped through large pipes containing turbines. The falling water impinges upon the blades of the turbines and turns them around rapidly. The turning turbines are used to spin electrical generators, and the resultant electricity is carried by wires to our industrial centers.

For the production of hydroelectric power, certain localities are considerably more favorable than others. First, there must be a

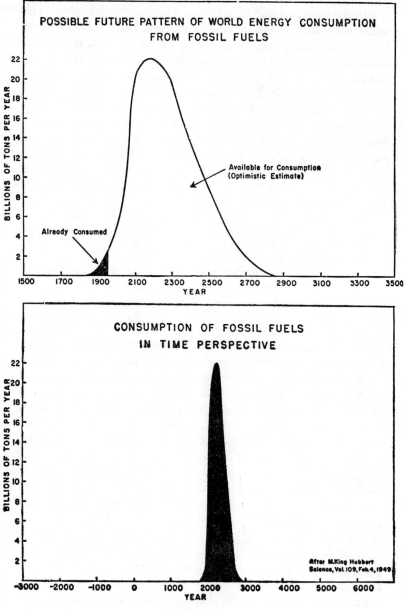

POSSIBLE FUTURE PATTERN OF WORLD ENERGY CONSUMPTION
FROM FOSSIL FUELS

Available for Consumption
(Optimistic Estimate)

Already Consumed

CONSUMPTION OF FOSSIL FUELS
IN TIME PERSPECTIVE

After M.King Hubbert
Science, Vol. 109, Feb. 4, 1949

FIGURE 31

relatively large volume of water of relatively steady flow. The water must drop a considerable height in a fairly short distance. Occasionally these conditions are met by waterfalls. If artificial dams have to be built in order to achieve the necessary conditions, the terrain must be such that large volumes of water can be impounded behind the dam. Similarly, sites for the dams must be available where the structures can be erected with capital investments that are not excessively high. When we take these factors into consideration, we find that the areas in which waterpower can be feasibly harnessed are limited. Nevertheless, the figures of the total potential power available in the world are impressive. Recent estimates give the following figures by continents (in millions of horsepower):

Africa	274
Asia	151
Europe	68
North America	84
Oceania	20
South America	67
Total	664

These estimates were based upon observations of "ordinary minimum flow" of the streams involved, which means, in effect, that the estimated power could be obtained for about 90 to 95 per cent of the time. If arrangements could be made for seasonal variations in industrial electrical consumption, or if the energy generated could in some manner be stored, the available waterpower would be increased approximately threefold, to 2000 million horsepower.

We can estimate the effective energy value of our potential waterpower resources by estimating the amount of coal that we would have to burn each year in order to produce the equivalent amount of electricity. When we take into account the fact that hydroelectric power stations produce power all the time—whether needed or not—while coal generating stations produce power only as needed, and the fact that steam generators are only about 20 per cent efficient in converting the energy of coal into electrical energy, we find that the energy obtainable from the potential waterpower supplies is equivalent to the burning of about 1.4 billion tons of coal per year—somewhat less than that at present generated from coal. If we take the threefold higher value rather than the value computed on the basis of ordinary minimum flow, we find that the world could produce hydroelectric power equivalent to that obtainable by burning 4.2 billion tons of coal per year. Thus we see that the development of all potential waterpower resources of the world would at best give us a twofold increase in world energy production if we depended entirely upon waterpower for our energy.

At the present time only a small fraction of the potential waterpower resources of the world has been developed. Europe, which has developed about 50 per cent of the total now used, and North America—about 40 per cent—lead in the use of waterpower. In the United States about 70 per cent of the available waterpower is now being utilized. But in other areas of the world the merest beginning has been made. In Africa, where the greatest sources are located, only 0.1 per cent is now being tapped. For the world as a whole, about 13 per cent of the estimated ordinary minimum flow potential has been developed.

Hydroelectric installations, requiring both dams and power plants, represent tremendous capital investments, and because of this fact major hydroelectric developments must take place slowly. Many interlocking factors must be taken into consideration when planning them—the prospects of long-range continuous power, land reclamation, flood control, and the feasibility of power distribution.

When we examine the potentialities of hydroelectric power on a regional basis, we can obtain a clearer picture of its inadequacy. Full development of potential hydroelectric sites in the United States would give a generating capacity—based upon ordinary minimum flow—of about 35 million horsepower, or an energy output of about 300 billion horsepower-hours per year. This would amount to little more than 2 per cent of our energy requirements at the present rate of consumption.

The waterpower resources of India are by no means negligible and are all the more important in view of the meagerness of that nation's coal resources. But even when fully developed, India's waterpower will yield no more than 2.5 per cent of the present energy production in the United States from all sources—and we must remember that the population of India is considerably larger than that of the United States.

About 25 per cent of the waterpower resources of Western Europe have already been developed. It is estimated that by 1975 approximately one-half of the potential will have been developed, and at that time it will contribute about 15 per cent of the total energy requirements. Even with full development of Europe's hydroelectric resources, it is doubtful that they will contribute more than 25 per cent of its energy requirements during the coming decades.

The waterpower resources of Africa, if fully developed, will provide annually about one-fifth the amount of the present energy consumption in the United States. Such power can indeed support sizable industrial development, but it is small when compared with over-all world needs.

It cannot be denied that waterpower is an extremely important source of energy. But if the time should arrive when we must rely largely upon it for our energy, the world's per capita rate of energy production would be very small. A world-wide civilization such as that which exists in the West could not be supported without a large reduction in population.

The prospect of satisfying more than a small fraction of our energy needs from other phenomena connected with atmosphere and water, such as the winds and the ocean tides, are so poor that lengthy discussion of them is unnecessary. Temperature differences which exist in the oceans can, in principle, provide considerable power, but the localities where energy extraction might be feasible are limited. Earth heat, contained in steam pouring from vents, might be important in a few restricted localities, and is utilized today, notably in Italy. But its over-all importance as a world energy source is destined to be small.

Clearly we must look to sources other than those discussed thus far if we are to find adequate replacements for fossil fuels.

8.

When the small fundamental particle known as a neutron strikes the nucleus of the uranium-235 atom, it is absorbed, and the nucleus splits into two fragments. Simultaneously a considerable amount of energy is released, and neutrons are ejected, making possible the chain reaction: a neutron strikes a uranium-235 nucleus; several neutrons are ejected; each of the new neutrons strikes a uranium-235 nucleus, and so on.

Fission of 1 pound of uranium-235 produces as much energy as can be obtained by burning 3 million pounds—or 1500 tons—of coal. One ton of ordinary uranium contains about 14 pounds of uranium-235, the balance of the element being composed of uranium-238, which does not undergo fission readily. However, an atom of uranium-238 can absorb a neutron, and a sequence of events follows, resulting in the transformation of uranium-238 into plutonium-239. This latter substance undergoes fission as readily as does uranium-235. In principle it is possible to transform all uranium-238 into fissionable plutonium. Thus, from the point of view of available energy, we can consider ordinary uranium, composed mainly of uranium-238, as being equivalent in releasable energy content to 3 million times its weight in coal.

The element thorium is somewhat more abundant than uranium, but, like uranium-238, it does not undergo fission readily. However, atoms of thorium can absorb neutrons, and a sequence of events follows resulting in the transformation of thorium into a fissionable isotope of uranium—uranium-233. Announcements from the Atomic Energy Commission lead us to believe that both plutonium-239 and uranium-233 emit sufficient numbers of neutrons per fission to permit us, in principle, to utilize all uranium and all thorium that can be mined.

The highest-grade deposits of uranium are in the form of pitchblende, and the largest known deposits are in the Belgian Congo and in Canada. The highest-grade thorium ores are in the form of monazite sands, which are found largely in India and in Brazil. Thus far, most uranium and thorium that has been mined has come from rich deposits. But it is likely that substantial quantities of uranium will be obtained in the near future from relatively low-grade deposits. It has been estimated that the "definitely mineable" reserves of uranium and thorium in the United States amount to about 50,000 tons. To this can be added about 500,000 tons which can probably be mined in the near future, with techniques that are yet to be developed. If atomic energy can be utilized as efficiently as can the energy derived from coal, the "probably mine-able" reserves would satisfy the present power requirements in the United States for over 1000 years—assuming complete recovery from the ores and complete fission of the uranium and thorium.

Actual world-wide reserves of uranium and thorium are unknown. Those which are known are unpublicized for reasons of military security. However, we can obtain some idea of the ultimate potentialities of atomic energy if we examine the distribution of uranium and thorium in ordinary rock. It is clear that if in the long-range future the industries of the world are to be operated primarily by atomic energy, existing high-grade deposits, and even intermediate deposits containing as little as 10 ounces of uranium per ton, would last but a short time. Large-scale utilization of atomic energy would eventually necessitate extraction of vast quantities of uranium and thorium present in extremely dilute concentration in ordinary rock.

One ton of average granite contains about 4 parts per million (0.0004 per cent) uranium and 12 parts per million (0.0012 per cent) thorium. These are admittedly tiny amounts, but the energy content is impressive. If all the uranium and thorium could be extracted from 1 ton of rock and "burned" in a nuclear reactor, the energy release would be equal to that obtained from burning about 50 tons of coal. Thus, from the point of view of releasable energy, 1 ton of ordinary rock is equivalent to about 50 tons of coal.

It would be extremely difficult to extract economically all the uranium and thorium that is present in ordinary granite, but it should be possible to extract about 15 per cent without undue difficulty. If a yield of approximately 15 per cent should prove to be attainable, then 1 ton of rock would be equivalent in energy content to about 7½ tons of coal. This figure must be decreased still further, because energy is required to quarry the rock, transport it to the mill, and carry out the physical and chemical operations necessary for the extraction of the uranium and thorium. It seems likely that these operations could be carried out with an energy expenditure no greater than half a ton of coal for each ton of rock. Thus, without stretching our imaginations unduly, we can visualize a "net profit" of energy from 1 ton of rock equivalent to that produced by about 7 tons of coal. Thus, in principle, from the point of view of obtaining usable energy, all of the granites of the earth's crust are at our disposal.

Under our present economy it might cost 10 dollars to process 1 ton of rock for the purpose of extracting uranium and thorium. If a yield of 15 per cent were obtained, about 200 tons of rock would have to be processed at a cost of 2000 dollars in order to obtain 1 pound of these elements. Although this might seem, at first glance, to be prohibitively expensive, particularly when compared with the existing uranium price of about 10 dollars per pound, the actual cost per unit of releasable energy would be quite modest. Since 1 pound of uranium and thorium is equivalent in energy content to about 1500 tons of coal, we see that, viewed solely from the point of view of energy content, uranium at existing price levels could compete successfully with coal costing less than 1 cent per ton, and, even at the high price of 2000 dollars per pound, uranium could compete with coal costing $1.50 per ton, if other factors were equal. In 1946, electric utilities in the United States paid about 5 dollars per ton for their coal.

It is clear that, per unit of releasable energy, the cost of nuclear fuel is already much less than the cost of coal, and that even when we are forced to process ordinary granite the cost per unit of releasable energy will be less than the cost of that obtained from coal today. Why, then, has atomic energy not already displaced coal as the major fuel in use in the world of the present time? The answer is that while the actual cost of extracting uranium and thorium from rock is modest, the process of converting them into usable energy is far more complex and requires a far larger capital investment and fuel inventory than does a power plant operating on coal. Indeed, in the present state of nuclear technology, the capital costs would be so large that the primary contribution to the cost of power would be the interest on the capital investment.

First, let us consider the matter of inventory. In a nuclear-power plant the fuel is not consumed rapidly, as it is in a coal-driven steam plant. A certain critical weight of uranium or thorium, mixed with fissionable material, must be present if the chain reaction is to occur under conditions where "breeding" of new fissionable material takes place. This weight depends upon the nature of the process—if it is a "fast-neutron" reactor, one weight will be required; if it is a "slow-neutron" reactor, another. The weight also depends upon the design and efficiency of the equipment for extracting the heat from the reactor and converting it into useful work.

Given the minimum weight for a reactor, at what rate can power be extracted? It seems unlikely that this will much exceed about 5000 kilowatts per ton of uranium and thorium present. At this rate of energy extraction, a plant would require an inventory of uranium or thorium over 500 times greater than its yearly consumption. If we take interest on capital to be 5 per cent, we see that the yearly interest on uranium inventories would be twenty-five times the cost of the uranium consumed (5 per cent of 500 = 25). If the interest rate were only 2 per cent, interest on inventories would still be 10 times greater than the cost of the uranium consumed (2 per cent of 500 = 10). To this there must be added the interest on the balance of the capital investment required for the power plant, in addition to the fuel inventory.

It is likely that electricity could be produced from atomic energy under existing economic conditions at a cost which would not exceed 1 cent per kilowatt-hour. With improved technology it is conceivable that the cost could be brought down to perhaps 0.6 cents per kilowatt-hour. This is to be compared with existing costs of coal-generated electricity in the United States, which average between 0.5 and 0.6 cents per kilowatt hour. Thus we can see that atomic power is not far from the stage where it might compete successfully with coal. As time goes on and the cost of coal increases further, and as nuclear technology improves, the cost differential between the two sources will become smaller, and will eventually vanish.

We have seen that the price of coal, relative to the general price level, is bound to rise considerably during the course of the next few decades. There will be a rapid rise when petroleum supplies approach depletion, and this will be followed by a continuous slow rise as it becomes necessary to mine more difficult seams. Coal will become increasingly a premium fuel, reserved, in the main, for use where other sources of energy are unsatisfactory: coke is needed for steel production; petroleum from coal will be needed for mobile power units; coal will be needed for a variety of chemicals which cannot be easily produced from other raw materials. It is entirely likely, barring unforeseen technical difficulties, that atomic energy will provide a substantial fraction of the world's energy by the time another century has passed. By 1975, when the end of the world's petroleum resources is more clearly in sight, we may well see the first major trend in this direction.

It must be emphasized that there are many technical difficulties that lie in the path of economical utilization of atomic energy. It is clear that its widespread use is dependent upon "breeding" that permits complete utilization of all uranium and thorium. But successful breeding of new fissionable material is in many respects incompatible with efficient conversion of atomic energy into useful work. Low conversion efficiency will in turn postpone the time at which atomic energy can compete successfully with coal.

Uranium and thorium in a nuclear reactor must be periodically treated and freed from the fission products which form and which decrease the efficiency of the operation. There are necessarily losses of material associated with the processing. Further, the problem of disposing of the radioactive products is considerable. They must be stored underground for many years, or transported to the oceans in such a way that people are not endangered in the process.

Another difficulty is associated with the usefulness of fissionable material in waging wars. Should all of the world derive the greater part of its industrial energy from uranium and thorium, the amount of fissionable material available for the production of atomic bombs would be enormous. Plutonium-239 and uranium-233 would be present at any time in sufficient quantity to permit the fabrication of hundreds of thousands of bombs. These aspects of atomic energy are discussed elsewhere in more detail.

In spite of the many difficulties, atomic energy now appears on the horizon as a major energy source of the future. If what now seems probable becomes actual, the operations involved will indeed be enormous. Let us imagine a world populated by perhaps 7 billion persons, who consume energy at a per capita rate equivalent to that derived from burning 10 tons of coal per person per year. Under such circumstances, uranium and thorium would be consumed at the rate of 23,000 tons per year, and yield losses might increase the consumption to 50,000 tons per year. The capital investment of uranium and thorium in the reactors would amount to over 10 million tons. Rock would be processed at a rate of nearly 20 billion tons per year, but an initial quantity amounting to perhaps 10 trillion tons of rock would have to be processed to provide the uranium and thorium "capital" required for the reactors. This capital investment would be equivalent to approximately 1000 cubic miles of rock.

Perhaps the main obstacle to world-wide utilization of atomic energy would be the enormous amounts of radioactivity that would be produced. The disposal problem would be tremendous. In a world powered largely by atomic energy, radioactivity will be without question a continuous major problem.

It should be stressed that supplies of uranium and thorium are finite; they should be looked upon, like coal and petroleum, as fossil fuels. If the world should come to rely largely upon these substances for its energy, the time would eventually arrive when the fuel would be exhausted. But at the rates of energy consumption foreseeable during the next century, the reserves in ordinary rocks should certainly last for tens of thousands of years, and more probably for millions of years.

In a way, since we know that our coal and petroleum will vanish in the near future, the prospect for atomic energy appears encouraging in spite of the purely technological difficulties. But, as we discuss in another chapter, there are other more serious difficulties to be considered.

7.

All the energy that can be obtained from fossil fuels is insignificant when compared with the amount of energy the earth receives from the sun during the course of a single year. Ayres and Scarlott [1] point out that in only 3 days we receive as much energy from the sun as could be obtained by burning all potential reserves of coal, petroleum, natural gas, and tar, together with all the earth's forests. To what extent might this enormous and constant supply of energy be utilized when our reserves of fossil fuels prove to be inadequate? Clearly we would need to tap but a tiny fraction of the energy received by the earth in order to provide the world

1. Ayres and Scarlott, loc. cit.

with an ample steady supply for the operation of its industries.

Until quite recently man derived practically all his energy requirements from vegetation, and it is generally recognized that this is the simplest and the most practical existing means of capturing a substantial fraction of the energy received from the sun. Over one-quarter of the land area of the earth is covered with forests, and about two-thirds of this area is considered "productive" in the sense that, given access and good management, a program of steady harvesting could be carried out at the present time. Only about one-half of the productive area, or one-third of the total forested area, is now considered economically accessible.

On the average, it appears possible to remove about 1 cord of wood from 1 acre of forested land each year without depleting the supply. This means that the productive forested areas of the world, if operated under sound management, could produce energy equivalent to approximately 5 billion tons of coal per year. This is indeed a significant quantity of energy, being nearly twice the present world-wide rate of energy consumption. Nevertheless, when we consider ultimate world energy needs, our forests will satisfy but a small fraction of the requirements.

By careful cultivation energy yields can be obtained from certain food crops which are greater than those obtainable from wood. Let us suppose, for example, that it is possible to obtain average yields of sugar amounting to 10 tons per acre. (See page 121.) These 10 tons, if burned directly, would give us as much energy as about 6 tons of coal. This is several times the energy yield per acre obtainable from wood—but on the other hand, a considerably greater effort is required to obtain this high yield. Wood and food crops such as sugar, corn, and potatoes can be converted into alcohol, which can be utilized satisfactorily as a liquid fuel, but energy losses are necessarily associated with the conversion. Wood yields of 1 cord per acre could result in alcohol production of about 70 gallons per acre. Sugar yields of 10 tons per acre could result in alcohol yields of about 150 gallons per acre.

Algae, like other foodstuffs, could be used as fuel, either by burning the material directly or by fermenting it under conditions whereby methane is produced. The yields per acre would be higher than those for sugar, but costs of energy would also be relatively high. Under existing conditions algae could probably not com-

pete with coal at a coal price of less than 30 dollars a ton, and perhaps the costs would be so high that it could be used as fuel only
at a price that would make it equivalent to 100-dollar-a-ton coal.

It appears at the present time that high yields of solar energy
can be obtained by directly utilizing heat from the sun's rays
rather than by going through the intermediate step of growing
vegetation. The heat from the sun can be trapped by permitting
it to impinge upon a blackened metallic surface after passing
through a pane of specially treated glass. The glass, which per-
forms the same function as does the glass of a greenhouse, minimizes the escape of heat into the air. If two or three panes of glass
are used, the trapping is all the more efficient. Such collectors,
properly arranged, are capable of trapping about one-third of the
solar energy which falls on them. One can also use focused mirrors
to concentrate the sun's rays, and produce a sufficiently high temperature to operate a steam boiler.

It has been estimated that solar engines with black-plate collectors might produce, on the average, 50 horsepower per acre in
Arizona, and less than half that amount in New York State. About
150 tons of coal would have to be burned annually in order to
obtain the average amount of power obtainable from an acre of
Arizona land. Under such circumstances the present power needs
of the United States could be met by solar engines occupying an
area of less than 50,000 square miles. To put the proposition in
other terms, 1 acre of Arizona land could provide sufficient power
to support 15 persons living at the present American level of per
capita energy consumption.

It must be emphasized, however, that cost of power from solar
engines would be quite high, largely because of the heavy capital
investment required. The main cost would be the annual charges
on the capital investment, but it appears at present that maintenance and operating charges would by no means be negligible. It
has been estimated that electricity might be produced directly
from solar energy in Arizona at a cost of about 2 cents per kilowatt-
hour, compared with costs from existing coal-operated generators
of about half a cent per kilowatt-hour.

A major difficulty with this method lies in the fact that power
is obtained only in the daytime and on clear days. If it is to be
available at night and during periods of inclement weather, facili-

ties must be provided so that a part of the energy produced when the sun shines can be stored.

The heat from the sun can be utilized successfully in other ways as a substitute for fossil fuels. We know that in the United States nearly one-third of the total energy requirement is for the heating of homes and offices. This is also true in England. In areas which are not industrialized, space heating is by far the most important energy demand. However, in many regions of the world it is possible to substitute solar heat for that now being obtained from coal, oil, natural gas, hydroelectricity, wood, and other organic materials, through special housing design which utilizes new techniques in glass-making and architecture. Solar heating of water supplies is being utilized with increasing frequency in the tropics and in the southern part of the United States.

There are purely practical limits to the extent to which solar heating can be applied. But with techniques that are in existence at present, an over-all saving of about 60 per cent in fuel for space heating could be obtained with proper design of solar-heated houses coupled with the application of the heat-pump—a device which works on the principle of the electric refrigerator, save that, instead of pumping hot air out of a box into a room for the purpose of cooling the box, it pumps hot air from out of doors into a house for the purpose of warming the house. Further, it seems likely that this saving could be increased in the future. But at the present time few houses are being designed to take advantage of these energy-saving features, for the reasons that the capital investments are high and costs of fossil fuels are still low. At present costs, interest on the additional investment exceeds somewhat the cost of the fuel saved. But as time passes the situation is bound to change.

There are other possibilities on the horizon for the efficient utilization of solar energy, but at present our information is so scanty that extrapolation into the future is difficult in the extreme. Electricity can be produced if one junction of two dissimilar wires is heated and the other is cooled. In the future, this effect might make possible the direct conversion into electrical energy of a small fraction of the solar energy which strikes a given area. Also, at some future time it might be possible to devise man-made chemical systems similar in principle to those in plants, by means of which solar energy could be converted efficiently into chemical or electrical energy. But it is difficult to say whether such a system can ever be made to operate more efficiently than photosynthesis or even than the "brute-force" method of converting solar energy to electricity by using solar-powered steam generators.

Eventually there will come a time when direct use of solar energy will be widespread. The development of atomic energy might postpone the arrival of solar-powered engines. But when the time arrives that there are no longer any fossil fuels and all accessible uranium and thorium have been consumed, we must turn to the sun for the fulfillment of our energy requirements.

8.

In the foregoing discussion I have tried to make it clear that, barring scientific discoveries or developments of which we have as yet no inkling, the broad outlines of the future world pattern of energy consumption are clear, though accurate estimates of time schedules for it are impossible. We have seen that, though fossil fuels would last us for many centuries at present world rates of consumption, and though most of our present needs could, if necessary, be met by hydroelectric power, energy requirements are rising rapidly and will doubtless continue to rise for decades because of population increases, the continuous spread of industrialization, the rise in per capita demands for material goods, and the increase in energy requirements necessary to process low-grade ores and to obtain the diminishing fossil fuels themselves.

Further, it has become apparent that, as fossil fuels disappear, increasing emphasis will be placed upon solar energy for space heating, and upon attempts to utilize it in other ways. At this time atomic energy may well come into its own as a major source of power, for it is likely that by then it will be able to compete economically with coal. The first major use for atomic energy—aside from the military one—might well be in central heating plants in northern regions where solar energy is not readily applicable. But in addition we can expect developments of combination electrical-generation and space-heating units. Further, we can expect that during the next phase of history the world will develop most of the remaining accessible hydroelectric sites.

Some regions of the world will enter the next phase of energy history sooner than others; indeed, in a sense, the transition has already started in some localities. As we know, solar water heaters are appearing on the scene with increasing frequency. During World War II, Germany was heavily involved in the production of liquid fuels from coal. Power-alcohol plants have already appeared in regions where petroleum must be imported, where coal is scarce, and where sugar is locally available. These regions include Brazil, India, Pakistan, Jamaica, and the Dominican Republic.

The third phase of energy history will come into existence when coal production passes its peak. When that point is reached, coal will be so expensive in relation to the general price level that its use will be confined to the production of a few important commodities where substitutes are not very satisfactory—such as the manufacture of steel. Space heating will be done primarily with atomic and solar energy. Practically all liquid fuels will be obtained from wood and vegetation. Increasing emphasis will be placed on the utilization of electricity produced from atomic energy for land transportation, and atomic-energy-powered vessels for ocean transportation.

On the basis of our existing technological experience, it seems likely that during this third phase atomic power will greatly exceed solar power in importance. This will be true if it develops that "breeding" on a large scale is compatible with reasonably efficient extraction of useful work. The assumption is also made that more energy can be extracted from a given weight of rock containing small amounts of uranium and thorium than is required for the processing. If it develops that these assumptions are correct, it seems likely that capital costs for production of atomic power will be less than those for the production of solar power. However, in time these assumptions might well prove to be wrong, in which case solar power will come into widespread use during the third phase of energy consumption.

Some regions of the world will probably enter the third phase while others are still living in the first and second phases. For example, as is pointed out in this chapter, India is very short of fossil fuels, and her waterpower cannot support major nation-wide industrial development. If India is to industrialize on a substantial scale, she must either extract considerable quantities of energy from her vegetation—which will be difficult in view of the severe food shortage—or she must adapt atomic energy and solar energy to industrial purposes.

If atomic power can be utilized on a large scale, and if it is possible to extract uranium and thorium from ordinary rock, this source of energy should last mankind for a very long time. But even the amount of uranium- and thorium-bearing rock on the earth's surface is not infinite, and some day those elements may cease to be available in quantities sufficient to meet the need. After the time when uranium and thorium production passes through its peak, man will become almost completely dependent upon solar power. He will have then entered the fourth and final stage of his energy-consumption history.

Although the broad pattern of future energy consumption is clear, it is difficult to place it in proper time perspective. The rapidity with which energy resources are consumed in the future will depend upon the rapidity with which regions of the world industrialize, the rate of population growth, the ultimate level of human desires to possess material goods—if there is such an ultimate level—and the effort that is made to accelerate production to fulfill those desires. Nevertheless, it is worth our while to examine a few figures to obtain some idea of the relative magnitudes of the various quantities with which we are dealing.

We have seen that the population of the world might well rise to nearly 7 billion persons by the time another century has passed. Let us imagine that those 7 billion persons consume energy at a per capita rate equivalent to the present per capita rate of energy consumption in the United States. This does not mean that each person would have as much in the way of material possessions as the population of the United States now has, for more energy would be required per unit of production. As we know, more energy will be consumed by conversion losses, and, as is pointed out in the next chapter, more energy will be required to obtain the raw materials from which the goods are manufactured. In general, it would appear that world-wide per capita consumption of energy equivalent to 10 tons of coal per year would be a conservative assumption.

At this assumed rate, total energy requirements would be equivalent to that derived from 70 billion tons of coal per year. Clearly, by the time this point is reached, natural petroleum will be but a dim memory of the distant past, much as home illumination by oil lamp is today. Coal would quickly vanish as a major source of energy, for at such a rate of consumption all reserves in the world would last but a few decades.

Approximately one-third of the total energy requirement would be for space heating. In a well-organized world, two-thirds of the space heating could be provided by solar heat, leaving the equivalent of 54.5 billion tons of coal annually to be provided from other sources. We can subtract from this the coal equivalent to the amount of energy that can be derived from waterpower. On the basis of minimum flow, this would amount to 1.4 billion tons; or, at a maximum, it would amount to 4.2 billion tons. Taking the larger figure, we would have a balance of energy equivalent to that available in 50 billion tons of coal to be provided annually from other sources.

Energy equivalent to 5 billion tons of coal would be obtained annually from forests. But somewhat over half of this would be required for lumber and paper manufacture, at the present American per capita level of wood consumption for these purposes, leaving wood equivalent to about 2.3 billion tons of coal to be converted into liquid fuels, chemicals, and directly into power.

Total demand for liquid fuel might be equivalent in energy to about 10 billion tons of coal annually. Conversion of the "surplus" wood into gasoline or alcohol would satisfy less than 10 per cent of the need. The balance of the liquid fuels would have to be obtained by conversion of agricultural products such as sugar or algae, or by a lengthy process, costly in terms of energy, involving production of carbon dioxide from limestone, production of hydrogen by the decomposition of water, and manufacture of hydrocarbons from these two raw materials. Even if we are optimistic and assume annual yields of gasoline from vegetation at an average of 500 gallons per acre, about 4 billion acres of land would have to be utilized for this purpose. As we can realize, this is a very large area indeed, particularly in view of the fact that an adequately fed population of 7 billion persons would require approximately 3.5 times as much food as is now being grown. Thus we must conclude that liquid fuels, if they are utilized in the quantities indicated, must be manufactured in the main by processes that are excessively expensive in energy, as, for example, the hydrogenation of carbon dioxide.

Thus, in our society of 7 billion persons, an amount of energy equivalent to between 40 and 50 billion tons of coal annually would have to be obtained from uranium and thorium or from the conversion of solar energy into useful power—the exact figure depending upon the intensity of conversion of agricultural products into useful power. If we assume the demand to be 45 billion tons annually, and if we assume that atomic energy corresponding to 7 tons of coal can be extracted from a ton of rock, approximately 6.4 billion tons of rock would have to be processed annually.

Should atomic-power production prove to be less feasible than solar-power production, enormous solar installations would be necessary to provide the mechanical energy equivalent to that obtained from 45 billion tons of coal. We have seen that an acre of southern desert land could provide mechanical energy equivalent to that obtainable annually from 150 tons of coal. Thus, our requirements could be met with solar-power plants covering a total area of about 30 million acres of suitable desert land. Although the capital investment would be high, the required acreage would not be unreasonably large.

In other words, we see that from the point of view of energy a population of 7 billion persons could, in principle, be supported at a fairly high consumption level for a very long period of time even in the absence of fossil fuels. But before we become too optimistic about the future of mankind, it should be emphasized that difficulties appear on the horizon to mar the otherwise hopeful prospects.

Chapter VI:

THINGS

> *The expansion of the machine during the past two centuries was accompanied by the dogma of increasing wants. Industry was directed not merely to the multiplication of goods and to an increase in their variety: it was directed toward the multiplication for the desire for goods. We passed from an economy of need to an economy of acquisition. . . .*
> LEWIS MUMFORD

1.

When man first learned to use tools, wood and stone were the only major raw materials available. But there is a limit to what can be accomplished with wood and stone alone, and it was not until the discovery of metallic copper that tool-making progressed beyond this limit. As the use of metals increased, the value of copper and tin—the two major constituents of bronze—resulted in extensive trade in those metals. We have seen that much of neolithic Europe was linked together by metal-trading.

But there were also limits to the extent to which bronze could be used. Ores of copper and tin are not very abundant, so that the limitations in techniques of both extraction and discovery prevented the utilization of metals from becoming really widespread.

Once man learned to produce metallic iron from ores—technologically a much more difficult job than producing copper—the use of metals increased rapidly, for high-grade iron ores are far more abundant than high-grade copper ores. Indeed, so abundantly has the earth's surface been endowed with iron that, in spite of huge production rates, we are still processing iron ores of high quality. By contrast, the copper that is so important to our modern industries must frequently be extracted from ores that contain less than 1 per cent of the element.

In considering copper and iron, we see the two major contrasting factors of scarcity and difficulty of extraction operating as major limitations to use. If copper had been as abundant as iron, and iron as scarce as copper, copper would now be our major material of construction. If the production of metallic copper had been as difficult as the production of metallic iron, the age of metals might have been postponed for many millennia. If metallic iron had been as readily obtainable from ores as metallic copper, the age of metals might have started at a much earlier time and would probably have spread more rapidly than it actually did.

The development of the technology of iron production eventually paved the way for the Industrial Revolution and the evolution of modern industrial society. Within that society there is an enormous production of goods which, for various reasons, people want to own. In order to produce the goods, raw materials and machines are needed. Machines are needed to produce machines, to extract the raw materials, and to transport machines, raw materials, and finished products. The result is a vast, complex, interlocking network of mines, factories, farms, and transportation facilities.

In order to manufacture the diverse products consumed by society, we mine iron ore, transport it to vast furnaces, and reduce it to pig iron. We take pig iron and transform it into varieties of steel. We shape the steel into many forms, which are in turn shaped into suitable end products. In similar fashion, we mine ores of copper and aluminum, extract the metals, and shape them to suit our needs. We quarry rock, cut trees, and mine the earth for sulphur, tin, vanadium, nickel, and tungsten. We evaporate seawater and produce salt and iodine. We convert the nitrogen of the atmosphere into ammonia and nitric acid. We carry out a multiplicity of operations, all of which are ultimately dependent upon the extraction of materials from the earth, the atmosphere, or the oceans.

Iron, which is abundant and which can be extracted easily, is by far the most widely used metal. In the United States approximately 1300 pounds of steel are produced per person per year. By contrast, per capita production of copper, which is the second most widely consumed metal, is only 23 pounds per year. Aluminum production is rising rapidly and will soon overtake copper production, but it is doubtful if per capita consumption will be greater than 50 pounds per year by 1975. Per capita production of all metals other than iron is only about 93 pounds per year—about one-fourteenth the production of steel. Per capita production of various metals in the United States in 1950 is shown in Table 6, together with the estimated requirements in 1975 as projected by the President's Materials Policy Commission.

TABLE 6

PER CAPITA CONSUMPTION OF METALS IN THE UNITED STATES

| METAL | POUNDS PER PERSON PER YEAR | |
	1950	PROJECTED 1975
Steel	1260	1550
Copper	23	26
Lead	16	20
Zinc	16	17
Aluminum	13	47
Chromium	13	20
Manganese	8.7	11
Nickel	1.3	2.1
Tin	1.2	1.2
Antimony	0.49	0.68
Magnesium	0.34	1–10
Molybdenum	0.17	0.36
Cadmium	0.07	0.13
Cobalt	0.06	0.21
Tungsten	0.04	0.08
Beryllium	0.04	0.08
Vanadium (1947)	0.02	?
Niobium	0.01	?
Bismuth	0.005	0.008

Many steps are necessary in order to obtain pure metals. First, a suitable ore deposit must be found. The ore must then be extracted from the earth—an operation that frequently requires drilling and blasting, followed by the excavation of large volumes of rock. Some ores, particularly iron ores, can be utilized directly for reduction to metal. But with depletion of high-grade ores, more low-grade ores are used, and it is necessary to concentrate the desirable constituents in these ores prior to the reduction. This in turn requires grinding and pulverizing, followed by a series of steps to concentrate the ores. The concentrated material can then be reduced to metals.

All of these steps require energy and labor. Costs go up rapidly with decreasing concentration of the desired metal in the ores, for the reason that much more material must be handled and processed. It has been estimated, for example, that the cost of treating iron ore that contains 30 per cent iron is well over twice the cost of treating ore that contains 60 per cent iron.

An industrial society consumes vast quantities of non-metallic minerals, as well as minerals which are used for the production of metals. As is shown in Table 7, for every person in the United States, over 7000 pounds of stone, sand, and gravel are consumed each year. Construction of highways, buildings, and dams results in the annual consumption of over 500 pounds of cement per person. Altogether, nearly 5 tons of materials, aside from food, water, fuels, and metal-bearing ores, are consumed in the United States each year for every person living in the nation.

TABLE 7

PER CAPITA CONSUMPTION OF NON-METALLIC MINERALS AT A HIGH
STANDARD OF LIVING

(*United States, 1949*)

	POUNDS PER PERSON PER YEAR
Stone, sand, and gravel	7300
Cement	520
Clays	380
Common salt	210
Phosphate rock	130
Gypsum	89
Lime (other than for cement)	85
Sulphur	71
Potassium salts	15
Pyrites	13

Outside of the Western World, per capita consumption of industrial raw materials, like per capita consumption of food, is low. Over 80 per cent of the world's steel, for example, is manufactured in the United States, the Soviet Union, the United Kingdom, France, and Germany. Outside those areas, per capita production in 1949 was only about $\frac{1}{40}$ of that in the United States. During the same year, per capita steel production in India averaged about $\frac{1}{150}$ that in the United States. Equally large differences can be seen if we compare production of other metals.

Per capita consumption of industrial raw materials is rising in the United States and even more rapidly in many other regions of the world. We must now inquire into the long-range aspects of supplies of industrial raw materials in relation to these rapidly increasing demands.

2.

With existing techniques, over 3 tons of raw materials are required to produce 1 ton of pig iron. The materials include $1\frac{3}{4}$ tons of high-grade iron ore, nearly 1 ton of coke, and close to $\frac{1}{2}$ ton of limestone. About 85 per cent of the pig iron produced in the United States is channeled into steel production, the balance being used for a variety of cast-iron products, such as railroad-car wheels, cast-iron pipe, and fittings. That portion which is consigned to the steel furnaces is melted with approximately an equal weight of scrap iron; the concentrations of alloying substances are adjusted, and the mixture is treated in a suitable manner to produce the desired variety of steel.

The output from the steel furnaces is shaped in the mills into a variety of finished products such as rails, tubes, bars, and sheets. Approximately 65 per cent of the iron in the steel furnaces ends up as finished products; about 25 per cent ends up as scrap, which is recycled; somewhat over 10 per cent is lost in the processing. The finished steel forms are then fabricated by other manufacturers into a variety of products, and during the course of manufacture a substantial fraction of the steel ends up as scrap, which is sold to the steel plants for recycling. The end products are sold and put to use, and after a period of time, which depends upon the nature of the product, they become obsolete or too worn for proper functioning, and frequently are returned to the steel mills as scrap for recycling.

Between the years 1870 and 1950 a total of about 2 billion tons of iron were produced in the United States. If all of this were now in use, our iron and steel industry inventory would amount to about 13.5 tons per person. But iron does not last forever—oxidation by the air, corrosion by liquids, and other general wear take heavy tolls. To this depletion must be added the losses which occur during steel production. It is impossible to estimate with any precision the amount of iron that has been lost never to be recovered. But if we make the reasonable assumption that annual irrecoverable iron losses, other than those involved in steel production, amount to about 1 per cent of the amount in use, and that losses involved in steel production amount to one-eighth the total annual production of steel ingots and castings, we find that about 60 per cent of the iron that has been produced during the last 80 years is still in use.[1] This corresponds to about 8 tons per person.

Clearly the amount of iron in use per person in our society is increasing, and if the projections of the President's Materials Policy Commission prove to be correct, the per capita amount of iron in use by 1975 may be as much as 15 tons.

We see that a substantial fraction of our pig iron production goes into the creation of new capital, the balance making up for various losses. If society ever reaches a condition of stability, then pig iron production need be only sufficient to make up for losses in use. The extent of these losses will ultimately be determined by the total amount of iron and steel in use, by the efficiency with which it is recycled, and by the extent to which it is protected during use.

For the purpose of our discussion, we will assume that the average life of end products containing steel will be approximately 20 years—in other words, on the average, 20 years will elapse from the time that an object is manufactured until it is returned to the steel mill as scrap. We will assume further that the average life of iron with respect to irrecoverable loss other than in steel production will be approximately 100 years. If we assume further that the stabilized per capita amount of iron in use will amount to 15 tons per person, and that the iron is primarily in the form of

1. This includes obsolete iron and steel equipment which has not yet been recovered as scrap.

steel, we see that per capita production of steel end products would average $1\frac{5}{20}$, or 0.75 tons annually. In order to produce this quantity of end products we would have to produce 0.88 tons of finished steel products such as castings, sheet, plate, and tubing per person. The production of this amount would in turn necessitate a total production of steel ingots and castings of about 1.2 tons per person annually. Annual iron losses during steel production would amount to about 0.15 tons per person. With 15 tons of steel in service per person, other irrecoverable losses would amount to an additional 0.15 tons per person. Thus, in order to maintain a balance, pig iron production would have to be about 0.3 tons per person annually.

We see that, as time goes on, it is well within the realm of possibility that per capita steel production will reach nearly double the level of production in 1950. On the other hand, per capita production of pig iron might eventually taper off to a level somewhat lower than that of today. Whereas the ratio of steel production to pig iron production during the period 1896–1900 was only 0.74, by 1950 it had reached 1.5. It seems likely that the ratio might eventually reach a level of 4.0 or more.

Let us assume that the population of the United States can eventually be stabilized at a level of 225 million persons, and that industry is stabilized at a point at which there are 15 tons of steel in existence per person. Under such circumstances, steel production would be about 270 million tons annually—nearly three times the 1950 level. Pig iron production would be about 68 million tons, an amount close to that produced in 1950. Per capita energy consumption for the production of finished steel products would be about the same as it is today, for although there would be considerable savings resulting from the reduced per capita pig iron production, this would be offset by the energy requirement of the enlarged steel production.

Reserves of iron ore in the United States containing 50 per cent or more of iron are dwindling rapidly and, at a pig iron production rate of 70 million tons annually, can last no more than about 15 years in the absence of other sources of supply. Since 1935 a growing proportion of iron ore has required treatment in order to raise the iron concentration to the high levels required by the steel mills, and the fraction of the ore requiring treatment is bound to increase even more rapidly in the future. But even reserves containing between 35 and 50 per cent iron ore, all of which require treatment, would last no more than an additional 25 years at a 70-million-ton annual production rate. Thus, by the time another half-century has passed, either most of the United States iron ore will be derived from deposits containing less than 35 per cent iron, or a substantial fraction will be imported.

In the Lake Superior region there is a widespread rock formation known as taconite, which contains between 25 and 35 per cent iron. Iron in the form of magnetite can be magnetically extracted from the rock if it is first ground exceedingly fine. Deposits of magnetic taconite, together with the non-magnetic variety, for which concentration processes are now being devised, are sufficiently abundant to supply 70 million tons of pig iron per year for about 300 years. The iron and steel industry, realizing the potential importance of taconites, is at present rapidly developing plans for the construction of facilities for processing these materials.

Once the supply of taconites approaches exhaustion it will be necessary to process ores containing less than 25 per cent iron. This could be done in principle, but of course more energy and effort would be required per ton of iron produced. It seems likely, however, that long before we reach such a point the changing energy picture will have already had a serious effect upon the steel industry. The end of fossil fuels, if not already at hand by that time, will be in sight, and rising prices of coal will have forced substitution of other sources of energy. Electrical energy provided by waterpower, atomic energy, or solar energy can be substituted for the heat provided by coal, but it would still be necessary to use a reducing agent that will combine with the oxygen of the iron ore. Such a process is now in operation in Sweden, where the Electro-Metal furnace produces pig iron from iron ore, using electric power as the source of heat and carbon as the reducing agent. In this process the carbon requirement—in the form of charcoal or coke—is only about one-third that required in the ordinary coke blast-furnace process.

It is possible to eliminate coal or charcoal entirely in pig iron production by using hydrogen gas as the reducing agent. Considerable research has gone into this process, by means of which reduction takes place at low temperatures, producing a sponge iron which can then be melted in the steel furnaces. The process has an advantage in that iron ore in almost any physical condition can be utilized. The over-all energy requirements would be largely those associated with the production of sufficient quantities of hydrogen gas by the electrolysis of water. Altogether, about 2400 kilowatt-hours of electricity per ton of sponge iron would be required, of which 2200 kilowatt-hours would be consumed in the production of hydrogen. This quantity of electricity could be produced by the consumption of 2100 pounds of coal, using modern, efficient generators. Comparing this with the 2600 pounds of coking coal required per ton of pig iron in ordinary blast-furnace production, we see that the hydrogen reduction process is actually somewhat less expensive than blast-furnace production from the point of view of energy consumed.

The fact that coal need not be considered an indispensable raw material for steel production has profound significance from the point of view both of world development during the coming decades and of the future of civilization during the coming centuries. It means that countries such as Brazil, which possess sizable deposits of iron ore but little coal, can produce steel, utilizing hydroelectric power or electricity generated from atomic or solar energy. It means that mankind as a whole, after the depletion of the world's coal reserves, will be in a position to continue steel production—assuming that other energy sources can be developed in time to produce the necessary electricity, following the disappearance of workable coal seams.

We have seen that about 8 tons of iron and steel per person are now in use in the United States, and that nearly 14 tons of iron per person have been produced from ore in order to achieve this working amount. We must now ask: What are the possibilities that such large amounts of metallic iron per capita will come into use in the world as a whole?

At the present level of world population, a total of nearly 20 billion tons of iron would be required for a high level of industrialization, assuming no losses in cycling and in use. But when we consider that the population of the world will probably continue to rise for many decades, and that there are actually many losses in cycling and in use, we see that the foregoing estimate is too low. Assuming a world population of 7 billion, the total pig iron capital essential to a high degree of world-wide industrialization would be something like 100 billion tons. The amount of metallic iron in the world today is a tiny fraction of this.

Production of steel in the relatively underdeveloped areas of the world where the greater part of humanity resides amounted in 1950 to less than 3 million tons annually. The production capacity of most areas is now being increased, and if all existing plans are realized, production may reach 6 million tons during the course of the next 20 years. This is a slow rate of increase, but even if steel production in those areas doubled in size every 10 years, nearly 150 years would be required for a high per capita level of steel production to be achieved.

Our knowledge of the total iron-ore resources of the world is severely limited. A survey published in 1938 [1] indicates that the iron content of all potential high-grade ores outside of the United States might amount to 25 billion tons. When we take into account the fact that ores containing as little as 25 per cent iron can be processed with known techniques, it seems likely that the production of 100 million tons is well within the realm of possibility, given adequate supplies of energy. It is clear, however, that long before the world as a whole becomes highly industrialized those iron-ore resources which can be easily mined and easily processed will have disappeared. From that point on, low-grade ores will have to be processed, with techniques of increasing complexity, which will necessitate the expenditure of ever greater quantities of energy.

3.

Steel is not suited for all uses to which metals are put in an industrial society. It cannot compete with lead in storage batteries, nor can it compete with copper in electrical wiring. If construction materials possessing a combination of lightness, strength, and corrosion resistance are required, metals such as aluminum and magnesium are substituted for steel. Every metal has a particular set of properties, including melting point, thermal and electrical

1. U.S. Tariff Commission, *Iron and Steel, 1938,* Report No. 128.

conductivity, density, and tensile strength, which makes it particularly suited for a specific function.

The development of the light metals made possible the design of machines and structures which could otherwise have been fabricated only with great difficulty. Aluminum, magnesium, and titanium are more expensive than steel, but their useful combinations of properties make them more valuable for many purposes. The situation is not unlike that which existed when metals first came into existence and competed with wood. They were more expensive than wood, but more useful, since their special properties enabled man to do things that would have been impossible by utilizing wood alone.

Aluminum is one of the more abundant elements in the earth's crust, and its most important ore, bauxite, is distributed widely. But because the difficulties of producing satisfactory aluminum metal from the oxide are much greater than those of producing metallic iron, metallic aluminum is a relative newcomer. In 1900 its production in the United States amounted to only about 3000 tons. By 1950 consumption exceeded 980,000 tons annually, having increased ninefold since 1925.

Demand for aluminum is still growing rapidly. With further increased use of it in power transmission, transportation, and building materials, it seems likely that by 1975 demand will have risen to a point at least five times higher than the 1950 level. It is extremely difficult to estimate the production level that might ultimately be reached, but it is conceivable that in another 50 years production will be fifty times greater than it is today.

World bauxite reserves probably amount to about 2 billion tons, the raw material for about 500 million tons of aluminum. At present rates of world production, this reserve could last for many centuries. But at the rates of increase in production suggested in the preceding paragraph, world bauxite reserves would not last for long.

Their depletion would by no means eliminate aluminum production, for there are many substances from which the element can be extracted in a form suitable for reduction to the metal. These substances include large deposits of clay and other aluminum-bearing minerals. Processing of these materials would involve greater expenditures of energy, and the processing would be more complex, than in the case of bauxite, but aluminum production need never be limited by availability of aluminum-bearing materials.

Once aluminum oxide has been extracted from its ore, the metal is produced by electrolysis. Approximately 18,000 kilowatt-hours of electricity are consumed in the production of 1 ton of aluminum metal. If all of this energy were generated from coal, approximately 9 tons of coal would be required per ton of metal. To this we can add the energy required in chemically processing the bauxite—an amount corresponding to about 1½ tons of coal. Thus, with existing technology, an amount of energy equivalent to about 10½ tons of coal is required to produce 1 ton of aluminum metal.

We have seen that the production of 1 ton of pig iron consumes about 1.3 tons of coking coal. Thus, on a weight basis, aluminum reduction requires about eight times the energy that is required by iron reduction. But we must remember that aluminum is considerably lighter than iron, with the result that fewer pounds are required for the construction of a given object. Calculated on a volume basis, 1 cubic foot of aluminum is ony 2.8 times as expensive in terms of energy as 1 cubic foot of iron.

From the point of view of money, aluminum is more expensive than iron—in part because of the greater energy requirement, and in part because more work must be done in order to obtain a product suitable for reduction to metal. Both industries are being driven to increasingly complex methods of ore processing, but when we take the major factors into consideration it seems likely that the treatment of aluminum ores will remain the more expensive process for a very long time in the future.

Eventually, as coal supplies dwindle and the world shifts to other energy sources, both iron and aluminum will be produced largely by electricity. The sponge-iron process requires about 2400 kilowatt-hours per ton, compared with the aluminum requirement of 18,000 kilowatt-hours per ton. When that time arrives, aluminum reduction will consume, pound for pound, about 7.5 times as much energy as iron production. Nevertheless, so great is the usefulness of the lighter metal that as time goes by it will become increasingly important in our economy. Indeed, it is conceivable that the amount of aluminum in use, together with the other light metals—magnesium and titanium—might some day in the distant future approach the amount of iron in use.

The magnesium industry is considerably younger than the aluminum industry, but there are indications that it will develop rapidly during the years to come. During World War II there was temporarily a large demand for magnesium, but peacetime uses were so meager that production dropped off enormously following the end of hostilities. In recent years there have been major advances in the techniques of fabricating magnesium alloys, with the result that demand is now increasing. In view of the fact that, volume for volume, magnesium weighs only two-thirds as much as aluminum, and of the excellent strength characteristics of many magnesium alloys, it seems highly probable that demand for magnesium will increase rapidly. Although it is more expensive than aluminum on a weight basis, on a volume basis it is actually less expensive.

Magnesium, like aluminum, can be reduced to metal by electrolysis. The energy requirement per pound is greater than that for aluminum, but on a volume basis the requirements are comparable. There are indications that other processes may eventually yield magnesium metal on a large scale with considerably greater energy efficiency.

The metal has been produced from a variety of magnesium-bearing ores. The most interesting source of supply, however, is seawater, which contains magnesium in solution at a concentration of 0.13 per cent. The magnesium can be removed by a series of simple operations and put into a form suitable for preparation of the metal. The only raw materials required in quantity, in addition to energy, are seawater, calcium carbonate—which exists abundantly on the surface of the earth—and hydrochloric acid, which can be made from seawater. Thus, with the exception of energy, the raw materials for magnesium production are of practically unlimited extent. It is clear that, given adequate sources of energy, mankind will be able to produce magnesium metal in quantity long after high-grade deposits of other metals have disappeared.

Titanium is the third light metal which shows considerable promise for the future. It possesses an unusual combination of advantageous properties, including light weight, resistance to corrosion, strength, and toughness. At present it has barely emerged from the experimental stage, and the rapidity with which the industry grows will depend upon the solution of a multitude of production and fabrication problems. At present the metal is expensive in terms both of money and of energy required for reduction. Reduction is carried out with molten magnesium metal.

Raw materials for titanium production are sufficiently abundant to make possible any production levels that may be achieved during the next few years. But if the problems of titanium production at low cost are satisfactorily solved, and production levels climb to 1 million tons or more annually during the next 25 years, the problem of supplies of high-grade ores may become serious.

4

Copper, one of the first metals known to man, has remained one of the most useful of metals throughout history, but its primary usefulness has changed considerably with time. Today its major uses are those which take advantage of its high electrical and thermal conductivity. Only one metal—silver—is superior to copper as an electrical conductor, but the small amount of silver in the earth's crust makes it prohibitively expensive.

In 1880 the world output of copper amounted to but 200,000 short tons. In 1949 world mine production amounted to about 2.2 million tons. After 1940 the United States, which had always been a net exporter of copper, became a net importer, and by 1950 we were bringing into the country approximately one-quarter of all the copper we used. In 1950 our total mine production amounted to about 900,000 tons—nearly 40 per cent of the world total—and our total consumption, including production from old scrap (475,000 tons), amounted to about 1.8 million tons.

Copper is a rare element in comparison to iron, aluminum, and magnesium. High production rates have been made possible only by the fact that demand for the metal has warranted the processing of extremely lean ores. In the eighteenth century ores that averaged less than 13 per cent copper were considered impracticable. As time passed and the rich ores disappeared, ores containing ever smaller concentrations of the metal were processed. By 1900 the average grade of copper ores of all types being processed was about 5 per cent. By 1950 the average grade of ore being handled had dropped to 0.9 per cent, and ores containing as little as 0.7 per cent copper were being processed.

According to the President's Materials Policy Commission, the total copper requirement of the United States in 1975 may amount to about 2.5 million tons—an increase of nearly 45 per cent over the 1950 level of consumption. Since it is highly unlikely that copper scrap can satisfy more than 30 per cent of the need, by 1975 we must either produce or import approximately 1.8 million tons. This is an amount roughly double the 1950 mine production.

The measured, indicated, and inferred reserves of recoverable copper in the United States now amount to about 25 million tons. Although there are some differences of opinion among geologists and mining engineers, it appears unlikely, in view of our diminishing resources, that an annual production rate greater than 800,000 tons can be maintained over the next 25 years. If these estimates are correct, by 1975 we will be importing approximately 1 million tons of copper annually—40 per cent of our enlarged demand.

World reserves of copper ore that can be mined, utilizing existing techniques, are probably not much greater than four times the reserve in the United States. It is conceivable that greater supplies will become available as techniques are improved, but it is clear that vanishing copper reserves will constitute a formidable barrier to world development. The situation will become increasingly difficult in view of the fact that areas which are already highly industrialized, such as the United States and Europe, are becoming ever more dependent upon the less developed areas for their supplies. If all potential reserves that can be processed with existing technologies were divided evenly among the people of the world, the quantity of copper allocated to each person would be far less than the per capita amount now in use in the highly industrialized regions of the world.

The acute situation can be relieved in the future only with considerable difficulty. Other materials can be substituted for copper, but frequently only at a considerable loss of efficiency both in fabrication and in operation. Aluminum can be substituted for copper in a variety of ways, but it must be admitted that there are many uses, involving the conduction of electricity and heat, in which copper would be very difficult to replace, especially in transformers and transmitting devices.

A second approach to an alleviation of the difficulty will lie in the direction of processing ores of still lower grade. Concerning this point, the President's Materials Policy Commission says:

Nor does there appear to be much chance that further technological progress in mining would increase reserves significantly by making lower-grade deposits profitable through lowering the minimum or cut-off grade of workable ore. The present loss of copper in milling is apparently at an irreducible minimum of 1 to 2 pounds per ton of ore. If the grade of ore being milled were lowered much more the percentage recovery would drop to an uneconomic level under present prices. But more important is the view that there is not a large quantity of copper left in ore below the current cut-off grade of roughly 0.5 per cent. In any event it is most likely that a number of important producing companies in this country will find it more advantageous to continue to expand their operations abroad where they have extensive holdings that are richer and cheaper to operate than to mine such low-grade deposits at home.

This statement, based upon existing copper economics, is probably unduly pessimistic. It seems highly likely that our present level of technology would permit the extraction of copper from ores far more lean than those now considered feasible. Of course the cost in money, and even more in energy, would be considerably greater than at present. But once the possibilities of importation dwindle, either because of increased industrialization of the less developed areas or because of depletion of foreign sources by the industrialized West, the United States will probably start processing "ores" containing as little as 0.1 per cent copper. As is discussed in more detail elsewhere, such processing of extremely lean ores would not be carried out for one major product; instead, the processing would be highly integrated and aimed at the extraction of a variety of products among which costs could be divided. Already we have seen the beginnings of such practices in the copper industry; an important aspect of copper economy today lies in the extraction of gold and silver from the ore as by-products.

In 1950 the average concentration of copper in the ore handled in the United States amounted to 0.9 per cent. In view of the fact that mine production of copper was somewhat over 900,000 tons, we see that more than 100 million tons of ore had to be processed. This corresponds in weight to the total amount of iron ore produced in the United States annually—from which we see that although consumption of copper is far less than that of iron, the actual mining operations are of the same magnitude. On this basis alone it is understandable why copper is, pound for pound, very much more expensive than iron.

In view of the vanishing reserves of copper in the world, it is clear that, unless ways and means are found for providing adequate substitutes and for processing ores of extremely low grade, the process of industrialization will be seriously impeded throughout the world. In any event, world copper requirements during the years to come will be met only by ever greater increases in the expenditure of energy.

5.

An industrial society requires large supplies of metals such as manganese, lead, zinc, tin, cadmium, and germanium, which, while not very abundant in nature, possess individual properties that make them particularly useful, and in some cases indispensable. The list of elements and the diversity of uses would be extremely long if we were to make it complete. It will be sufficient for our purposes at this point to examine but a few of the more important minor elements and their patterns of use, from which we will be able to appreciate the broad aspects of future supply and demand.

In 1950 approximately 800,000 tons of manganese were consumed by the steel industry in the United States. The greater part of the amount used is lost in the slag in a form which makes recovery of the metal difficult. Reserves of manganese ore in the United States are of low grade, and if we were to add together all measured, indicated, and inferred reserves containing 1 per cent or more of the element, the total would amount to no more than 100 million tons—approximately a 100-year supply at the present rate of consumption.

Manganese ores of high grade are available in other regions of the world, with the result that both the United States and Western Europe are heavy importers. In 1950 the United States imported nearly 95 per cent of its requirements, and Western Europe imported about the same fraction. Africa and Asia are the largest exporters. Russia possesses over half of the known manganese reserves of the world, but has ceased exporting. Known reserves outside of the Soviet Union, averaging 25 per cent manganese or higher, amount to about 200 million tons.

It is clear that the known manganese reserves of the world will last for many decades, but the time will come when low-grade material will have to be processed. Indeed, if for any reason imports of manganese ore by the United States are curtailed, it will be necessary to start a major low-grade-ore processing program.

As the demand for alloy steels increases, demands for alloying metals such as chromium, nickel, molybdenum, cobalt, nisbium, and tungsten will increase. Deposits of these metals are widely distributed throughout the world, but, with the exception of molybdenum and, to a lesser extent, tungsten, reserves in the United States are meager. For the rest we are virtually completely dependent upon imports. In all of these cases the situation will become increasingly acute as more regions of the world become industrialized. Within a few decades it is likely that either all of these elements will be produced from low-grade ores or the nations of the world will do without.

Consumption of lead in the United States amounted to 278,000 tons in 1900, and domestic production was sufficient to take care of almost all the demand. By 1950 we were consuming 1.2 million tons annually, and net imports had risen to a level corresponding to nearly half of the total. The President's Materials Policy Commission estimates that by 1975 demand for lead may rise to nearly 2 million tons annually. As is true of many rare elements, heavily industrialized areas cannot produce sufficient quantities of lead to satisfy their needs. Western Europe and the United States together produce 42 per cent of all new lead in the world, but they consume 85 per cent of the total world production. Mexico, Canada, Australia, and New Zealand are major exporters.

Dwindling lead reserves in the United States have resulted in dwindling production. According to the President's Materials Policy Commission:

The decline in lead mine output from 1925 to 1950 was general throughout the country. Production from the southeast Missouri district, for example, the largest contributor throughout the present century, fell from an average of 199,000 tons in the 1924–27 period to 123,000 tons in the years 1946–49, a decline of 38 per cent. Similar proportionate declines were registered in the Coeur d'Alene, Idaho, and Bingham, Utah, districts, two of the four leading producers, while output from the fourth, the Tri-State district, declined about 70 per cent. . . .

As this general fall in productive capacity took place, the number of smaller producers increased. About 1925 the first fruits of selective flotation began to be realized—many small deposits of mixed lead-zinc ores, especially in the West, were made economic by this technological innovation and were brought into production to meet the high level of demand. But many of the smallest were relatively short-lived. Consequently, even though there were more small mines, the net effect on total capacity was not sufficient to offset the decline of production in the larger districts; indeed, it was insufficient to counteract the decline of total output among the small producers themselves, for the aggregate decline of the big producers did not account for the total national decline.

In 1950 measured, indicated, and inferred reserves of lead in the United States amounted to 7 million tons of recoverable metal. Actual proved working reserves amounted in 1950 to the equivalent of less than 3 years' production. Measured and indicated reserves outside the United States and outside the Soviet sphere amount to about 27 million tons of recoverable lead. Making due allowance for future discoveries, it seems unlikely that total world reserves of lead recoverable under our existing technology amount to much more than 100 million tons, or roughly a 70-year supply at the current rate of world production. But we have seen that world demand for lead, like the world demand for other elements, is increasing rapidly.

Scrap represents an important part of the total lead production in the United States. In 1950 approximately 35 per cent of the total requirements were met by production from old scrap. But many of the uses to which lead is put are of such a nature that the element is lost in irrecoverable form. Out of every 100 pounds of lead used each year by the United States, 24 pounds are dispersed in gasoline, paints, ceramics, and in diverse other uses. Of the 76 pounds which are potentially recoverable, 16 pounds are lost and 60 pounds are eventually recycled. Thus, out of every 100 pounds of lead brought into use each year, 40 pounds are lost never to be recovered.

During the coming decades, increasing care will be taken to recycle potentially recoverable lead, and we can expect that as time goes on less and less lead will be used in products which result in dispersal of the element. The day is probably not far distant when tetraethyl lead will no longer be used extensively in gasoline as an anti-knock substance, and paint containing lead pigment will be but a memory of more abundant days in the past. In addition to these measures, efforts will probably be made to extract lead from low-grade ores. This is quite feasible in principle, but, as with other elements, more effort and, in particular, more energy will be required.

The tin situation is similar. The United States has always been dependent on imports for nearly all of her supplies. In 1950 we imported 109,000 long tons, produced 22,000 tons from old scrap, and produced only 94 tons domestically. There is nothing to indicate the possibility of production on any significant scale either in the United States or in any of its possessions. Resources of tin in Western Europe are also meager, with the result that approximately 95 per cent of new tin must be imported.

At present rates of consumption, known tin reserves, primarily in Malaya, Indonesia, Bolivia, the Belgian Congo, Thailand, and Nigeria, would last about 30 years. But it is clear that world tin demands are increasing rapidly in spite of technological advances that decrease wastage in use.

The situation with respect to many other metals follows a similar pattern. Increasing demands in industrial areas, coupled with decreasing reserves of high-grade ores, result in increasing shortage and the inevitable need for importation. The President's Materials Policy Commission estimates that by 1975 net zinc imports by the United States will have doubled, cadmium imports will have increased fivefold, bismuth imports will have doubled, and beryllium imports will have increased by 35 per cent.

Eventually the high-grade reserves of nearly all of the minor elements will vanish. That does not mean that use of those elements will stop. But it does mean that we will be forced to meet all of our requirements by extracting the elements in the main

from very low-grade ores. The penalties will be ever greater expenditures of energy.

6.

The chemical industry represents an extremely important part of
an industrialized society—indeed, fully as important from many
points of view as the metals industry. From the chemical industry
spring the vast quantities of solvents, medicines, fertilizers, dyes,
refrigerants, bleaching agents, and plastics which enter, in one
way or another, into practically every area of our existence.

The basic raw materials of the chemical industry are coal, water,
air, sulphur, salt, and limestone. From coal we obtain energy, ammonia, coal tar, and coke; from solutions of brine plus energy,
hydrogen, chlorine, and caustic soda; from limestone, plus energy,
quicklime and carbon dioxide. We burn sulphur with air and obtain sulphur dioxide and sulphuric acid. From the nitrogen of the
air we obtain ammonia and nitric acid. From water and coke we
obtain carbon monoxide and hydrogen. From combinations of
these various basic substances with other less widely used materials
we obtain the enormous variety of chemicals which together make
up the output of the chemical manufacturing and processing industries.

Energy is without question the most important raw material of
the chemical industry, for most other basic materials exist in virtually unlimited quantities. Carbon can, if necessary, be obtained
entirely from limestone. Chlorine, hydrogen, and sodium hydroxide
can always be obtained from seawater. Nitric acid and ammonia
can always be obtained from the air. But energy is an indispensable ingredient for any process designed to produce them.

At one time the chemical industries of the world obtained their
fixed nitrogen essentially without energy expenditure, by mining
deposits of potassium nitrate in India. As the Indian deposits
waned, early in the nineteenth century, vast deposits of nitrate were
found in Peru. Peruvian nitrate, later taken over by Chile, quickly
became one of the most coveted of the earth's possessions. But the
great distance from Chile to Europe, with the consequent dangers
during periods of hostility, spurred considerable effort in the direc-

tion of producing fixed nitrogen from other sources. The development of the by-product-coke oven led to recovery of ammonia from gases which had formerly been wasted. Small quantities of nitrogen were recovered from animal and vegetable waste. But it was not until it became evident that the Chilean deposits were not inexhaustible that major progress was made. During the opening years of the twentieth century three major commercial processes were developed for fixing atmospheric nitrogen. Since that time consumption of fixed nitrogen has increased with enormous rapidity and has reached the point where production of Chilean nitrate is negligible when compared with the total.

The history of the fixed-nitrogen industry is an excellent example of the path man must follow when a substance which is not abundant in nature becomes essential to him. The procedure, in a somewhat different form, is being repeated in the case of sulphur, the major raw material used in the production of sulphuric acid. Until early in the twentieth century most of the world's supply came from pyrites, notably from Spain, and from native sulphur deposits in Sicily. The pyrite industry virtually collapsed when the Frasch process was developed for extracting elemental sulphur inexpensively and simply from the salt-dome formations of Texas and Louisiana. Prior to the introduction of this process in 1903, the United States depended largely upon the roasting of imported and domestic pyrites for its supply of sulphur. By 1910 production of native sulphur exceeded domestic production from all other sources. By 1920 the United States had become a net sulphur exporter. By 1950 production of native sulphur had exceeded 5 million tons annually, and the United States was exporting more than 1.5 million tons. As the United States became a major supplier for the world, the output of sulphur from other natural sources contracted or ceased to expand.

The end of inexpensive sulphur production by the Frasch process is now in sight. Known deposits will probably not last much longer than another quarter-century at existing production rates, and production is keeping pace with demand only with difficulty. It is estimated that by 1975 the demand in the United States and in Western Europe will have risen to twice the 1950 level.

In 1950 only about one-seventh of the sulphur supply in the

United States came from non-Frasch sources. But in Western Europe pyrites provided the larger part of the sulphur that was produced, though most countries outside the Soviet sphere received nearly one-fourth of their supply from the United States. In great measure the large imports by the rest of the world resulted from the fact that United States sulphur delivered in England was considerably less expensive than that obtained from pyrites from Spain.

The world need never be deprived of sulphur for lack of availability of the element in some form. By the end of another two decades it is likely that the greater part of our own supply will be derived from pyrites and from smelter fumes. Long before another century has passed it is likely that a large fraction of the world's sulphur requirement will be met by extracting the element from calcium sulphate, large deposits of which are widely distributed throughout the world. Costs in terms of money and in terms of energy will be considerably higher than at present. But the basic raw material will last indefinitely.

Approximately three-quarters of all sulphur that is produced is converted into sulphuric acid—a substance which is one of the most widely used reagents in industry. Approximately 40 per cent of that which is produced in the United States is consumed in the production of phosphate fertilizers, consumption of which is increasing rapidly and must increase for many decades in the future if food production is to expand. At the present time almost all of the phosphate fertilizer used in the United States is produced by the action of sulphuric acid upon phosphate rock.

In 1950 world production of phosphate rock totaled about 22.5 million tons, of which 10.5 million were produced in the United States, 8.5 million for domestic use, and 2 million for export. The earth's phosphate rock deposits, estimated at 35 billion tons, are located chiefly in the United States, North Africa, the Soviet Union, Europe, and the Pacific islands. Asia, Australia, and South America do not possess large known deposits, but it is likely that substantial reserves will eventually be uncovered in Venezuela, Brazil, and Indochina. If we include in known reserves low-grade material which is not economically minable under present conditions but which will eventually be, as high-grade reserves are depleted, the world total would amount to a 10,000-year supply at

present rates of consumption. However, rates of consumption are
increasing rapidly as fertilizers become more generally used. It
seems likely that consumption will at least double in the next 25
years; by the end of another century it might well be twenty times
the existing rate. Even at this greatly expanded rate, reserves would
last several centuries, and by processing ores containing still less
phosphorus, supplies should last for millennia.

But with phosphorus, as with all other materials that enter into
our civilization, continued extended use will result in ever greater
rates of energy expenditure. As lower-grade rock is processed,
more energy is required for mining and extraction. Further extended use of phosphate fertilizers will result in depletion of
sulphur reserves at an accelerated pace and will hasten the approach of sulphuric acid production at increased energy costs. As
sulphur resources dwindle, it is likely that increasing quantities
of phosphate fertilizers will be produced by the electric-furnace
process or by substituting nitric acid for sulphuric acid in the
treatment of the rock.

In recent years polymeric materials, or plastics, have come into
widespread use, and during the years to come the consumption of
such materials will probably increase rapidly. From carbon, hydrogen, oxygen, and chlorine, and, to a lesser extent, from silicon and
fluorine, a wide range of products can be made which can substitute for a number of materials in current use, ranging from natural rubber, wood, glass, and natural fibers to such materials as
copper, lead, zinc, tin, aluminum, and even iron.

The raw materials for plastics are obtained, at present, primarily
from by-products of coke production and from petroleum and
natural gas. During the next 25 years demand for plastics will
probably increase far beyond the levels that can be supplied by
the coke industry, with the result that production of plastics from
materials supplied by the petroleum industry will probably rise
considerably. As petroleum supplies dwindle, plastics, together
with an increasing variety of chemicals, will be made from coal
hydrogenation processes, and, as coal supplies are exhausted,
from limestone, provided that adequate sources of energy are
available.

We see that the future course of the world's chemical industry
depends almost entirely upon the development of the world's

energy resources. With the exception of energy, basic raw materials are widely distributed and of practically infinite extent. Today the production of chemicals rests largely upon the production of coal, petroleum, and natural gas. As fossil fuels diminish in abundance it is likely that the use of coal by the chemical industry, as a starting point in the production of complex molecules, will diminish less rapidly than the use of coal solely as a source of heat.

7.

In addition to the requirements of food, energy, and minerals, our civilization is dependent upon adequate and reliable supplies of water, not only for drinking, hygienic purposes, and the growth of crops, but also in prodigious quantities for the manufacture of the diversity of products which are consumed in industrial society.

The average person in the United States drinks about 200 gallons of water annually. For washing, cooking, laundering, and operating heating and air-conditioning equipment he consumes about 15,000 gallons a year. But these quantities are dwarfed by industry, which uses 40 per cent of our total consumption, or about 160,000 gallons annually for every person in the nation. In our great factories water is used in quantities for cooling, for heat exchange, for washing, in the preparation of various solutions, in the disposal of industrial waste.

Five gallons of water are required to process 1 gallon of milk, 10 gallons to produce 1 gallon of gasoline, 100 gallons to make 1 gallon of alcohol, 10 to 75 gallons for every pound of finished fabric, 80 gallons for each kilowatt-hour of electricity generated, 300 gallons in the manufacture of 1 pound of synthetic rubber, and over 65,000 gallons in the manufacture of 1 ton of steel. The list could be many pages long.

But even more greedy than industry in its use of water is irrigation, which on 26 million acres in 1950 used over 50 per cent of the total water consumed in the United States. Further, it is estimated that by 1975 an additional 6 million acres will be irrigated, thus increasing water consumption for this purpose by an additional 20 or 25 per cent.

Each day billions of gallons of water are evaporated from the oceans and distributed over the land masses of the world. Each year the mean rainfall over the United States amounts to 30 inches —corresponding to a total daily rainfall of about 4300 billion gallons.

Approximately 70 per cent of the water that falls on the land area of the United States returns to the atmosphere as the result of evaporation or transpiration of vegetation. The remaining 30 per cent runs off the land areas and flows down streams and rivers into oceans. This amount, which totals about 1300 billion gallons of water daily, represents the maximum rate at which water can be consumed in the United States, unless the water is re-used, or unless fresh water is obtained from some other source, such as seawater.

The earth's mantle contains large reservoirs of water, known as ground water, which have accumulated as a result of the circulation of rainwater down through cracks and crevices and through porous rocks and sands. The force of gravity causes the the water to move downward until lack of porosity prohibits further penetration. The upper limit of the zone of water saturation is known as the "ground-water table," and its depth below the land surface may be zero, as in the case of localities near springs, or it may be hundreds or even thousands of feet.

Ground water can be tapped by drilling wells to depths below the ground-water table and pumping the water to the surface. Such wells provide the major part of the water used by the two-thirds of the people in the United States who live on farms or in towns and cities with less than 100,000 population. In addition, wells supply much of the water used in many of the metropolitan areas. However, the greatest single use for ground water is in irrigation. Each day about 18 billion gallons of water are pumped to irrigate fields in arid regions or to provide supplemental irrigation in other regions. This amounts to about 20 per cent of all water used for irrigation in the United States.

Underground reserves of water are tremendous but not limitless. Over a long period of time water cannot be removed from ground-water reservoirs at a rate greater than that of replenishment. If the rate of withdrawal is consistently greater than the rate of replenishment, of course, the reservoir becomes dry.

However, some of the heaviest consumers of ground water are

regions that receive insufficient rainfall to replenish their reservoirs. Tucson, Arizona, which receives an annual rainfall of only 11.5 inches, is pumping water from the ground at rates far greater than rates of replenishment. Overuse of ground water in the Los Angeles area has resulted in greatly lowered water tables, followed by encroachment of salt water from the ocean. In addition, land surfaces have sunk as much as 8 feet in some spots. In many arid and semi-arid regions one can see pump after pump bringing water to the surface for irrigation at rates that are far greater than rates of replenishment. As there is no hope of materially raising the level of ground water in most such areas, the alternatives are either to abandon the land eventually or to obtain water from distant points.

Only a small fraction of the water used for irrigation purposes can be re-used. Most of the water which is poured over the land is ultimately evaporated, and very little percolates through the soil and returns to the underground reservoirs. However, a large part of the water used for industrial purposes can be re-used, and indeed often is.

We have seen that a major industrial use of water is for cooling. When water is so used it is unaltered and can be used by another plant downstream for the same purpose. However, there is a limit to the extent to which such practices can be carried out without penalty, as was demonstrated recently when it was found that so many industries were using and re-using the water of the Mahoning River near Youngstown, Ohio, that it became too hot to be used for cooling.

On the average, cities and industries return as waste over 90 per cent of the water withdrawn. But frequently the returned water is accompanied by huge quantities of destructive chemicals, garbage, excreta, and many other elements of pollution. Virtually every industry contributes noxious stuff to streams for disposal, and the sewage of 30 million people is dumped into rivers without treatment. The net result of these practices is that the cities and industries downstream must purify the water before it can be re-used. Without treatment it is frequently too contaminated for human or livestock consumption, and the impurities make it unsuitable for many industrial operations.

As the population of the United States increases and industrial activity expands, problems of water supply and stream pollution will become even more acute than they are at the present time. Increasing efforts will have to be made to remove noxious materials, to reclaim water once it has been used, to regulate the flow of streams, to develop new ground-water reservoirs, to avoid contaminating ground water with noxious substances, and to recharge existing reservoirs.

As time goes on we will see an ever expanding network of aqueducts, dams, reservoirs, sewage-treatment plants, and water-purifying units. The penalties for the improvements will be greatly increased cost of water and, above all, increased per capita expenditures of energy. Energy must be consumed to construct and maintain water systems and to separate waste from water so that it can be re-used.

As more areas begin programs of public health, extended agriculture, and industrialization, the world water situation will become increasingly acute. Eventually, as the populations become larger and larger, we may reach the time when practically no water that falls on land will reach the oceans via streams. Every gallon will be conserved, used, purified, and re-used, and the process will be repeated again and again until nearly all has been evaporated.

There is, of course, an abundance of seawater, but it cannot be used directly for human or animal consumption or for irrigation. Also the salt concentration prohibits its use for most industrial purposes other than for cooling and waste disposal, and the corrosive effects of undiluted seawater makes use of the liquid for cooling purposes often rather uneconomic. Nevertheless, increasing quantities are being utilized for this purpose; in 1950 about 15 billion gallons of brackish water were used by industry in the United States for cooling purposes.

Eventually it is likely that large quantities of fresh water will be obtained in many regions of the world by removing the salt from seawater. This process is costly from the point of view of energy, but in an industrial society the energy costs are not fantastically large when compared with energy expenditures for other purposes. It appears possible to obtain fresh water from salt water at energy costs equivalent to about 60 pounds of coal per 1000 gallons of water. This means that all of the fresh water consumed in the United States in 1950 could have been produced at an energy cost equivalent to about 2 billion tons of coal, a little more than the total contemporary energy consumption in the United States.

Economically, the production of fresh water from seawater cannot compete successfully with other water supplies at the present time. The average cost of water used for irrigation is now no more than 1 cent per 1000 gallons. The cost of industrial water averages only about 4 or 5 cents per 1000 gallons. Cost of treating even the poorest grades of water now used by cities probably is no greater than 5 cents per 1000 gallons. With our present technology, costs of distillation in large units might be as low as 50 cents per 1000 gallons, but it is doubtful that they can be brought much lower. This figure is some ten times greater than the present average cost.

Nevertheless, as the world becomes more heavily populated, as the necessity for irrigation increases, as industry spreads over the several continents, water will be in increasingly short supply. Seawater will be treated, first for municipal consumption in coastal regions of low rainfall, and probably eventually for agricultural purposes as well. By combining seawater-treatment plants with chemical plants for the production of salt, magnesium, caustic soda, fluorine, hydrogen, and various other substances that can be extracted from seawater, net costs can probably be reduced to the point at which seawater will be a major water source and will make it possible to grow food economically in arid coastal areas in California, Peru, and North Africa.

8.

The procurement of raw materials for industry and agriculture has followed a consistent pattern throughout the greater part of history. Man has always done the easiest things first. His agriculture started in the fertile, automatically nourished river valleys and gradually radiated outward into areas more difficult to cultivate. The first ores he processed contained high concentrations of desired elements. The first fuels he utilized existed abundantly on the earth's surface.

As time has gone by, both population and individual desires

have increased, with the result that he has now consumed the ores that could be obtained easily and has expanded into areas where the production of the necessities of life is increasingly difficult. Whereas once he found ores at the surface of the earth, he now follows seams deep underground. Whereas once he processed high-grade ores, he now processes ores containing tiny concentrations of desired metals. Whereas once he confined his agriculture to river valleys or to regions where rainfall was abundant, he now builds dams, transports water for long distances, and cultivates desert lands. Whereas once he cultivated soil that remained fertile generation after generation, he now cultivates land that must be fertilized each year.

With each passing year his material desires have increased. Industrialization has spread from Western Europe to America to Japan to the Soviet Union to Oceania and to South Africa. It is now spreading to South America, to the rest of Africa, and to Southeast Asia. Eventually it is possible that industrialization will have spread, like agriculture, over the entire surface of the earth.

As more and more areas become industrialized, and as the population of the earth increases still further, ever increasing demands will be placed upon mineral resources. All high-grade ores will eventually disappear, and man will be forced to extract the raw materials for his industry from the leanest of substances that exist on the surface of the earth. He need not be deprived of the elements from which he fabricates his tools and his possessions, for the oceans and all the rock of the earth's crust are at his disposal. But as time goes by, everything he does will be more costly in terms of energy, and human affairs will necessarily become more highly organized in order to carry out the increasingly complex tasks.

In the future we shall undoubtedly see major changes in basic industrial processes, changes which reflect the quantity and quality of resources in each locality, and, as a result, practices will differ in different places. Some regions will begin processing low-grade iron ores while others are still able to process high-grade ores. Some regions will eliminate coal from iron processing, while others are still using coal as the major energy source in steel production; some will process aluminum-bearing clays while others are still able to process bauxite; some will manufacture sulphuric acid from calcium sulphate while others are still able to manufacture it from pyrites; some will distill seawater for their municipal water systems while others will have an abundance of natural fresh water available.

We can expect that the industries of the world as a whole will pass through several stages, at the end of which time mineral resources will cease to be important factors in world economy. As high-grade ores diminish in abundance, we will consume our energy resources more rapidly. As coal dwindles and becomes more expensive, its use will be reserved for premium functions such as reducing iron ore and producing organic chemicals. Eventually iron will be produced entirely without coal, by reduction with hydrogen in electric furnaces, and coal will be reserved entirely for the production of chemicals. At some time in the future aluminum will be produced in the main from anorthosites and clays. Consumption of magnesium will increase, partly as the result of its ready availability in seawater. Sulphuric acid will be produced entirely from calcium sulphate. Increasing emphasis will be placed on the utilization of nitric and hydrochloric acid, largely as the result of the ready availability of raw materials for both. Minor elements such as copper, tin, lead, nickel, and germanium will be extracted from ores containing lower and lower concentrations of the elements, and increasing emphasis will be placed on the extraction of co-products among which costs can be divided, and on the utilization of substitutes.

Eventually the time will come when ordinary rocks such as granite will be looked upon as ores. We have already seen that average granite contains sufficient uranium and thorium to pay, energy-wise, for the processing of the rock and still leave a substantial energy profit. In addition, without unduly increasing the energy expenditure, one can probably extract from the rock a multitude of elements that are essential to an industrial society. One hundred tons of average igneous rock contain, in addition to other useful elements, 8 tons of aluminum, 5 tons of iron, 1200 pounds of titanium, 180 pounds of manganese, 70 pounds of chromium, 40 pounds of nickel, 30 pounds of vanadium, 20 pounds of copper, 10 pounds of tungsten, and 4 pounds of lead. It is doubtful that all of these quantities could be conveniently extracted, but it seems likely that a sizable fraction could be isolated without undue difficulty.

The basic raw materials for the industries of the future will be seawater, air, ordinary rock, sedimentary deposits of limestone and phosphate rock, and sunlight. All the ingredients essential to a highly industrialized society are present in the combination of those substances. From seawater we will obtain water for agricultural and industrial purposes, hydrogen for iron-ore reduction, chlorine, caustic soda, magnesium, salt, bromine, iodine, and potassium, together with minor supplemental quantities of other elements. From the air we will obtain nitric acid and ammonia, which will be used for food production and industrial processing. From the air we will also obtain oxygen and other gases which are needed in various industrial operations. From ordinary rock we will satisfy the greater part of our requirements for essential metals and fissionable materials. From limestone we will derive the greater part of the carbon that will be a major starting point for the organic chemical industry and a starting point for the manufacture of liquid fuels. From phosphate rock we will obtain fertilizer. From sunlight we will obtain electricity and a variety of organic substances that will be used for food and as a starting point for various chemical industries.

The industries of the future will be far more complex and highly integrated than those of today. The "sea industries" will dwarf all existing mining operations. One can visualize vast assemblages of plants in coastal regions where rock is quarried, uranium and other metals are isolated, nitric acid is manufactured, atomic power is generated, hydrogen is produced, iron ores are reduced to pig iron, aluminum and magnesium metals are prepared, and vast quantities of liquid fuels and organic chemicals are manufactured. As time goes on it is likely that the single-purpose plant will diminish in importance, eventually to disappear from the scene.

With increasing necessity and demand for efficiency, integration, and minimizing of waste in the economic world, there will be increasing demand for efficiency, integration, and minimizing of waste in the social world. These changes will have marked effects upon the ways in which men live. It seems clear that the first major penalty man will have to pay for his rapid consumption of the earth's non-renewable resources will be that of having to live in a world where his thoughts and actions are ever more strongly limited, where social organization has become all-pervasive, complex, and inflexible, and where the state completely dominates the actions of the individual.

Chapter VII:

PATTERNS OF THE FUTURE

Ah Love! could you and I with Him conspire
To grasp this sorry Scheme of Things entire,
Would not we shatter it to bits—and then
Re-mould it nearer to the Heart's Desire!
.OMAR KHAYYAM

1.

We have seen that the resources available to man are being rapidly consumed, but that, at the same time, new resources are being made available by our increased knowledge and improved technology. Given adequate supplies of energy, man can, in principle, extract everything that he needs for his existence at a high standard of living from substances which exist abundantly on the earth's surface—air, seawater, and ordinary rock. We have seen that within the rock itself there is sufficient energy to carry out the processing and also to provide power for the operation of industrial machinery. At the same time, man can extract energy from sunlight and use it to operate his factories. When we look at the situation solely from the point of view of technological and energetic feasibility, we must conclude that the resources available to man permit him, in principle, to provide adequately for a very large population for a very long period of time.

There are, of course, physical limitations of some sort which will determine the maximum number of human beings who can live on the earth's surface. But at the present time we are far from the ultimate limit of the number of persons who could be provided for. If we were willing to be crowded together closely enough, to eat foods which would bear little resemblance to the foods we eat today, and to be deprived of simple but satisfying luxuries such as fireplaces, gardens, and lawns, a world population of 50 billion persons would not be out of the question. And if we really put our minds to the problem we could construct floating islands where people might live and where algae farms could function, and perhaps 100 billion persons could be provided for. If we set strict limits to physical activities so that caloric requirements could be kept at very low levels, perhaps we could provide for 200 billion persons.

At this point the reader is probably saying to himself that he would have little desire to live in such a world, and he can rest assured that the author is thinking exactly the same thing. But a substantial fraction of humanity today is behaving as if it would like to create such a world. It is behaving as if it were engaged in a contest to test nature's willingness to support humanity and, if it had its way, it would not rest content until the earth is covered completely and to a considerable depth with a writhing mass of human beings, much as a dead cow is covered with a pulsating mass of maggots.

For population densities to reach levels much higher than those which exist in present-day agrarian cultures, a great deal of technology is required. India, for example, could not possibly support her existing high population density without the benefit of the knowledge and materials she obtains from the industrialized society of the West. Without the existence of an industrialized society somewhere in the world, disease could not be effectively controlled and transportation would not be in existence which would permit shipment of food from areas of surplus to areas of deficiency. In the absence of the availability of the products of industrialization, the population of the Indian sub-continent would probably not exceed about 100 million persons. Similarly, if industrialization should for some reason cease to exist in the world, and human life were to be supported entirely by intensive agriculture, the population of human beings would probably never exceed about 5 billion persons. This represents about the maximum number that could be supported on a bare subsistence basis in the absence of the means to construct elaborate transportation and irrigation systems, and provide artificial fertilizers and chemicals and other weapons for combating animals and insects which compete with man for food.

2.

As is indicated in an earlier chapter, within a period of time which is very short compared with the total span of human history, supplies of fossil fuels will almost certainly be exhausted. This loss will make man completely dependent upon waterpower, atomic energy, and solar energy—including that made available by burning vegetation—for driving his machines. There are no fundamental physical laws which prevent such a transition, and it is quite possible that society will be able to make the change smoothly. But it is a transition that will happen only once during the lifetime of the human species. We are quickly approaching the point where, if machine civilization should, because of some catastrophe, stop functioning, it will probably never again come into existence.

It is not difficult to see why this should be so if we compare the resources and procedures of the past with those of the present.

Our ancestors had available large resources of high-grade ores and fuels that could be processed by the most primitive technology—crystals of copper and pieces of coal that lay on the surface of the earth, easily mined iron, and petroleum in generous pools reached by shallow drilling. Now we must dig huge caverns and follow seams ever further underground, drill oil wells thousands of feet deep, many of them under the bed of the ocean, and find ways of extracting elements from the leanest of ores—procedures that are possible only because of our highly complex modern techniques, and practical only to an intricately mechanized culture which could not have been developed without the high-grade resources that are so rapidly vanishing.

As our dependence shifts to such resources as low-grade ores, rock, seawater, and the sun, the conversion of energy into useful work will require ever more intricate technical activity, which would be impossible in the absence of a variety of complex machines and their products—all of which are the result of our intricate industrial civilization, and which would be impossible without it. Thus, if a machine civilization were to stop functioning as the result of some catastrophe, it is difficult to see how man would again be able to start along the path of industrialization with the resources that would then be available to him.

The situation is a little like that of a child who has been given a set of simple blocks—all the blocks of one type which exist—with which to learn to build, and to make the foundation for a structure, the upper reaches of which must consist of more intricate, more difficult-to-handle forms, themselves quite unsuited for the base. If, when the foundation was built, he conserved it, he could go on building. But if he wasted and destroyed the foundation blocks, he would have "had it," as the British Royal Air Force would say. His one chance would have been wasted, his structure of the future would be a vanished dream, because there would be nothing left with which to rebuild the foundation.

Our present industrialization, itself the result of a combination of no longer existent circumstances, is the only foundation on which it seems possible that a future civilization capable of utilizing the vast resources of energy now hidden in rocks and seawater, and unutilized in the sun, can be built. If this foundation is destroyed, in all probability the human race has "had it." Perhaps there is possible a sort of halfway station, in which retrogression stops short of a complete extinction of civilization, but even this is not pleasant to contemplate.

Once a machine civilization has been in operation for some time, the lives of the people within the society become dependent upon the machines. The vast interlocking industrial network provides them with food, vaccines, antibiotics, and hospitals. If such a population should suddenly be deprived of a substantial fraction of its machines and forced to revert to an agrarian society, the resultant havoc would be enormous. Indeed, it is quite possible that a society within which there has been little natural selection based upon disease resistance for several generations, a society in which the people have come to depend increasingly upon surgery for repairs during early life and where there is little natural selection operating among women, relative to the ability to bear children—such a society could easily become extinct in a relatively short time following the disruption of the machine network.

Should a great catastrophe strike mankind, the agrarian cultures which exist at the time will clearly stand the greatest chance of survival and will probably inherit the earth. Indeed, the less a given society has been influenced by machine civilization, the greater will be the probability of its survival. Although agrarian societies offer little security to the individual, they are nevertheless far more stable than industrial ones from a long-range point of view.

Is it possible to visualize a catastrophe of sufficient magnitude to obliterate industrial civilization? Here the answer must clearly be in the affirmative, for, in 1954, it takes no extraordinary imagination to foresee such a situation. Practically all major industrial countries are now aligned on one side or the other of a major dispute. Weapons of such power that whole cities can be destroyed in a few minutes are in the hands of the disputants, and, should a major war break out, those weapons, which become more powerful every year, will almost certainly be used. It is clearly within the realm of possibility that another war would so disrupt existing industrial societies that recovery would be impossible and the societies would either revert to agrarian cultures or become extinct. Indications of the possibilities that confront us are offered by the catastrophe which paralyzed Western Europe in World War II, and the slow process of its postwar recovery—a process which would have been very much slower had the highly industrialized United States not been in existence, relatively unscarred and prepared to give aid. And the damage and disruption of industrial activity we witnessed then are insignificant when compared with the disruption that might be suffered by all participants in an "atomic" war.

It is quite possible that a war fought at the present time, even with existing powerful weapons of mass destruction, would not bring industrial civilization to an end. With America and Europe prostrate, the people of Asia would have room into which they could expand and thus accelerate the evolution of their own industrial society. It is also quite possible that the West would recover from a major war, although admittedly recovery would be a far slower process than it was after World War II. But with each passing year, as populations become larger, as the industrial network becomes more complex, and as high-grade resources dwindle, recovery from a major war will become increasingly difficult.

It must be emphasized, however, that industrial civilization can come to an end even in the absence of a major catastrophe. Continuance of vigorous machine culture beyond another century or so is clearly dependent upon the development and utilization of atomic or solar power. If these sources of newly applied energy are to be available in time, the basic research and development must be pursued actively during the coming decades. And even if the knowledge is available soon enough, it is quite possible that the political and economic situation in the world at the time the new transition becomes necessary will be of such a nature that the transition will be effectively hindered. Time and again during the course of human history we have seen advance halted by unfavorable political and economic conditions. We have seen societies in which technical knowledge and resources were both present, but where adequate capital and organization were not in existence and could not be accumulated sufficiently rapidly.

3.

At the present time a part of the world is agrarian and another part is either already industrialized or in the process of industrialization. It appears most unlikely that these two greatly different ways of life can co-exist for long. A world containing two major patterns of existence is fundamentally unstable—either the agrarian regions of the world will industrialize or, in the long run, the industrial regions will revert to agrarian existence.

That the agrarian regions of the world will attempt to industrialize is unquestionable. We see about us today signs of revolution, of reorganization, and of reorientation of goals leading toward the creation of local counterparts of Western machine culture. The reasons underlying the trend are obvious. It is in the nature of man not to want to die early and to look enviously at his neighbor who possesses greater wealth than his. A longer life, greater personal security, and more material comforts are looked upon as harbingers of greater happiness, and although this premise is by no means necessarily true, the fact that the individual believes it to be true is the important consideration that confronts us.

The search for greater personal security, longer life, and more material possessions will force the agrarian regions of the world to attempt to industrialize. But, as is indicated here, the probabil-

ity of their succeeding in the absence of a major world catastrophe
in the near future is small. There are clearly paths that could be
taken which would lead to a successful transition in the world as
a whole. But the nature of man makes remote the possibility that
the steps necessary for complete transition will be taken. The
picture would change considerably if Western machine civilization were to collapse, thus giving the present agrarian cultures
room into which they could expand. But the collapse of Western
culture would have to come well in advance of the time when
high-grade ore and fuel deposits disappear. We have seen that a
collapse of machine civilization after the disappearance of high-
grade ore deposits would probably be irreversible, and the world
as a whole would be covered with people living an agrarian existence.

It is clear that machine civilization as it is organized at the
present time may revert to agrarian culture. In view of this possibility, the most probable pattern for the future of mankind is that
sooner or later the entire world will become an agrarian one. This
could come about in one of several ways. The status quo could be
maintained with abortive attempts on the part of agrarian regions
to industrialize, leading eventually to depletion of ore deposits,
followed by the decline and eventual decay of machine culture.
The regions of advanced machine culture might fight one another and so disrupt the elaborate machine network that recovery
would be impossible. The greater part of the world might actually
succeed in industrializing, but a catastrophe could bring about
reversion to agrarian existence.

Collapse of machine civilization would be accompanied by
starvation, disease, and death on a scale difficult to comprehend.
In the absence of adequate sanitation facilities, the ability to
inoculate against disease, facilities for food transportation and
storage, factories for producing items which are essential for the
maintenance of life, the death rate would reduce the population
to a level far below that which could be supported by a stable
agrarian society which practices intensive agricultural techniques.
There would be such violent competition for food that savagery
would be the heritage of the survivors. Human life would be
confined once again to those areas which can be most easily cultivated, watered, and fertilized, and the principles enunciated

by Malthus would once again become the major force operating upon human populations. Only very slowly would the number of persons climb to the level which could be supported by a world-wide agrarian culture—about 5 billion.

The characteristics of the agrarian society of the future would probably be very much like those of most parts of China today or like those of societies which existed in Europe as late as the early eighteenth century. The ratio of available food to total population would be low. There would be no large-scale industries, for metals would be practically non-existent and the only sources of energy would be wood and waterpower. Lack of adequate supplies of metals would prevent the widespread use of electricity. Although parts of society would benefit from accumulated knowledge concerning public health and human biology, death rates would be high. Antibiotics and vaccines would be non-existent. Birth rates would almost certainly lie close to the biological maximum.

In the agrarian world of the future, as in the world prior to 1750, there would be very little difference in the manner of life of all civilized people. This fact is vividly illustrated by a story told recently by a well-known demographer:

I remember walking down a street in Nanking, China, one afternoon nearly twenty years ago with the eminent English economic historian, R. H. Tawney, and remarking to him that Chinese cities often reminded me of his description of early eighteenth-century English economic life. He replied in effect: "I was just thinking that the English workmen of that age would have been very much at home in the economy as well as in the living conditions we have just been observing, but so also would the Frenchman from Paris or the Italian from Florence. The farmers would have wondered at some of the crops raised here, but they would have understood the Chinese methods of cultivation and the care given the soil." [1]

Although the world as a whole would be predominantly agrarian, it is possible that small pockets of semi-industrialized society would survive. These would be centered largely around areas where waterpower is available and limited quantities of metals such as magnesium from seawater could be produced. But in the absence of a broader industrial base, per capita production of

1. Warren R. Thompson, "Population," in *Scientific American*, February, 1950, p. 11.

such materials would be extremely small. These semi-industrial areas, centered around regions of waterpower, might well become the wealthiest regions of the world, and it is in such regions that we might expect the traditions of the arts and the sciences to be perpetuated. But in such a world the sciences almost certainly would not flourish to the extent to which they do today or even to that which distinguished the ancient empires. Material wealth would be too rare and the struggle for food too intense to permit many persons to engage in such activities.

Much of the knowledge existing at the time when industrial civilization reached its peak would probably be preserved, taught in schools, and passed on from generation to generation. But much of it would be valueless and, as time went on, would be lost. We know from observations of past societies that knowledge and techniques can be lost rather quickly. In order to appreciate this, we have only to contrast the superb engineering techniques of the Romans with those of the residents of the Italian peninsula early in the Renaissance.

It is of course possible that, starting from a base of knowledge accumulated by previous society, and the abilities to utilize waterpower and to extract magnesium from seawater, man might once again learn to process rock, harness solar power, and extract energy from uranium. In such an eventuality a world-wide industrial civilization would arise once again and cover the earth, perhaps later to crumble under pressures similar to those which now confront humanity. But the probabilities of a second emergence would be remote. The advantages gained by the existence of previously accumulated knowledge would probably be offset by the scarcity of the number of raw materials necessary for the smooth functioning of an industrial society.

4

Although machine civilization as it exists at the present time is unstable and may revert to agrarian culture, it is important that we examine ways and means whereby stability in a world industrial society might be achieved. Can we imagine a sequence of events that might lead eventually to industrialization of all peoples of the world? And can we further imagine political, economic, and social structures that would permit the resultant society to maintain a long-range stability? When we enumerate all the difficulties in which the human species can become embroiled, it would appear *a priori* that the probability of successful transition along any path would be extremely small. Yet the fact that we are able to imagine patterns that might lead to successful transition is, in itself, significant. If stability is possible, it is achievable, although the probability of achievement may be small.

Perhaps the most immediate danger to confront machine civilization is war. A world filled solely by agrarian cultures is a stable one, and in such a world the various groups can fight among themselves as much as they please without endangering human population as a whole to any great extent. War in an agrarian world decreases individual security, and in like manner it decreases national security. But the world is so large that in the absence of machines that permit both rapid transportation over long distances and truly large-scale destruction, the existence of war would constitute no great danger to humanity. As in the past, nations, empires, and universal states would rise only to fall as new ones rose in turn.

But, as we can see, industrial society as a whole is extremely vulnerable to disruption by war, and the vulnerability is increasing rapidly as weapons become more effective, as the range of warfare increases, as the people become more dependent upon the smooth functioning of the industrial network, and as the reservoir of easily obtainable resources decreases. It is clear that industrial civilization cannot afford the luxury of many more wars. It is conceivable that the next war could so shatter it that it would be unable to recover. On the other hand, it is also conceivable that it could survive two or three more. But in any case, the number which can be tolerated is finite, and each conflict will decrease further the probability that industrial civilization will continue to exist.

Wars in the past have been fought for varieties of causes, for resources such as water, agricultural land, and ore deposits, for outlets to markets, to discard yokes of enslavement and to sever colonial bonds, to further religious, economic, and political creeds, to obtain power for power's sake. They have been fought over the pursuit of military security and over real or imagined threats to security. The causes of past wars have indeed been manifold, and the potential causes of future wars are equally numerous.

An agrarian region cannot wage a successful major war by itself against an industrial region; the weapons in the hands of the latter are too powerful to permit this. To be sure, agrarians can be trained and armed by industrialists and thus enabled to prosecute a war, as was the case with Russian-armed Chinese Communists fighting in Korea. But in a partially industrialized world the main dangers of war spring from the areas which are already industrialized and from those which have undergone partial transition.

History shows that wars between cities, states, and geographic regions cease once the originally independent units have amalgamated under the leadership of a single government with the power of making and enforcing laws that are binding upon individuals. One might reason on this basis that if all of the industrialized and semi-industrialized regions of the world were to federate under a common government, the probability of another war would be greatly decreased. It seems likely that this conclusion would be valid if the resultant federation were as complete as was the federation formed by the original thirteen colonies in America. On the other hand, it is extremely unlikely that such a highly centralized federation could come into existence at the present time; nationalistic feelings of individual men and groups of men, and conflicts of economic interests, are too strong to permit rapid transition. Also, those nations which have high per capita reserves of resources and high per capita production would be most reluctant to delegate their sovereignties to higher authority and to abandon the economic barriers that now exist.

It is possible that a federation possessing jurisdiction only over those features of society that determine the immediate ability of a nation to engage in war—the production of munitions and the creation and deployment of armed forces, for example—would decrease the probability of war. But it is extremely doubtful that such a system would really eliminate war as an instrument of national policy. Just as the existence of the United Nations decreases somewhat the probability of war today, so a universal government with jurisdiction limited solely to matters connected with armament and armed forces might decrease the probability of war still further. But it seems highly likely that nothing short of complete federation—of the creation of a true universal state possessed of the power to make and enforce laws dealing with a wide range of international economic and social matters—can really eliminate war in the long run.

The factors which increase the probability of war among industrialized and semi-industrialized areas are, in the main, the factors which prevent federation—desires on the part of the "haves" to maintain the status quo; desires on the part of the "have nots" to improve their position; enthusiasm for a particular economic or political creed; desire for power. As time goes on the effects of increasing population, decreasing resources, disappearing markets, and waning possibilities of importing food and raw materials from abroad should produce leveling effects that will simultaneously decrease the probability of war and increase the possibility of obtaining federation. A century ago the creation of a federation of the nations of Western Europe by means other than force would have been unthinkable. Today the fact that the predicaments of the nations involved are very nearly the same makes possible serious discussion of the subject.

Thus far we have spoken in terms of federation of those areas which are industrialized. The first reason for speaking in such terms is that the major danger of war springs directly from the war-making potential of industrialized countries. Secondly, true federation between countries of high population growth potentials and those of low is extremely difficult to imagine if abolishment of economic barriers is to be an integral feature of federation. For example, although a federation between the United States and Canada would produce relatively little dislocation in either social structure or economy and could possibly be consummated easily should both countries agree, a federation between the United States and Mexico at the present time could have disastrous consequences. Although the standards of living in Mexico would probably be improved by such a move, at least temporarily, the standard of living in the United States would almost certainly be lowered, and, far more important, the sudden incorporation in our society of a major group possessed of high growth potential would lead to an accelerated rate of population increase, together with the numerous difficulties associated with an accelerated rate of increase. Examination of the Puerto Rican situation provides

an excellent clue to the difficulties which could be created by federation of areas of high and low growth potentials. Fortunately
Puerto Rico is small, but even so the difficulties she creates are out
of all proportion to her size. To take but one example, the high
growth potential of Puerto Rico swells the relief rolls of the city
of New York, largely as a result of the steady emigration from
the island to the city and of the difficulties encountered by the
Puerto Ricans when they attempt to support themselves in their
new environment.

The creation of a true federation of the world, containing no
economic barriers, indeed appears to be remote at the present
time, but at least a pathway can be discerned which might lead
eventually to this goal. One of the first steps might be the creation
of a broad federation, including elimination of economic barriers
between industrialized areas whose growth potentials are low.
Concurrently, the United Nations could be strengthened and given
adequate powers to control the production of armaments and
sizes and locations of armed forces. Simultaneously, the industrialized areas of the world could take concerted action to help
the unindustrialized areas build factories, increase crop yields,
lower birth rates and death rates, and generally improve their
standards of living. Once the net reproduction rates of such areas
reach unity within a framework of low birth rates and low death
rates, the areas would become eligible for admission to the broad
federation of industrialized areas, and economic barriers would
be removed. Continuation of this process could lead eventually
to a completely industrialized world under a common government.

It should be emphasized again at this point that the author does
not suffer from the illusion that there is much probability that a
pattern of evolution such as is described in the preceding paragraph
might actually come into existence. But, as is stressed earlier, that
which can be imagined by man becomes possible, provided the
achievement of what is imagined does not require violation of
fundamental physical and biological laws. Time and again during
the history of man major changes have taken place that would have
been considered impossible during earlier times. Human beings
have demonstrated frequently that they can unite against common
threats to their existence and against common threats to their ways

of life. And battles against common dangers have frequently created strange bedfellows.

5.

Time, the spread of industrialization, and depletion of resources will tend to equalize the relative positions of nations and will tend to diminish the importance of many of the potential causes of war. But two will remain for many decades to come, independent of most leveling effects. The first is the pursuit of military security. The second is the desire to spread a particular political, economic, or religious creed, and, related to it, the pursuit of power for power's sake.

Today, in 1954, we see these particular influences toward war in vigorous operation. Both the Soviet Union and the United States are in positions which, from the raw-material point of view, are better than the positions of any other regions of the globe. Both nations have ample fossil-fuel resources to power their machines for many decades. Agricultural resources are sufficient to accommodate considerably expanded populations at advanced levels of technology. Although both nations import raw materials from other regions they do so more as the result of economic convenience than as the result of actual necessity. If high impenetrable fences were placed around both the Soviet Union and the United States, so that the two nations were forced to exist in isolation on their individual resources, there is little question that they would continue to exist comfortably from the material point of view for many years. Yet the two nations have for many years been engaged in bitter conflict which may, in the very near future, become a full-scale war.

Why is it that the two nations that are better off, from the resources point of view, than other regions of the globe are on the verge of war—and, as a corollary, are jeopardizing their future welfare and existence? A part of the difficulty appears clearly to be connected with the pursuit of security. Both nations appreciate that there is a real possibility that they will be at war, and, knowing this, each wants to place itself in the most favorable position from the strategic point of view. The Soviet Union attempts to

extend her buffer zone; the United States attempts to confine the
Soviet Union by building up the military forces of countries which
border the Soviet Union and her satellites. In the absence of circumstances such as threats from the outside, which might relieve
the situation, the vicious circle remains unbroken—action leads
to counteraction, which leads to further action, which leads eventually to war.

Superimposed upon the struggle for security is a conflict of
ideology which helps further to keep the vicious circle tightly
closed. The government of the Soviet Union is clearly a totalitarian
one, and many actions taken by the Soviet government are dis-
turbing to the people of Western countries. So conditioned are
most Western people to life divorced from despotism that they
would prefer to have no world rather than a world dominated by
Soviet rulers.

By contrast, the Soviet rulers appear to be confident that their
existing philosophy of government and economics is in the long
run the only one which gives promise of stability. There is good
reason to believe that they feel compelled to spread their philosophy, and some students are convinced that this evangelical compulsion dominates the actions of Soviet leaders. The relative proportions in which the pursuit of security, the compulsion to spread
Communist doctrine, and the search for power determine Soviet
actions are unknown, and much time could be spent debating the
problem. If the pursuit of security largely dominates the nation's
actions, ways and means of creating a stable peace can be imagined. On the other hand, if her actions are dominated largely
by the search for power and a zeal to spread Communist doctrine
—by force if necessary—the possibility of avoiding war in the
long run would appear to be very small.

In addition to the dangers created by the pursuit of security
and the desire to spread particular creeds, a third danger will remain with the world until such time as all regions are industrialized
and the population transition is complete in the world as a whole.
The danger arises from the enormous pressures produced by rapid
population growth during the process of industrialization. Japan,
for example, invaded several areas for the purpose of obtaining
raw materials for her machines and additional food for her people,
and to provide space into which some of the excess population

could be drained. To be sure the conquests were relatively pain-less for her, as long as she confined her attentions to agrarian regions. But eventually she came into conflict with other indus-trialized areas, and her attempt to form the "Greater East Asia Co-Prosperity Sphere" was halted.

Today Japan is confined once again to her home islands, and the pressure of her population is now far greater than it was prior to World War II. She must import a substantial portion of her food and raw materials, yet she is cut off from many of her former sources of supply. In the long run her situation is unstable in the extreme, and it is highly likely that serious trouble lies ahead. The Japanese now express the desire to live in peace with other nations, but as time goes on and the pressures become still more intense, it is likely that they will attempt again to extend their area to the point where they can attain some measure of self-sufficiency.

The industrialization of India and Pakistan will result in equally severe internal pressures. India at the present time is a peaceful nation and, knowing the temperament and traditions of the people, we are inclined to believe that she will remain so. But during the process of industrialization the greatest pressures occur at about the time the nation suddenly finds itself possessed of the power to wage war. This combination of circumstances can conceivably turn a peaceful nation into a warlike one. Indeed, if the process of industrialization in India proceeds rapidly it is conceivable that in another four or five decades she might be as great a threat to the world as Japan was prior to World War II.

No matter how we look at the picture, the threat of war is the greatest immediate danger confronting industrial civilization. The possibility of man's eliminating war as an instrument of national policy indeed appears remote, and to the extent that this is so it seems likely that industrial civilization is doomed to extinction. Nevertheless, the picture is not completely black, for we can con-ceive of ways and means not only of eliminating specific causes of war but of eliminating war itself. The fact that we are able to recognize these problems and conceive of solutions gives some hope that man's intelligence may save him in the future as it has saved him in the past. Remote though this possibility may be, it is the one hope to which those of us can cling who are unprepared to admit that man's destiny is, *a priori*, an ignominious one.

6.

For the purpose of our discussion, let us assume that war and the possibility of war between existing industrialized nations disappear from the earth, though this seems most unlikely. Would the problems of survival of industrial civilization be solved? It is clear that they would not. Elimination of war, although it is an absolutely necessary condition for survival, is by no means a sufficient condition. In truth, the task of eliminating war, difficult though it may appear, pales into insignificance beside the further problems that will confront us.

One of the most important, from both a short-range and a long-range point of view, is that of controlling rates of population growth and at the same time permitting human beings to take full advantage of the benefits of public health and modern medicine. Here there can be no escaping the fact that if starvation is to be eliminated, if the average child who is born is to stand a reasonable chance of living out the normal life span with which he is endowed at birth, family sizes must be limited. The limitation in birth rates must arise from the utilization of contraceptive techniques or abortions or a combination of the two practices.

We know that by proper application of technology the earth could support a considerably larger population than now exists. But no matter where we place the limit of the number of persons that can be comfortably supported, at some point in history population growth must stop. And if population growth is to stop without our having excessively high death rates, we must reconcile ourselves to the fact that artificial means must be applied to limit birth rates. This conclusion is inescapable. We can avoid talking about it, moralists may try to convince us to the contrary, laws may be passed forbidding us to talk about it, fear of pressure groups may prevent political leaders from discussing the subject, but the conclusion cannot be denied on any rational basis. Either population-control measures must be both widely and wisely used, or we must reconcile ourselves to a world where starvation is everywhere, where life expectancy at birth is less than 30 years, where infants stand a better chance of dying than of living during the first year following birth, where women are little more than machines for breeding, pumping child after child into an inhospitable world, spending the greater part of their adult lives in a state of pregnancy.

The extent to which human beings avoid discussing conception control is truly incredible. Volume after volume has been written, and conference after conference has been held, on the subject of increasing world food production, and arguments have raged over whether or not food production can be increased sufficiently rapidly to keep pace with population increase. Huge efforts have been made to improve public health in many of the underdeveloped areas. Yet if anyone, in an official or semi-official capacity, is so bold as to suggest that the approach is one-sided, paralysis sets in. The minority pressure groups start to work on the hapless individual, and soon he claims that his remarks were misinterpreted.

Some of those who fight against conception control do so on the grounds that it is "unnatural." Yet what could be more unnatural than appendectomies or injections of penicillin? And, for that matter, is not agriculture itself unnatural? Certainly a potato field growing in Western Europe is one of the most unnatural things in the world. The plant is not indigenous; forests were removed so that the plot could be cultivated; plants which prefer to grow there are uprooted so that the potato can thrive without competition; artificial fertilizers are applied to the ground; insecticides disturb the balance of insect life. Clearly, once man invented agriculture he moved into an unnatural world, and, as his knowledge has increased, his dependence upon unnatural surroundings has increased. Those who maintain that conception control should not be used because it is unnatural would be far more convincing if they urged simultaneously abolishment of all clothing, antiseptics, antibiotics, vaccinations, and hospitals, together with all artificial practices which enable man to extract food from the soil.

A second sector of the world which vigorously opposes contraception is the group which maintains that such practices are contrary to the precepts of religion. This concept indeed places man in an interesting light, representing him as one who, though he was created with the means of alleviating suffering by modifying the effects of natural processes (as he proves every time he puts on an overcoat or takes a pill), yet believes that he is obeying the will of his Creator when he refuses to establish and maintain a balance between resources and population by the simplest and most humane of all possible ways. The outlook is all the more interesting in view of the fact that it is the children who suffer the most in regions where the ratios of food to population are very low. When I walk through such regions, where birth rates are at a biological maximum, and I see dirt-encrusted, malnourished, disease-ridden children, I know that this is not the sort of world advocated by the One who said, "Suffer little children to come unto me, and forbid them not, for of such is the Kingdom of Heaven."

The Roman Catholic Church knows this too, but offers only these choices to underprivileged groups: an almost impossible degree of continence, the difficult spacing of intercourse according to the principle of the highly unreliable "rhythm theory" (reluctantly accepted but not encouraged by some religionists), or the spawning of children who, *a priori,* cannot be supported and are doomed to die in filth and misery.

Who, then, are the guilty ones in this grisly drama? Are they the parents, whose love for each other is perhaps the one tolerable aspect of an otherwise bleak and miserable existence? Or are they those who pass laws and issue edicts prohibiting the spread of contraceptive knowledge and, in so doing, help to perpetuate the misery and unhappiness which exists? Or, perhaps, are they the persons, whose names are legion, who are frightened by the creedists and in their fright refuse to take action?

The members of the third group which actively opposes contraception do so not because of any deep conviction that such practices are either sinful or "unnatural," but rather for the straightforward and unfortunate reason that they want their particular group, whether it be nation, race, or adherents to a creed, to become more populous. This motivation was partly responsible for many of the actions and attitudes in Italy during Mussolini's time and is responsible for existing official attitudes toward birth control in the Soviet Union. The leaders of the Catholic Church undoubtedly recognize that if adherents to the faith are able to maintain a substantial difference in birth rate between Catholics and non-Catholics, the proportion of Catholics in the population as a whole is likely to increase. Similar thoughts probably determine in part the attitudes of numerous groups of people.

In recent years a new attitude toward birth control has appeared in several underdeveloped areas—the fear that industrialized nations are attempting to exterminate them by propagandizing contraceptive techniques. This, of course, is a blind, unreasoning fear —but no more unreasoning than most other attitudes which prevail. This particular attitude will probably increase in importance in years to come, nurtured by existing race struggles and by the conflict between the Soviet Union and the West.

In view of the diversity of the attitudes which result in active opposition to family-limitation techniques, there is serious question that human populations in the world as a whole will ever be stabilized. Indeed, a convincing argument can be presented to the effect that the population of the world can never be stabilized over a long period of time by a willful decrease of the birth rate. At the moment, however, important though the problem of ultimate stabilization is, the most pressing problem confronting us is whether or not the growth potentials of the underdeveloped areas can be decreased to the point where such areas can undergo industrialization without undue population pressure being built up in the process.

We have seen that in the absence of a world catastrophe it is highly improbable that the "traditional" process of industrialization will ever again be repeated. This process, characterized by growth of the machine network, decreasing mortality, rapid growth of population, expansion of the population into new areas, assimilation of the resources of new areas, and, finally, reduction of birth rates leading eventually to population stabilization, can take place only if there is at the beginning of the process an adequate resource base and a favorable ratio of people to available land. It is a process which one can visualize as having been possible in India had it been started in that country prior to the middle of the nineteenth century. But today—so one-sided has been the application of certain of the benefits of machine civilization—the process would appear to be inapplicable. Successful industrialization and population stabilization in modern India require a drastically new approach.

There are persons who deny this, and say that areas such as India can industrialize successfully without particular attention to contraceptive techniques. This point of view was emphasized recently in a book by Josué de Castro entitled *The Geography of Hunger*,[1] which is a remarkable example of confusion between cause and effect. De Castro points to the fact that areas of low per capita animal-protein intake have high birth rates, while areas of high per capita animal-protein intake have low birth rates. He succumbs to the temptation to conclude emphatically that fertility is primarily a matter of nutrition—if we would but feed the people of the world adequate quantities of animal protein, fertility would decrease, and population stability would be achieved. We need not contradict the thesis here beyond pointing to two facts. First, a similar correlation exists between birth rates and per capita ownership of automobiles. Secondly, perhaps the most rapid rates of population increase in the history of the world occurred in England and in the United States during periods when meat consumption was extraordinarily high. It would be tempting to conclude from these facts that ownership of automobiles rather than animal-protein intake is responsible for the decrease in fertility in the Western World. But of course innumerable such correlations are possible—plumbing fixtures, radios, motion-picture theaters, miles of railroad track, and availability of newspapers and books. Although it would be pleasant to believe de Castro's thesis, there is not a shred of evidence which indicates that the rate of population growth would be decreased appreciably by providing adequate nutrition.

It is possible to imagine a process whereby areas such as India might industrialize at a rate greater than the rate of population increase, but it is possible to imagine such a process only if the rate of population increase normally associated with industrialization is in some way greatly lessened. Let us make the drastic assumption, for the purpose of discussion, that organized opposition to dissemination of birth-control information can be ignored, and let us attempt to visualize a program whereby birth rates might, under the circumstances, be lowered more rapidly than death rates within the framework of an industrialization process.

As is pointed out in Chapter III, new techniques of birth control which are on the horizon offer considerable promise of being both inexpensive and applicable within the social structures of many

1. J. de Castro, *The Geography of Hunger* (Boston: Little, Brown and Company, 1952).

of the underdeveloped areas. It is quite possible that within the next few years injections will be available similar to that of protein from the umbilical cord mentioned in Chapter III, which will produce sterility for a period of several months. Further, it is quite possible that drugs will be available which will prevent, without serious side effects, implantation of a fertilized egg in the wall of the uterus. Let us assume that such drugs are available—as they almost certainly can be, given adequate research and development. We must then ask: Is it possible to establish techniques that would secure both widespread use and widespread acceptance?

The degree of personal opposition to contraceptive techniques will vary greatly from culture to culture and from area to area. In Jamaica, for example, one would have to combat the belief that "a woman must give birth to all of the babies she has in her" if she is to remain healthy. In Puerto Rico one would be confronted with the desire for children as symbols of virility. In Asia one would be confronted with the desire for male children, for additional farm hands, and for the security which is believed to be brought by large families. Nevertheless, in spite of such individual opposition, it seems likely that in most such areas there is a large proportion of women who do not want to become pregnant—or at least not so frequently. One has but to see estimates of the frequency of crude "stick abortions" in places such as Puerto Rico and Jamaica, and of the sale of worthless potions and amulets in Asia, in order to appreciate this.[1] If large numbers of women are willing to obtain dangerous and crude abortions in order to avoid having additional children, it is only reasonable to assume that even larger numbers of women would gladly use contraceptives *if* they could afford to buy them, *if* the contraceptives would not

1. For example, a patent-medicine firm in Kapurthala, India, which advertises diverse talismans and tonics for increasing wealth and improving health, also advertises a preparation of dubious effectiveness known as "Stop Con." The advertising copy reads: "With the keen struggle for existence ahead, it is perfectly rational for parents to have children when they want them and not when they may happen to arrive. The apprehension of yet another child is not to enforce abstinence and to refrain the couple from coition even after they have had enough children to feed and look after. Stop Con is a harmless vegetable product providing a great relief for such cases. Taken for seven days by the lady, it stops permanently without in any way affecting the general health or interfering with the healthy flow of monthly course. It is a boon for couples with large families. RESULT GUARANTEED. Ten shillings for full course. (Postage free.)"

interfere with the pleasures of the sexual act, and *if* use of the contraceptives would not require elaborate facilities that are unavailable in most such areas. Periodic painless injections which produce temporary sterility and which could be administered in conjunction with other public-health services could well satisfy a part of this need. Inexpensive pills which prevent implantation and which could be taken when it becomes evident that the menstrual cycle is delayed could well satisfy another part of the need.

Although effective contraceptives can probably be made quite inexpensively by Western standards, it is doubtful that the cost will ever be brought down to the point where they can be easily afforded by persons who are as poverty-stricken as those in the greater part of India today. This means that if birth control is to be really effective prior to the completion of the industrial transition it must be made a part of government policy, and, in particular, birth-control programs should be incorporated as integral parts of the public-health programs that are established.

Costs of contraceptives will probably remain prohibitively high for a majority of the individuals in underdeveloped areas for many years to come. But the governments of such areas could well afford, if necessary, to spend substantial fractions of their incomes on the manufacture and dissemination of contraceptives and on mass education concerning birth-control techniques. Money spent on securing widespread use of birth-control techniques can be returned many-fold as the result of the greater differential obtained between rate of population increase and rate of increase of industrial and agricultural production. Actually, however, the cost of comprehensive birth-control programs in underdeveloped areas need not be prohibitively high, particularly when compared with the cost of establishing general public-health programs, of increasing agricultural production, and of industrialization. Attention can be confined to women who are in the fertile age group, which altogether makes up only 20 to 25 per cent of the total population. Intensive educational efforts can be confined to young girls. If all girls were carefully educated for a 1-year period following their fifteenth or sixteenth birthdays, the training program would embrace fewer than 2 per cent of the total population at a given time and by the end of 25 years the vast majority of fertile females would be thoroughly familiar with contraceptive techniques.

Major birth-control programs can rationally be given priority over many aspects of public-health programs, for lowered birth rates automatically result in improved public health. Less frequent exposure to childbearing results in lowered female mortality. Smaller family sizes result in better nutrition and lowered infant mortality. In addition, the lowered food requirement for an individual family results in generally lowered adult mortality. Thus, a major birth-control program can in itself be looked upon as a major public-health program.

In each area where comprehensive family-limitation programs are established, considerable social research will be necessary in order to ascertain the most satisfactory approaches for gaining general acceptance of the new ideas. Incentives must be devised and new educational approaches must be used. There must be social experimentation on a vast scale. There will be failures, of course, but, given sufficient imagination and effort, it is likely that there will also be successes.

There are persons who maintain that no amount of effort can succeed in lowering birth rates more rapidly than the rate of decrease that has been associated with industrialization processes in the past. Such views might well prove to be correct, but it seems more likely at the present time that such views are wrong. In any event, sound predictions of success or failure on the basis of existing knowledge are impossible. We shall never really know whether or not success is possible until a vigorous effort is made and our ingenuity and imagination have been wholeheartedly applied to the problem. If we succeed there will be hope. If we fail, the prospects for successful transition of the underdeveloped areas to stable industrial societies will be so remote as to border on the impossible.

7.

Industrialization of the underdeveloped areas of the world is perhaps the most formidable task confronting mankind today. We must now ask: Can we visualize ways and means by which existing primitive agrarian societies can be transformed reasonably rapidly and smoothly into modern industrial societies? Thus far we have discussed primarily the importance of family limitation as a neces-

sary feature of such a transition. But we must recognize that even
if family-limitation techniques should receive widespread acceptance, the path of industrialization would still be extremely difficult,
and it would still be fraught with innumerable dangers.

An industrialization program must possess many interlocking
features, no one of which can be divorced from the others. The
ultimate goal of such a program would be to manufacture goods
in sufficient quantity so that every person would have adequate
housing, clothing, education, medical and public-health facilities,
and at the same time receive adequate nutrition. In order to ac-
complish this, factory buildings and production machines must
be built, building materials must be produced, machines must be
fabricated which in turn can be used to fabricate machines, metals
must be produced, ores must be mined, fuels must be obtained,
and transportation systems must be extended. Men must be trained
to build and to operate the factories and transportation systems.
These men must come from the farms, but they cannot leave the
farms until food production per man-hour has been increased
without decreasing crop yields—otherwise there would be a lowering of food production and more widespread starvation. In turn,
a significantly increased food production per man-hour requires
mechanization of farms. Mechanization of farms in turn requires
machines, which in turn require a certain degree of industrialization if they are to be manufactured and properly maintained. Thus,
in a sense, the inhabitants of underdeveloped areas find themselves in a vicious circle which cannot easily be broken.

Industrialization requires enormous investments of materials
and labor before goods can actually be produced, transported, and
used. Obviously, if all persons in a given society must spend all
of their working hours producing food for their own consumption,
accumulation of a surplus becomes impossible. We have seen that
if a surplus of food can be produced, some members of the society
can engage in occupations other than farming and can manufacture goods. But unless a mechanism is available whereby a part
of the effort can be channeled into the production of capital goods
such as machines and factory buildings, which are not consumer
items but which will later enable greater production of such items,
industrialization cannot expand. In other words, mechanisms must
be available which enable persons to deprive themselves of con-

sumer goods and instead to use a part of the surplus food and goods
which they have produced for the purchase of capital items which
are not immediately useful but which will eventually result in
increased consumer production. Translated into terms of money,
persons must refrain from spending all the money they derive from
the sale of goods and other services, and the "savings" must be
invested in capital goods that will result in increased production.

We can obtain some idea of the amount of capital investment
that is required in a highly industrialized society by examining
the capital resources of the United States. Prior to World War II,
the real capital resources, exclusive of land, amounted to about
250 billion dollars, corresponding to an average of 200o dollars for
every person in the country. At the same time the average per
capita income in the United States amounted to about 550 dollars
per year. Simultaneously, the average per capita income in the
underdeveloped areas of the world amounted to little more than
40 dollars per year.

The greater part of the incomes of the inhabitants of the underdeveloped areas must be spent on food, and there is practically no
surplus that can be saved for capital investment. In India, for
example, voluntary savings amounted to only 2 to 3 per cent of
the national income, compared with savings rates of between 10
and 15 per cent in the United States, the United Kingdom, and
Canada. When we couple the respective savings rates with the
respective per capita income we see that available capital per
person can increase in the United States at a rate about 70 times
more rapid than the rate in India.

In many underdeveloped areas only a small fraction of the
voluntary savings available are channeled into productive uses at
home. Many savings are hoarded in the form of precious stones,
gold, and silver. Other funds are often sent abroad for investment
in industrialized countries. For example, during the period 1936–
1947, there was a net inflow to United States banking funds of over
2 billion dollars from Latin America and from the Far East. An
additional handicap in the underdeveloped countries is the lack
of adequate facilities for collecting and investing voluntary savings. Commercial bank facilities do not exist in most such areas,
and there are few investment banks and other forms of private
credit institutions.

If all underdeveloped areas at their existing population levels were to possess the per capita capital investment enjoyed by the United States immediately prior to World War II, the total investment in those countries would amount to about 3600 billion dollars. It has been estimated that a sum corresponding to about one-seventh that amount—about 500 billion dollars—would suffice over a 50-year period to switch about one-fourth of the labor force and their families from agricultural to industrial and commercial occupations. This would give them an economic situation similar to that which existed in prewar Japan.

In view of the low incomes of underdeveloped areas, it is clear that industrialization requires either outside financing during the initial stages, or forced savings well above the voluntary rate, similar to the compulsory savings in the Soviet Union. However, even with strict totalitarian regimes of the Russian type, industrialization would necessarily proceed slowly in the absence of help from the outside, largely as the result of the unfavorable population-land-resource situations in most underdeveloped areas.

The most difficult part of an industrialization program is that of getting started. Once industrialization is well under way and goods begin to flow in increasing quantity, both per capita incomes and savings can increase rapidly. Substantial help from the outside can contribute greatly toward overcoming the initial hurdles and can accelerate the whole industrialization process.

It seems likely that, given concerted efforts of both the underdeveloped areas and the industrialized regions of the world, the standards of living of the underprivileged two-thirds of humanity could be raised significantly in about 50 years, and standards of living characteristic of the industrialized West of today might be attained in an additional 50 years without resorting to totalitarian methods. But it is equally likely that in the absence of concerted efforts and vigorous application of imagination and ingenuity to the problem, the programs would be doomed to failure. The chance of success of a vigorous program is much greater than that of a half-hearted one.

Let us assume for the purpose of discussion that a degree of industrialization in the underdeveloped areas equivalent to that which existed in prewar Japan could be attained with an investment of about 500 billion dollars over a 50-year period. Let us assume further that an additional 100 billion dollars would be required for increasing agricultural production to the point where all persons would receive adequate nutrition. The average annual investment would then be somewhat over 10 billion dollars, of which perhaps one-half could be furnished over the entire period by the underdeveloped regions. During the initial years the domestic savings would provide but a small proportion of the required sums, but, as incomes increase in the underdeveloped regions, they would be able to provide an increasing proportion of the investment. On this basis, foreign investments averaging about 5 billion dollars annually over the 50-year period would be required. The annual requirement for foreign investments might be less than this during the initial years because of the limited existing capacity of most underdeveloped areas to absorb new capital. But the requirements for outside financing would rise rapidly. After about 30 years the requirements for foreign investment would begin to decrease as the result of increased local savings.

If the industrialized areas of the world were to join in recognizing the overwhelming importance of the problem, and would agree to take common action to speed the industrialization of the underdeveloped areas, the problems of financing would not be prohibitive. Largely because of the risk involved and the uncertain profits to be gained, it is difficult to visualize large amounts of private capital from Western nations contributing substantially to the development program. For this reason it seems likely that the greater part of the outside funds, at least during the initial stages, must be public funds. On the basis of a policy of investing in proportion to ability to pay, the United States would at first carry the greater part of the financial burden—perhaps as much as three-quarters of the international investment during the first decade. But as the economic situation of Western Europe improves, the share from the United States might well decrease appreciably.

The average cost to the United States of a world development program over a 50-year period might amount to between 4 billion dollars and 5 billion dollars annually. When we compare this to our national income, to our present federal budget, to the funds required for armament, and to the cost of waging war, the amount required does not appear to be excessive. When we compare it to the potential gains that can result from a successful development program, it appears even smaller. And when we compare the cost to that of inaction and to the consequences of attempting to maintain the status quo, it is indeed insignificant.

It is clear that the nations of the West possess sufficient resources and productive capacity to catalyze a successful world development program at the present time. Our physical ability to bring about successful transition is not one of the unknowns. We have the ability to do it; whether we have the vision and the will is another matter. Have the people of the industrialized areas the foresight to launch a major effort to elevate standards of living in the underdeveloped regions? Will they be able to subordinate immediate selfish interests to the goal of achieving an abundant life for humanity as a whole? Will the people of the underdeveloped areas in turn have the vision to guide their own destinies wisely? Will they be able to discourage detrimental action of self-seeking minority groups? Will they be able to plan intelligently their own programs of development of basic industries, transportation, agriculture, public health, education, and culture?

We have seen that areas which attempt to industrialize within the framework of the existing world situation will experience many difficulties that have not been experienced heretofore by nations undergoing the industrialization process. These difficulties stem from the unfavorable ratios of men to easily cultivable land and to resources. The difficulties will be offset to a certain extent by our increased knowledge and technological development. But even so, problems will quickly arise which will be far outside the realm of our previous experience. As we know, for example, India cannot maintain a large per capita production level for a prolonged period of time with her existing energy resources. This means that if India's transition is to be successful she must utilize atomic or solar energy long before the United States is forced to take equivalent steps. Similarly, in order to produce sufficient food, the people of India will have to utilize new types of agricultural technology such as algae culture and food-yeast production long before the United States is in a similar position of necessity. Similar problems will be encountered in practically all areas of resource development.

Problems such as these will create many serious economic and political situations. On the economic side, is it possible for a region, in the interests of self-sufficiency, to devise ways and means of manufacturing and utilizing fuels and foods if they are more expensive than those which are used elsewhere in the world but which would otherwise have to be imported? Is it possible for a nation such as India to organize her economic and political structure in such a way that she can utilize on a large scale power which might cost her perhaps two to three times as much as power derived from imported coal? Such steps will clearly be necessary if the industrial transitions in most such areas are to be successful, for in general there is little that can be exported which will not be needed, in the long run, at home.

From the point of view of long-range world stability, regional self-sufficiency would appear to be a goal toward which all major areas of the world should move as rapidly as possible. If the world as a whole were to have a common government and a political and economic structure that would permit India to produce food and Iraq to produce oil for the great world industrial centers, much as Iowa produces food and Texas produces oil for the industrial centers of the United States, stability might be achieved. But in the absence of such structures and in view of the fact that surpluses of any description are becoming rarities on the world scene, regional self-sufficiency appears to be a highly desirable goal even at the expense of utilizing resources temporarily more expensive than those used in other parts of the world at the time.

8.

New technological developments will have considerable effect both on the processes of industrialization in underdeveloped areas and upon the economies and social structures of those nations which are already industrialized. Perhaps the most far-reaching of the new developments is the rapid trend toward automatization of industrial production.

Most persons are familiar with simple automatic-control devices, such as governors for controlling engine speeds and thermostats for controlling temperatures in rooms. Few of us appreciate the rapidity with which similar robots are replacing human activity in practically every area of industrial endeavor. The first major phase of the Industrial Revolution involved the replacement of human and animal energy with energy derived from fossil fuels and waterpower. The second major phase—which has but barely begun—involves the replacement of a very large proportion of the human operators of the machines by mechanisms which possess faster reaction times, can make operative selections more rapidly, and can make the necessary process adjustments more efficiently.

Our communications system is already highly controlled and interlocked. Intricate networks of instruments now supervise the production of a diversity of products ranging from plastics and drugs to petroleum, steel, and textiles. One of the results of thus eliminating the necessity for human control from large areas of industrial technology has been increased production per unit of capital investment. And equally important, it is now possible to carry out procedures which heretofore have been impossible because of limitations inherent in the make-up of human beings.

The petroleum industry is a leading example of an industry which has rapidly extended the use of automatic control in production. A refinery built recently near Tyler, Texas, has been vividly described by Eugene Ayres as follows:

It is a bewildering kind of factory, with metallic towers rising 20 stories high, hundreds of miles of pipe, and only an occasional modest building. A few lonely men wander about the spectral monster doing supervisory or maintenance tasks here and there. The plant is almost noiseless, all but devoid of visible moving parts. Despite its apparent inertness, however, the plant is throbbing with internal heat and motion. Every day a quarter of a million barrels of oil flow unobtrusively into its maw, and about as many flow out in the form of dozens of finished petroleum products—all profoundly and specifically altered by processing. Forty tons of catalyst are being circulated every minute of the day and night. Great volumes of chemicals are being consumed in processing, and greater volumes of chemical intermediates are being manufactured. Scores of unit processes are interlocked, with a meticulous balance of energy distribution.

The nerve center of this mechanical organism is the control room with its control panel. Here are ensconced the human operators—attendants upon the little mechanical operators of the plant. The human operators watch, they sometimes help or correct the instruments, but only occasionally do they take over the major part of operating responsibility. Barring emergencies, they take over completely only when the plant is starting up or shutting down—normally only about once a year. . . .[1]

Use of automatic controls in industry has expanded only in part because of rising labor costs. The primary impetus has arisen from the need for processing under conditions of speed, temperature, and pressure which make human control impossible, and from the need for turning out products of unprecedented uniformity and quality. Nevertheless, although rising labor costs contributed but little to the impetus, the new trend is bound to have considerable effect upon working hours and unemployment—and the consequences of these effects can be only dimly perceived at the present time.

Between the years 1880 and 1938 the number of man-hours required for a given unit of industrial production decreased by about two-thirds. The greater part of this increased efficiency has been reflected in greatly increased per capita consumption, but a considerable part has been reflected in shortened working hours. During the period between 1870 and 1950 the average work week in the United States decreased from about 67 hours to 42.5 hours. Rapid extension of the use of automatic controls will certainly bring about a further rise in the efficiency of production, which will be reflected in increased per capita consumption or shortened working hours or unemployment or combinations of the three effects.

It is doubtful that machines will ever completely supplant human beings in industrial control and management. Yet when we examine the potentialities of the full range of control possibilities, even as they exist in their present crude forms, the ultimate gain in production efficiency that might be realized appears to be enormous. It is by no means outside the realm of possibility that the man-hour requirements per unit of production might decrease to one-fifth, or even one-tenth, those of the present during the course of the next century. Such a change would, of course, necessitate major economic readjustments.

During the immediate future it is unlikely that the extension of automatization will create severe dislocations, largely because at present capital requirements for a given unit of output are falling

1. Eugene Ayres, "An Automatic Chemical Plant," in *Scientific American*, September 1952, p. 82.

about as rapidly as are labor requirements. This means that labor's share of the production relative to capital's share is remaining approximately constant. However, one can foresee the time when investment requirements per unit of output will cease to fall, while labor requirements will continue to decrease. If such a situation were actually to come into existence it is clear that there would be considerable dislocation and major steps would have to be taken in order to insure widespread distribution of goods.

As time goes on and automatization is expanded, the character of the labor forces in industrial societies will change considerably. The proportion of unskilled labor will dwindle to a negligible percentage, that of semi-skilled labor will rise and then fall, and that of highly skilled workers, professional personnel, and clerks will continue to rise steadily. These changes will have profound effects upon the social structure of our society.

Existing automatic controls—as, for example, those in the petroleum refinery described above—will function satisfactorily as long as the unexpected does not happen—as long as the plant is working under equilibrium conditions. At other times, human operators must take over, with the result that control rooms must be designed so that human beings can see symptoms of trouble and take the necessary corrective steps. It is quite likely that this difficulty, or bottleneck, will eventually be eliminated by replacing the human control supervisors with automatic computing machines which can be instructed, which can react in emergencies much more rapidly than can human operators, which can "learn," and which can seek out better ways of accomplishing tasks once they have been given proper sets of criteria. We can visualize factories under the regulation of central computing machines which govern the activities of all plant components. The computers would receive information from the various controls, process the information, compute the most satisfactory corrective measures, and issue instructions to the controls they regulate. In addition, the central computers would issue reports of the day's performances and issue accounting records.

Modern computers, or information machines, will have considerable effect upon our lives during the years to come. We have seen that they can control factories. Similarly, it is likely that they can control economies.

The economy of an industrial society consists of a vast interlocking network of causes and effects. The mathematical relationships between the various parts of the network are extremely complicated, and similar to the relationships that exist between the component parts of a variety of interlocking systems ranging from ecological assemblages of living things to the assemblages of controls in a modern oil refinery. Once the fundamental principles of the economic network of a given society are clearly understood, it is possible that computing machines will take over the task of timing investment expenditure, forecasting business activity, and plotting the economic course of a nation in such a way that major economic oscillations can be avoided.

It is likely that automatization can be put to good use in speeding the industrialization of underdeveloped areas. We have seen that capital investments per unit of production are considerably less for fully automatic plants than for plants utilizing human control. This means that, in principle, it should be possible for existing underdeveloped areas to undergo the industrial transition more rapidly than has been possible heretofore. A further aspect of automatization which might accelerate the process is that fewer men need be trained to operate the plants. "Instead of trying to lift the whole economy by the slow, painful methods of the past," says Wassily Leontief, "an industrially backward country may take the dramatic short cut of building a few large, up-to-date automatic plants. Towering up in the primitive economy like copses of tall trees in a grassy plain, they would propagate a new economic order."

But the same author warns:

In the rising new countries economic efficiency may at least temporarily run far ahead of progress towards social maturity and stability. Much of the stimulus for the educational advancement of the Western nations came from economic necessity. Automatization may weaken that powerful connection. It remains to be seen whether the backward countries will find a driving force to help them develop the social, cultural and political advances necessary to help them cope with the new economic emancipation.[1]

1. Wassily Leontief, "Machines and Man," in *Scientific American*, September 1952, p. 160.

9.

If industrial civilization eventually succumbs to the forces that
are relentlessly operating to make its position more precarious,
the world as a whole will probably revert to an agrarian existence.
In such an event history will continue for as long a time as man
exists. Empires, republics, and military states will rise and fall.
There will be wars, migrations, and revolutions. Art, music, and
literature will flourish, wane, then flourish again. As in the histories
of the past and of the present, there will be unceasing change. Yet,
looked upon over a period of thousands of years, history will have
a sameness like the repeated performances of a series of elaborate
epic plays in which, over the centuries, the actors change, the lan-
guages change, the scenery changes, but the basic plots remain
invariant

But if industrial civilization survives--if wars are eliminated, if
the population of the world as a whole is stabilized within a framework of low death rates and low birth rates—will there continue
to be a human history? The terms "stability" and "security" imply
predictability, sameness, lack of change. And these terms further
imply a high degree of organization—universal organization to
avoid war, local organization to produce goods efficiently, and
organization to control the distribution of goods. Organization in
turn implies subjugation of the individual to the state, confinement
and regimentation of the activities of the individual for the benefit
of society as a whole.

Today we see about us on all sides a steady drift toward increased human organization. Governments are becoming more
centralized and universal. In practically all areas of endeavor
within industrial society—in our systems of production, in the fields
of labor, capital, commerce, agriculture, science, education, and
art—we see the emergence of new levels of organization designed
to coordinate, integrate, bind, and regulate men's actions. The
justifications for this increasing degree of organization to which
man must accommodate himself are expressed in terms such as
"stability," "security," and "efficiency." The end result of this rapid
transition might well be the emergence of a universal, stable, efficient, industrial society within which, although all persons have

complete personal security, their actions are completely controlled. Should that time arrive, society will have become static, devoid of movement, fixed and permanent. History will have stopped.

Here we indeed find ourselves on the horns of the dilemma. To what purpose is industrialization if we end up by replacing rigid confinement of man's actions by nature with rigid confinement of man's actions by man? To what purpose is industrialization if the price we pay for longer life, material possessions, and personal security in regimentation, controlled thoughts, and controlled actions? Would the lives of well-fed, wealthy, but regimented human robots be better than the lives of their malnourished, poverty-stricken ancestors? At least the latter could look forward to the unexpected happening—to events and situations which previously had been outside the realm of their experiences.

In a modern industrial society the road toward totalitarianism is unidirectional. In days gone by men could revolt against despotism. People could arise against their governments in the absence of legal recourse, and with muskets, sticks, knives, and stones as their weapons they could often defeat the military forces of the central authorities. But today our science and our technology have placed in the hands of rulers of nations weapons and tools of control, persuasion, and coercion of unprecedented power. We have reached the point where, once totalitarian power is seized in a highly industrialized society, successful revolt becomes practically impossible. Totalitarian power, once it is gained, can be perpetuated almost indefinitely in the absence of outside forces, and can lead to progressively more rapid robotization of the individual.

Thus we see that, just as industrial society is fundamentally unstable and subject to reversion to agrarian existence, so within it the conditions which offer individual freedom are unstable in their ability to avoid the conditions which impose rigid organization and totalitarian control. Indeed, when we examine all of the foreseeable difficulties which threaten the survival of industrial civilization, it is difficult to see how the achievement of stability and the maintenance of individual liberty can be made compatible.

The view is widely held in our society that the powers of the machine will eventually free man from the burden of eking out an existence and will provide him with leisure time for the development of his creativity and enjoyment of the fruits of his creative efforts. Pleasant though this prospect may be, it is clear that such a state cannot come into existence automatically; the pressures forcing man into devising more highly organized institutions are too great to permit it. If he is to attain such an idyllic existence for more than a transitory period he must plan for that existence carefully, and in particular he must do everything within his power to reduce the pressures that are forcing him to become more highly organized.

One of the major pressures that give rise to the need for increasing numbers of laws, more elaborate organization, and more centralized government is increase of population. Increase of numbers of people and of population density results in greater complexities in day-to-day living and in decreased opportunities for personal expression concerning the activities of government. But even more important, as populations increase and as they press more heavily upon the available resources there arises the need for increased efficiency, and more elaborate organizations are required to produce sufficient food, to extract the necessary raw materials, and to fabricate and distribute the finished products. In the future we can expect that the greater the population density of an industrial society becomes, the more elaborate will be its organizational structure and the more regimented will be its people.

A second pressure, not unrelated to the first, results from the centralization of industrial and agricultural activity and from regional specialization in various aspects of those activities. One region produces textiles, another produces coal, another automobiles, another corn, and another wheat. Mammoth factories require mammoth local organizations. Centralized industries must be connected, and this requires elaborate transportation systems. Regional localization of industries gives rise to gigantic cities, which in turn give rise to elaborate organization for the purpose of providing the inhabitants with the necessary food, water, and services. All of these factors combine to produce vulnerability to disruption from the outside, increased local organization and regimentation, more highly centralized government, and increasing vulnerability to the evolution of totalitarianism.

A third pressure results from increasing individual specialization and the resultant need for "integration," "coordination," and "direction" of activities in practically all spheres of vocational and leisure activity. It results in the placing of unwarranted trust in "integrators," "coordinators," and "directors." Early specialization results in lack of broad interests, lessened ability to engage in creative activity during leisure hours, decreased interest in the creative activities of other individuals, and lessened abilities to interpret events and make sound judgments. All of these factors combine to pave the way for collectivization, the emergence of strong organization, and, with it, the great leader.

Strong arguments can be presented to the effect that collectivization of humanity is inevitable, that the drift toward an ultimate state of automatism cannot be halted, that existing human values such as freedom, love, and conscience must eventually disappear.[1] Certainly if we used the present trends in industrial society as our major premises, the conclusion would appear to be inescapable. Yet is it not possible that human beings, recognizing this threat to the canons of humanism, can devise ways and means of escaping the danger and at the same time manage to preserve those features of industrial civilization which can contribute to a rich, full life? Is it really axiomatic that the present trends must continue and that in the long run industrial civilization and human values are incompatible? Here, in truth, we are confronted with the gravest and most difficult of all human problems, for it is one that cannot be solved by mathematics or by machines, nor can it even be precisely defined. Solutions, if they exist, can arise only in the hearts and minds of individual men.

The machine has divorced man from the world of nature to which he belongs, and in the process he has lost in large measure the powers of contemplation with which he was endowed. A prerequisite for the preservation of the canons of humanism is a reestablishment of organic roots with our natural environment and, related to it, the evolution of ways of life which encourage contemplation and the search for truth and knowledge. The flower and vegetable garden, green grass, the fireplace, the primeval forest with its wondrous assemblage of living things, the uninhabited hilltop where one can silently look at the stars and wonder —all of these things and many others are necessary for the fulfill-

1. These views have been forcefully and eloquently expressed by Roderick Seidenberg in his book *Post-Historic Man* (Durham: University of North Carolina Press, 1950).

ment of man's psychological and spiritual needs. To be sure, they are of no "practical value" and are seemingly unrelated to man's pressing need for food and living space. But they are as necessary to the preservation of humanism as food is necessary to the preservation of human life.

I can imagine a world within which machines function solely for man's benefit, turning out those goods which are necessary for his well-being, relieving him of the necessity for heavy physical labor and dull, routine, meaningless activity. The world I imagine is one in which people are well fed, well clothed, and well housed. Man, in this world, lives in balance with his environment, nourished by nature in harmony with the myriads of other life forms that are beneficial to him. He treats his land wisely, halts erosion and over-cropping, and returns all organic waste matter to the soil from which it sprung. He lives efficiently, yet minimizes artificiality. It is not an overcrowded world; people can, if they wish, isolate themselves in the silence of a mountaintop, or they can walk through primeval forests or across wooded plains. In the world of my imagination there is organization, but it is as decentralized as possible, compatible with the requirements for survival. There is a world government, but it exists solely for the purpose of prevent-ing war and stabilizing population, and its powers are irrevocably restricted. The government exists for man rather than man for the government.

In the world of my imagination the various regions are self-sufficient, and the people are free to govern themselves as they choose and to establish their own cultural patterns. All people have a voice in the government, and individuals can move about when and where they please. It is a world where man's creativity is blended with the creativity of nature, and where a moderate de-gree of organization is blended with a moderate degree of anarchy.

Is such a world impossible of realization? Perhaps it is, but who among us can really say? At least if we try to create such a world there is a chance that we will succeed. But if we let the present trend continue it is all too clear that we will lose forever those qualities of mind and spirit which distinguish the human being from the automaton.

10.

We have seen that population stabilization within a framework of low birth rates and low death rates is a major key to the avoidance of collectivization and robotization of humanity and to the perpetuation of machine civilization. However, powerful arguments can be made to the effect that stabilization within such a framework over a long period of time is impossible, that sooner or later the starving margin will appear in all areas, and that populations will again be controlled by high death rates. These arguments have recently been expressed forcefully by Sir Charles Galton Darwin in his stimulating and highly provocative book entitled *The Next Million Years*.[1]

Sir Charles's argument takes the following form:

1. Any nation which limits its population becomes less numerous than nations which do not limit their populations. The former will then sooner or later be crowded out of existence by the latter.
2. A nation which limits its population forfeits the selection effects of natural biological competition and as a result must gradually degenerate.
3. The tendency of civilization to sterilize its ablest citizens accelerates this process of degeneration.
4. The possibility that statesmen, perceiving these dangers, might agree upon a world-wide policy of limitation appears remote. How can they be expected to agree among themselves in this area when they have failed to solve the far easier problem of military disarmament?
5. Even if agreements among nations could be obtained, there would be great difficulty in establishing limits to the numbers admissible for the various populations.
6. The problem of enforcement of population-limitation agreements would be extremely difficult.
7. The probabilities of fanatical opposition to population limitation would be enormous. Although existing opposition is not, in the main, strongly emotional, it is likely that once population growth is forbidden by law, new creeds will emerge which will regard the practice as sinful.
8. The creedists, by multiplying more rapidly than the others, will

1. New York: Doubleday and Company, 1953.

make up an increasingly large fraction of the population, thus making enforcement increasingly difficult.

9. Natural selection will operate in favor of parental, as distinct from sexual, instincts. Those persons who want large families will in general have more children than others, and to the extent that this characteristic can be inherited, it would spread throughout the population.

These are indeed powerful arguments and, when considered together, they make the possibility of ultimate population stabilization within a framework of low birth rates and low death rates appear so remote as to border on the impossible. Nevertheless, we must ask ourselves: Can we visualize ways and means whereby these difficulties might be minimized?

In the first place, it is amply clear that population stabilization and a world composed of completely independent sovereign states are incompatible. Populations cannot be stabilized by agreement any more than levels of armament can be stabilized by agreement. And, as in the latter case, a world authority is needed which has the power of making, interpreting, and enforcing, within specified spheres, laws which are directly applicable to the individual. Indeed, population stabilization is one of the two major problems with which a world government must necessarily concern itself.

Given a world authority with jurisdiction over population problems, the task of assessing maximum permissible population levels on a regional basis need not be prohibitively difficult. A rancher in Nevada usually puts no more cattle on a range than he believes can be adequately supported. Similarly, working on the basis that individual regions of the world should be self-sufficient both agriculturally and industrially, indices of potential productivity can be computed for all regions of the world, and maximum permissible population levels can be calculated on this basis.

The more serious difficulty is that of creating a situation in which the birth rate more or less automatically adjusts itself to the death rate. In nature, the death rate automatically adjusts itself to the birth rate, and the adjustment requires no conscious directed effort. In the artificial world that has been created by man, an artificial mechanism must be devised which can be incorporated with man's culture, which can operate automatically with a minimum of conscious effort, and which will permit birth rates to be determined by death rates.

If all babies were born from test tubes, as in Aldous Huxley's *Brave New World,* the solution would be fairly simple: The number of babies produced on the production line each year could be made to equal the number of deaths. In years of unusually high death rates, the production line could be speeded up; in years of low death rates, the line could be slowed down. Further, if we cared little for human emotions and were willing to introduce a procedure which most of us would consider to be reprehensible in the extreme, all excess children could be disposed of much as excess puppies and kittens are disposed of at the present time. But let us hope it will be a long time before a substantial number of our babies are born from test tubes. And let us hope further that human beings will never again be forced to resort to infanticide in order to avoid excessive population pressure.

We know from experience that social and economic pressures, coupled with widespread knowledge concerning birth-limiting techniques, can result in net reproduction rates that are very close to unity. We have seen that the net reproduction rate in England and Wales dropped to well below unity for a period of about 25 years, and that the net reproduction rate in the United States hovered around unity during the great depression. We have seen further that the net reproduction rate is a very sensitive index to social and economic pressures, and that these pressures can change greatly in but a short span of time.

Clearly a prerequisite for long-range population stabilization is stabilization of economic and social conditions to the point where birth rates will not fluctuate as widely as they do in industrial societies at the present time. Complete stabilization of such conditions is obviously difficult to achieve, and, from the point of view of individual freedom and human advancement, it is undesirable. Nevertheless, if economic and social pressures can be stabilized to the point at which the natural net reproduction rate does not fluctuate upward or downward by more than a few per cent from year to year, adequate control mechanisms are conceivable.

Birth rates obviously cannot fluctuate widely if population stabilization is to be achieved. Net reproduction rates which are constantly greater than unity, or which are only slightly less than unity, can quickly lead to enormous population pressures or to the danger of extinction. Ideally, the net reproduction rate should be kept at unity with a precision which borders on the fantastic: 1.0000. In the light of this rigid requirement, we must ask: If the natural uncontrolled net reproduction rate fluctuates by several per cent, how can the actual net reproduction rate be controlled with such accuracy?

Here we must examine the actual conception rate as distinct from the natural conception rate and as distinct from the birth rate. The actual conception rate can be divided into two parts—the conception rate which occurs as the result of the natural course of events, plus the addition to the natural rate which results from special treatments such as artificial insemination or hormone injections. Secondly, the birth rate depends upon the abortion rate, which we know is fairly high in most industrialized areas. It is clear that by maintaining rigid control over aids to conception, in particular artificial insemination, and rates of induced abortion, birth rates could be controlled with high precision—provided, of course, that the fluctuations in natural rates of conception do not exceed the requests for aids to conception and for abortions.

Briefly, such a control system would operate in the following manner. Let us suppose that in a given year the birth rate exceeds the death rate by a certain amount, thus resulting in a population increase. During the following year the number of permitted inseminations is decreased, and the number of permitted abortions is increased, in such a way that the birth rate is lowered by the requisite amount. If the death rate exceeds the birth rate, the number of permitted inseminations would be increased while the number of abortions would be decreased. The number of abortions and artificial inseminations permitted in a given year would be determined completely by the difference between the number of deaths and the number of births in the year previous.

It can be argued that such a procedure would be ruthless and would deprive many people of their individual liberties. Yet would it be any more ruthless than the policy which is now followed in the United States? Only a small fraction of the population would be affected. The vast majority of persons who might want to conceive would be able to do so, and the majority of those who might desire to terminate unwanted conceptions would be able to do so under hygienic conditions. Contrast this with the status quo, where abortions must be obtained frequently on kitchen tables, usually at great expense and under circumstances where the victims have the "freedom" to choose between giving birth to unwanted children and endangering their lives by subjecting themselves to illegal operations under insanitary conditions.

Control of aids to conception and of abortions could also provide a mechanism for slowing down the deterioration processes associated with the elimination of biological competition. Priorities for artificial insemination could be given to healthy women of high intelligence whose ancestors possessed no dangerous genetic defects. Conversely, priorities for abortions could be given to less intelligent persons of biologically unsound stock.

Such steps would undoubtedly contribute substantially to a slowing down of species deterioration. But it is clear that they would by no means be sufficient. A broad eugenics program would have to be formulated which would aid in the establishment of policies that would encourage able and healthy persons to have several offspring and discourage the unfit from breeding at excessive rates. Here, of course, we encounter numerous difficulties— what would constitute "fit" and what would constitute "unfit"? Where is the boundary between the mentally deficient person and the genius?

These are indeed grave problems, and the probability is high that they will never be solved. Yet the possibility cannot be excluded that solutions may be found. Our knowledge of human genetics, of human behavior, and of human biochemistry is fragmentary. Two or three generations of intensive research aimed at understanding the functioning of the human machine might well enable us to define terms such as "fit" and "unfit," as applied to human beings, with considerable precision. Although we realize that there is little likelihood that human beings will ever be able consciously to improve the species by carrying out a process of planned selection, there appears to be a finite possibility that, given adequate research and broad planning, deterioration of the species might eventually be halted.

Precise control of population can never be made completely

compatible with the concept of a free society; on the other hand, neither can the automobile, the machine gun, or the atomic bomb. Whenever several persons live together in a small area, rules of behavior are necessary. Just as we have rules designed to keep us from killing one another with our automobiles, so there must be rules that keep us from killing one another with our fluctuating breeding habits and with our lack of attention to the soundness of our individual genetic stock. On the other hand, although rules of behavior which operate in such areas are clearly necessary if our civilization is to survive, it remains to be seen whether or not such rules can be reconciled satisfactorily with the ideal of maximum individual freedom.

11.

When we look into the dimness of the distant future we see the possibility of the emergence of any of three possible patterns of life. The first and by far the most likely pattern is a reversion to agrarian existence. This is the pattern which will almost certainly emerge unless man is able to abolish war, unless he is able to make the transition involving the utilization of new energy sources, and unless he is able to stabilize populations.

In spite of the difficulties that confront industrial civilization, there is a possibility that stabilization can be achieved, that war can be avoided, and that the resource transition can be successfully negotiated. In that event, mankind will be confronted with a pattern which looms on the horizon of events as the second most likely possibility—the completely controlled, collectivized industrial society.

The third possibility confronting mankind is that of the world-wide free industrial society in which human beings can live in reasonable harmony with their environment. It is unlikely that such a pattern can ever exist for long. It certainly will be difficult to achieve, and it clearly will be difficult to maintain once it is established. Nevertheless, we have seen that man has it within his power to create such a society and to devise ways and means of perpetuating it on a stable basis. In view of the existence of this power, the possibility that the third pattern may eventually emerge cannot be ignored, although the probability of such an emergence, as judged from existing trends, may appear to be extremely low.

Existing industrial society did not arise as the result of any concerted effort on the part of mankind. Rather, industrial society emerged as the result of a series of accidental circumstances and events, many of which were quite unrelated to one another. Just as new biological species arise to fill niches in the scheme of life, so industrial civilization arose to fill a niche in the scheme of human existence. And just as biological species may thrive, then die, as the result of changing environment, so industrial civilization may thrive, then die, as a result of rapid changes in its environment—changes which civilization itself is creating.

Although the emergence of industrial society required no concerted, planned effort, perpetuation of that society will require effort of a magnitude which transcends all previous human effort. And upon this we must superimpose the wise action that will be required to avoid robotization and to preserve freedom and human dignity.

In our survey of the situation in which man now finds himself, we see that, although our high-grade resources are disappearing, we can live comfortably on low-grade resources. We see that, although a large fraction of the world's population is starving, all of humanity can, in principle, be nourished adequately. We see that, although world populations are increasing rapidly, those populations can, in principle, be stabilized. Indeed, it is amply clear that, if man wills it, a world community can be created in which human beings can live comfortably and in peace with each other. But it is equally clear that the achievement of this condition will require the application of intelligence, imagination, courage, unselfish help, planning, and prodigious effort. And it is equally clear that the time for decision is the present. With the consumption of each additional barrel of oil and ton of coal, with the addition of each new mouth to be fed, with the loss of each additional inch of topsoil, the situation becomes more inflexible and difficult to resolve. Man is rapidly creating a situation from which he will have increasing difficulty extricating himself.

If man is to find his way successfully through the labyrinth of difficulties that confront him in the years ahead, he must, above all, use his intelligence. He can no longer rely upon the unforeseeable fortunate circumstance; future mistakes will have consequences far more dangerous than past ones have been. He must divorce himself from unreasoned slogans and dogma, from the soothsayer, from the person whose selfish interests compel him to draw false conclusions, from the man who fears truth and knowledge, from the man who prefers indoctrination to education. Man must rapidly accumulate knowledge concerning both his environment and himself, and he must learn how to use that knowledge wisely. He must encourage the emergence of new ideas in all areas. He must learn not to fear change, for of one thing he can be certain—no matter what happens in the world of the next few decades, change will be the major characteristic. But it is within the range of his ability to choose what the changes will be, and how the resources at his disposal will be used—or abused—in the common victory—or ignominious surrender—of mankind.

We have surveyed briefly the extra-human resources with which he has to work. The values of these are, for all practical purposes, known to science, and they are potentially adequate for a richness of living as yet unexperienced. The unknown values are those of what, in the last analysis, will prove to be the critical resources—those within the mind and spirit of man himself, the "human resources." To what extent can man subjugate selfishness to generosity, ignorance to wisdom, and hate to love? To what extent will he be able to realize in time that if he continues to follow the present path he will soon be confronted by disaster?

We in the United States are in a position of overwhelming responsibility at the present time, for in a very real sense the destiny of humanity depends upon our decisions and upon our actions. We still possess freedom, our resources, and our knowledge, to stimulate the evolution of a world community within which people are well fed and within which they can lead free, abundant, creative lives. Or we can refuse to take constructive action, in which case man will almost certainly start down the steep incline which divides and leads, on the one hand, to the world of robots and, on the other, to that of agrarian slaves. Never before in history has so much responsibility been inherited by a group of human beings. Where in previous times the lives of individual nations and cultures were at stake, today the stake is the destiny of all humanity.

In this time of grave decision, when all the goodness in man must be called forth to subjugate the bad, when our survival depends upon the victory of wisdom and knowledge over stupidity and dogma, we would do well to pay heed to the words of a poet who has expressed the inarticulate thoughts of many of us who look forward hopefully to a more meaningful future for mankind. If the words of Rabindranath Tagore were to become the creed of all men, there would be little doubt that our civilization, and with it our freedom, would survive.

Where the mind is without fear and the head is held high;
Where knowledge is free;
Where the world has not been broken up into fragments by narrow domestic walls;
Where words come out from the depth of truth;
Where tireless striving stretches its arms toward perfection;
Where the clear stream of reason has not lost its way into the dreary desert sand of dead habit;
Where the mind is led forward by thee into ever widening thought and action—
Into that heaven of freedom, my Father, let my country awake.[1]

1. Rabindranath Tagore, "Gitanjali" (1912).

BIBLIOGRAPHY
AND INDEX

BIBLIOGRAPHY AND SUGGESTIONS
FOR FURTHER READING

Anything approaching a complete bibliography concerning the subjects discussed in this book would be of far greater length than the book itself. However, in order to enable the reader to study specific topics in more detail, an attempt has been made to list a few general reference works, together with other works which are readable summaries and which will provide the reader with additional keys to the available literature.

For a discussion of the course of evolution, the reader is referred to *The Meaning of Evolution* by George Gaylord Simpson (New Haven: Yale University Press, 1949), an abridgment of which has been published by Mentor Books (1951). The reader is also referred to Julian Huxley's *Evolution, the Modern Synthesis* (New York: Harper and Brothers, 1943). George Gamow's *Biography of the Earth* (New York: The Viking Press, 1941) is a stimulating popular account of earth-history, but unfortunately it is overly dogmatic concerning a number of debatable questions. Detailed descriptions and pictures of the diverse forms of animal life that have existed in the past and which exist to-day can be found in *Animals without Backbones* by R. Buchsbaum (Chicago: University of Chicago Press, 1948), and in *Man and the Vertebrates* by A. S. Romer (Chicago: University of Chicago Press, 1941).

Readers who are interested in ecology would profit by reading Alfred J. Lotka's *Principles of Physical Biology* (Baltimore: Williams and Wilkins, 1925), and *Animal Ecology* by C. Elton (London: Sedgwick and Jackson, 1947). The fundamentals of genetics are discussed lucidly by H. Kalmus in his book *Genetics* (London: Penguin Books, 1948).

For accounts of human evolution, the reader is referred to *Mankind So Far* by O. Howells (New York: Doubleday and Company, 1945), *Apes, Giants and Men* by H. Weidenreich (Chicago: University of Chicago Press, 1946), and the books of Sir Arthur Keith, particularly his *New Discoveries Relating to the Antiquity of Man* (New York: W. W. Norton and Company, 1931).

Many aspects of early primitive cultures can be deduced from implements, cave paintings, and bits of pottery that have been uncovered. The reader can find an interesting account of artifacts in paleolithic times in M. C. Burkitt's *The Old Stone Age* (New York: The Macmillan Company, 1933). Another approach to an understanding of early human culture is to study the cultures of contemporary primitive peoples. For interesting discussions of primitive cultures, the reader is referred to *General Anthropology* by Franz Boas and others (Boston: D. C. Heath and Company, 1938) and to *Patterns of Culture* by Ruth Benedict (Boston: Houghton Mifflin Company, 1935). Geographical and cultural factors are brought together and discussed clearly in *Human Ecology* by J. W. Bews (London: Oxford University Press, 1937).

For a stimulating and extensive account of the emergence of civilization, the reader is referred to *The Great Cultural Traditions* (Volume I: The Ancient Cities, and Volume II: The Classical Empires) by Ralph Turner (New York: McGraw-Hill Book Company, 1941). Other works of interest concerning the emergence of agriculture, animal domestication, urban culture, and the ancient empires are V. Gordon Childe's *Man Makes Himself* (London: C. J. Watts and Company, Ltd., 1941), recently reprinted by Mentor Books, and his *What Happened in History* (London: Penguin Books, Inc., 1946). The reader should also consult *The Study of History* by Arnold J. Toynbee, six volumes (1934–1939), or the one-volume abridgment of the work by D. C. Somervell (London: Oxford University Press, 1947), but this should be accompanied by a reading of Shepard B. Clough's stimulating, clearly written, and highly readable *The Rise and Fall of Civilization* (New York: McGraw-Hill Book Company, 1951). Detailed discussions of the great civilizations can be found in these books, and the reader will also find in them an abundance of suggestions for additional reading.

For discussions of the evolution of science and engineering, the reader should consult George Sarton's *The Study of the History of Science* (Cambridge: Harvard University Press, 1936), and his five-volume *Introduction to the History of Science* (Baltimore: The Williams and Wilkins Company, 1927–1947). The best short history of technological development is R. J. Forbes's *Man the Maker* (New York: Henry Schuman Company, 1950). For a critical study of the machine and its effects upon civilization, the reader should consult Lewis Mumford's *Technics and Civilization* and his *The Culture of Cities* (New York: Harcourt, Brace and Company, 1934, 1938).

C. Curwen's *Plough and Pasture* (London: Corbett, 1947) is an excellent short history of agriculture. For a fascinating account of changing food habits, the reader should consult *The Englishman's*

Food by J. Drummond and A. Wilbraham (London: Jonathan Cape, 1939).

For English historical background, the reader should consult G. M. Trevelyan's *History of England* (3rd Edition, 1945) and his *English Social History* (1942), both published by Longmans, Green and Company. Information on the evolution of economic life in the United States can be obtained from *The Rise of American Civilization* (four volumes) by Charles A. Beard and Mary R. Beard (New York: The Macmillan Company, 1933).

Colin Clark's *The Conditions of Economic Progress* (New York: The Macmillan Company, 1940), and the chapters dealing with underdeveloped and transition areas in *World Population* edited by P. K. Hatt (New York: The American Book Company, 1952), provide much useful information concerning the present economic condition of man. Kingsley Davis's *The Population of India and Pakistan* (Princeton: Princeton University Press, 1951), and Harvey S. Perloff's *Puerto Rico's Economic Future* (Chicago: University of Chicago Press, 1950), provide detailed pictures of conditions as they exist at present in those areas.

A recent edition of T. R. Malthus's *An Essay on the Principle of Population*, edited by Ernest Rhys, is available in Everyman's Library. The growth of world population has been discussed by A. M. Carr-Saunders in *World Population; Past Growth and Present Trends* (London: Oxford University Press, 1936). More recent works which discuss the growth of world population are Raymond Pearl's *Natural History of Population* (London: Oxford University Press, 1939), Warren S. Thompson's *Population Problems* (New York: McGraw-Hill Book Company, 1942), and *Studies in Population*, edited by G. F. Mair (Princeton: Princeton University Press, 1949). Robert C. Cook's *Human Fertility: The Modern Dilemma* (New York: William Sloane Associates, 1951) is a highly readable account of the factors that determine how rapidly human populations grow, and determine the quality of the population that results.

Changes in death rates in the Western World resulting from increased medical knowledge have been discussed at length by Louis Dublin and Alfred J. Lotka in *Length of Life* (New York: The Ronald Press, 1936). B. J. Stern's *Society and Medical Progress* (New York: Princeton University Press, 1941) is an excellent short history of the evolution of modern medical and public-health techniques. Data on mortality in the Roman Empire can be found in an article by W. R. Macdonell, *On the Expectation of Life in Ancient Rome and in the Provinces of Hispania and Lusitania, and Africa,* published in *Biometrika*. Volume 9, page 370 (1913).

For a fascinating acount of the evolution of contraceptive techniques, the reader should consult *A Medical History of Contraception* by N. E. Himes (Baltimore: The Williams and Wilkins Company, 1936). Modern techniques are described by R. L. Dickenson in a booklet, *Techniques of Conception Control*, and sterilization techniques are discussed by R. L. Dickenson and C. J. Gamble in *Human Sterilization*, both published by the Planned Parenthood Federation of America (1950). Future possibilities for conception control are discussed by Paul Henshaw in an article which can be found in *Science*, Volume 117, page 572 (1953).

The Human Species by Anthony Barnett (New York: W. W. Norton and Company, 1950) is a lucid account of the biology of man and contains highly readable sections on heredity, reproduction, evolution, race, nutrition, death, and population. The sexual behavior of human beings is discussed by C. S. Ford and Frank A. Beach in *Patterns of Sexual Behavior* (New York: Harper and Brothers, 1951) and by A. C. Kinsey, W. B. Pomeroy, and C. E. Martin in *Sexual Behavior in the Human Male* (Philadelphia: W. S. Saunders Company, 1948).

Curt Sterns's *Principles of Human Genetics* (Freeman, 1949) is a useful source book for information in that area, as is *Genetics and the Races of Man* by W. C. Boyd (Boston: Little, Brown and Company, 1950). Effects of differential birth rates are discussed by Cyril Burt in *Intelligence and Fertility; the Effect of the Differential Birthrate on Inborn Mental Characteristics* (London: Hamish Hamilton, 1947). A description of Swedish policy can be found in *Nation and Family; the Swedish Experiment in Democratic Family and Population Policy* by Alva Myrdal (New York: Harper and Brothers, 1941).

World vital statistics can be found in the *Demographic Yearbook* of the United Nations.

For further information concerning world food production, the reader is referred to *World Resources and Industries* by Erich W. Zimmermann (New York: Harper and Brothers, 1951), to the annual reports of the Food and Agricultural Organization of the United Nations and in particular to the F.A.O. *World Food Survey* (Washington, 1946). *The Soils That Support Us* by Charles E. Kellog (New York: The Macmillan Company, 1941) is an excellent introduction to soil science. W. G. Moore's *The World's Wealth* (London: Penguin Books, 1947) gives a lucid description of the present sources of world food. The problem of feeding the world's population has been discussed at considerable length by a variety of authors and from a variety of viewpoints. Among the more important books designed to be read by the general public are: *Our Plundered Planet* by Fairfield Osborn (Boston:

Little, Brown and Company, 1948), *The Road to Survival* by William Vogt (New York: William Sloane Associates, 1948), *The World's Hunger* by Frank A. Pearson and Floyd A. Harper (Ithaca: Cornell University Press, 1945), and *Let There Be Bread* by Robert Brittain (New York: Simon and Schuster, 1952). The reader will also find much of interest in *Food for the World,* edited by T. W. Schulz (Chicago: University of Chicago Press, 1945).

Problems of soil conservation are discussed in *Natural Principles of Land Use* by E. H. Graham (London: Oxford University Press, 1944), *Soil Conservation* by H. H. Bennett (New York: The McGraw-Hill Book Company, 1939), *Deserts on the March* by Paul B. Sears (Tulsa: University of Oklahoma Press, 1935), and *Vanishing Lands* by R. O. Whyte and G. V. Jacks (New York: Doubleday, Doran and Company, 1939).

E. Glesinger's *The Coming Age of Wood* (New York: Simon and Schuster, 1950) is an outstanding discussion of the possibilities of forest utilization. *World Population and Future Resources* edited by Paul K. Hatt contains considerable information on the possibilities of improving crop yields, of extending agriculture to greater areas, of extending the acreage of irrigated land, and of increasing the yield of food from the oceans.

Robert Brittain's *Let There Be Bread* is the only book that has come to my attention which seriously discusses drastically new techniques of food production. W. F. Gericke's *The Complete Guide to Soilless Gardening* (New York: Prentice-Hall, 1940) might prove of interest to some readers, but discussions of the applications of microbiology and algae culture are available primarily in technical periodicals. The reader is referred to an article by A. C. Thaysen, "The Value of Micro-Organisms in Nutrition (Food Yeast)," in *Nature,* Volume 151, page 406, and Volume 152, page 526 (1943), and to an article by R. L. Meier, "The Industrialization of Photosynthesis and Its Social Effects," in *Chemical and Engineering News,* Volume 27, page 3112 (1949).

The outstanding discussion of the world energy situation is that of Eugene Ayres and Charles A. Scarlott in their book *Energy Sources, The Wealth of the World* (New York: The McGraw-Hill Book Company, 1952). The reader will find there detailed discussions of fossil fuels, conversion of energy from one form to another, solar energy, energy from vegetation, and energy from wind and water. Their discussion of the possibilities of atomic energy is, in the opinion of this author, overly pessimistic. For a stimulating discussion of fossil fuels in time-perspective, the reader is referred to an article by M. King Hubbert, "Energy from Fossil Fuels," which appeared in *Science,* Volume 109, page 103 (1949), and which has been reprinted in the

Smithsonian Report for 1950 (U.S. Government Printing Office). A series of essays by F. E. Simon entitled *The Neglect of Science* (Oxford: Basil Blackwell, 1951) contains interesting discussions of the energy situation with particular reference to Great Britain. For discussions of the economic aspects of atomic energy the reader is referred to *Economic Aspects of Atomic Power* by S. H. Schurr and J. Marschak (Princeton: Princeton University Press, 1950), and to *Atomic Power* by V. H. Whitney and W. Isard (Philadelphia: The Blakiston Company, 1952). The reader is also referred to a stimulating essay by Farrington Daniels, "Atomic and Solar Energy," which appeared in the October 1950 issue of *The American Scientist*.

For information on energy and other mineral resources, together with discussions of possible future technological developments, the reader is referred to the comprehensive report of the President's Materials Policy Commission entitled *Resources for Freedom* (five volumes; Washington: U.S. Government Printing Office, 1952). Statistics can be found in the Bureau of Mines' *Minerals Yearbook* (Washington: U.S. Government Printing Office, published annually). Descriptions of processing techniques and basic raw-material requirements of major industries can be found in Erich W. Zimmermann's *World Resources and Industries*.

The water resource situation is discussed in *Resources for Freedom*, but the reader is referred further to *Water, Land and People* by B. Frank and A. Netboy (New York: Alfred A. Knopf, 1950), *Water or Your Life* by A. H. Carhart (Philadelphia: J. B. Lippincott Company, 1951), and *The Conservation of Ground Water* by Harold E. Thomas (New York: The McGraw-Hill Book Company, 1951).

During the last few decades there has been much written speculation concerning man's future. The most recent serious discussions are Charles Galton Darwin's *The Next Million Years* (New York: Doubleday and Company, 1953) and Roderick Seidenberg's *Post-Historic Man* (Durham: University of North Carolina Press, 1950).

The economic possibilities of industrializing underdeveloped areas are discussed in a series of pamphlets entitled *Bold New Program Series* published by the Public Affairs Institute (1950).

A wealth of information covering all areas of science can be found in the postwar issues of *Scientific American*. Also the reader will find stimulating essays on the interrelationship between science and society in the *Bulletin of the Atomic Scientists* and in *Impact,* a quarterly published by UNESCO.

INDEX